Foreign Fields

Sir Peter Wilkinson, KCMG, DSO, OBE was born in 1914, educated at Rugby and at Corpus Christi College, Cambridge, and commissioned in the Royal Fusiliers in 1931. He served as a military officer on a number of quasi-political missions in pre World War II Eastern Europe and in the war was one of the Special Operations Executive founders in the Baker Street Headquarters later serving in the Middle East, Italy, the Balkans and Central Europe, and commanding No. 6 Special Force (SOE) from 1943 to 1945. After the war he became a diplomat with appointment as Under Secretary at the Cabinet Office, as senior civilian instructor at the Imperial Defence College and as Ambassador in Saigon and Vienna. On retirement in 1972, he succeeded the late Sir Dick White as Co-ordinator of Intelligence at the Cabinet Office. Sir Peter Wilkinson died on 16 June 2000.

FOREIGN FIELDS:
The Story of an SOE Operative

P ETER W ILKINSON

I.B. Tauris Publishers
LONDON · NEW YORK

Paperback edition published in 2002 by I.B. Tauris & Co Ltd
6 Salem Road, London W2 4BU
175 Fifth Avenue, New York NY 10010
www.ibtauris.com

First published in 1997 by I.B. Tauris

In the United States and Canada distributed by
St Martin's Press, 175 Fifth Avenue, New York NY 10010

ISBN 1 86064 779 0

A full CIP record for this book is available from the British Library
A full CIP record for this book is available from the Library of Congress

Set in Berthold Baskerville by Ewan Smith, London
Printed and bound in Great Britain by MPG Books, Bodmin

Contents

Foreword

THIS splendidly crisp war autobiography is prefaced by a few chapters on the childhood that helped to form the man. Peter Wilkinson was born in India into the old officer class. While he was still a baby his father was killed at Ypres early in 1915; he thus grew up, through the routine mills of preparatory school, Rugby and Cambridge, envisaging a regular officer's career. Into this he was indeed admitted by the original of Siegfried Sassoon's 'cheery old card' whose staff blundered at the battle of Arras. Yet there were variants: aunts who painted, a step-father with whom he spent school holidays in Egypt.

He thus had a more original view of life than many regimental officers; plain regimental life bored him. Through his skills as a linguist and through luck, he got a job at the War Office. This led him swiftly to adventures that might have figured in an Eric Ambler thriller of the late 1930s, when war clouds were gathering over central Europe; vividly described below, and quite true.

The great Colin Gubbins, of whom he and Joan Bright Astley recently published a life, picked him to attend the first secret course on clandestine war; and held on to him. He was with Gubbins in Poland when the Germans conquered it in 1939 and escaped; escaped again when the Germans conquered France in the following spring; and worked under Gubbins in the secret stay-behind parties that were to have sabotaged the invasion of England that Hitler cancelled.

He then moved forward with Gubbins into the hectic early stages of that still underestimated secret service, the Special Operations Executive, in which he spent the rest of the war. Several fascinating and hitherto unpublished aspects of SOE's working system come out in these pages, as seen by a particularly keen-eyed and well-placed observer.

Though for much of the war he was a staff officer, he was not one of those *embusqués* who never went up the line. On the contrary, danger seemed to attract him. Hence his presence in Crete, from which an imperious signal rescued him just in time in May 1941; and hence his venture on the 'Clowder' Mission into German-occupied Yugoslavia in 1943.

Following an established SOE drill – deal first with the man at the top – he began by seeing Tito, whose intellect impressed him. Armed with a signed photograph of Tito, he pressed forward; from Bosnia into Croatia; then into Slovenia; then right into the Third Reich itself, in its Austrian province. He is justly proud of being the first man in the army since 1940 to have taken part in an offensive patrol on German territory.

He returned safely from it, to receive an immediate DSO. He left behind in Austria his friend Alfgar Hesketh-Prichard, who never came back; not the least of Wilkinson's achievements in this book is to remind the nation of Hesketh-Prichard's heroic personality, which has never received the publicity that has washed over so many less deserving figures in the resistance struggle.

He also makes it clear, by his matter-of-fact accounts of mountainous scrambles over ghastly terrain, how tough the countryside actually was in the 'Ljubljana Gap' through which so many amateur strategists have marched so many armies. His journeys make 'yomping' in the Falklands sound more like a picnic than an operation of war.

He was back in Austria again, right at the end of the war, with the advancing Allied armies; able to detect the fear felt locally for the Cossack bands, about whose fate also there has since been some under-informed speculation.

The Foreign Office, an essentially peaceable body, seldom saw eye to eye with SOE, and helped to have it put down soon after the war's end; but snapped up Wilkinson from it, for a career of high distinction, tragically cut short by accident. If his diplomatic memoirs are half as interesting as his military ones, they too will make enthralling reading.

M. R. D. Foot

NORWAY

Bergen

Oslo

Stavanger

SWEDEN

FINLAND

Helsinki

Stockholm

Leningrad

ESTONIA

DENMARK

Copenhagen

Riga

LATVIA

GREAT
BRITAIN

Hamburg

LITHUANIA

London

HOLLAND

Danzig

Konisberg

Rotterdam

E.PRUSSIA

Brussels

Cologne

Berlin

BELGIUM

Warsaw

Paris

GERMANY

Leipzig

POLAND

Dijon

Stuttgart

Prague

Cracow

FRANCE

Munich

CZECHOSLOVAKIA

USSR

SWITZERLAND

Vienna

AUSTRIA

Budapest

BESSARABIA

Milan

HUNGARY

ITALY

Zagreb

ROMANIA

YUGOSLAVIA

Belgrade

Bucharest

CORSICA

Sarajevo

Rome

SARDINIA

BULGARIA

Sofia

ALBANIA

ALGERIA

GREECE

SICILY

TURKEY

TUNISIA

MALTA

Athens

CRETE

EUROPE

BEFORE THE SECOND WORLD WAR

——— International boundaries

LIBYA

EGYPT

CHAPTER I

Early Years

I N any biography the difference between factual truth and biographical truth is nowhere more evident than in the pages devoted to the subject's childhood. This generalization applies particularly to an auto-biography in which the incidents that the author omits are often more revealing than those he chooses to include. If only to explain some of the peculiarities in my subsequent behaviour, I offer my puerile reminis-cences for what they are worth. *Tout comprendre, c'est tout pardonner.*

I was born on 15 April 1914 at Pach Marhi in the Central Provinces of India where my father, a captain in the East Yorkshire regiment, was an instructor at the Army Musketry School. My mother, who had married eighteen months previously, was no stranger to India; she had been born at Darjeeling, her father, Sir Alexander Wilson, having been President of the Bengal Chamber of Commerce and a member of the Viceroy's Legislative Council. However, her parents and their five children had returned to England when she was three years old.

I arrived early. The station medical officer was at a guest night at the officers' mess when summoned to attend my mother and was too drunk to mount his horse. By the time he had been conveyed to our bungalow in a rickshaw, I had been safely delivered by my Indian ayah. My mother, exhausted by her efforts and weakened by malaria and heart disease, was unable to nurse me and I was reared on a mixture of Benger's Food and diluted buffalo's milk with the consequence that I was soon seriously ill with gastroenteritis. By the time both my mother and I were out of danger, the Archduke Franz Ferdinand and his wife had been assassinated at Sarajevo and the Great War had begun.

I was nearly five months old when my father's regiment was ordered to France. In those days officers' wives were not allowed to travel in the same troopship as their husbands and it was several weeks before my mother and I said goodbye to my ayah and embarked at Bombay with the other regimental wives and their children. It seems to have been a

I

hideous voyage. For some reason, instead of going through the Suez Canal, the ship was routed via Cape Town and it was over six weeks before we reached England. My mother was fully occupied in looking after me for I was still seriously ill and she had the distressing experience of overhearing the ship's doctor telling the colonel's wife that I had little chance of reaching Plymouth alive. However, he had underrated my resilience and my mother's determination.

When we rejoined my father in December, his regiment was undergoing training near Winchester and we were billeted in the house of a canon of Winchester Cathedral. He and his wife had a large young family and my mother would often recall the sweetness of those small children singing carols on Christmas Eve. During these last few weeks together, my father and mother seemed to have been aware that their time was running out. The New Year came in very cold; winter uniforms were scarce and officers and men had to make do in their tropical kit. In mid-January the battalion embarked for France. Almost immediately they were sent up the line and, on 6 February, my father died in hospital at Hazebrouck of wounds received in the Ypres salient on the previous day. He was aged thirty-seven years and I was not quite ten months old.

The official telegram reporting his death was followed a few days later by a letter from the Army Pay Office demanding the refund of the balance of his February pay, paid in advance. Still dazed with grief my mother repaid the money by return of post though it left her almost completely without funds. Recalling this incident with some bitterness many years later, she said that it was this incredibly heartless act on the part of the Paymaster General which had brought her up short with the realization that henceforward she and I would be on our own.

My mother had no one to turn to. Her father and mother were both dead and her step-mother was now commandant of a Red Cross hospital at Eastbourne organized by her sister, the Duchess of Hamilton. My mother scarcely knew my father's family at all. On return from their honeymoon, which they had spent fishing in Ireland, she and my father had embarked almost immediately for India. Like two of his brothers, my grandfather was a retired major general. He was born in 1828 in the reign of George IV and as a young officer he had commanded the Chestnut Troop of the Royal Horse Artillery during the Crimean War. By now he was slightly senile and was looked after by his two devoted daughters, my aunt Edith and my aunt Eleanor, both destined to play an important role in my upbringing. My father's eldest brother, Frank, formerly a major in the Royal Fusiliers, had retired from the army some years previously and was now living in London. His other brother, Claud, also a bachelor, had joined the Royal Naval Division on the outbreak of war and was shortly to transfer to the Grenadier Guards. My mother had not met these relations since her wedding.

My grandfather and his family lived in a rambling mock-Tudor house at Thorpe, near Egham in Surrey. The large vegetable garden, so valuable in wartime, was managed by my aunt Eleanor while my aunt Edith ran the household. Both sisters also worked part-time as VAD nurses in the local Red Cross hospital. One of my few memories of Thorpe is of being got out of bed to watch the searchlights on St Anne's Hill playing on a marauding Zeppelin but there was also a memorable breakfast when I was about four years old at which my grandfather, in a moment of senile irritation, had poured a full plate of porridge over the unfortunate manservant who was serving him. Shortly after this incident, the old General died, unlamented by my mother who had never been accepted by him.

My father had been the baby of the family and my aunts' favourite brother and, though they offered my mother their sympathy, they had no wish to share their personal grief with a comparative stranger. My mother found this attitude hard to understand, as she did the fact that, having been strictly brought up to hide their personal feelings, my father's family were temperamentally incapable of giving her the sort of emotional support that she so desperately needed.

Material support was more readily forthcoming. Since we now had nowhere to live and my mother had yet to receive the first instalment of her War Widow's Pension of one hundred and fifty pounds a year, she thankfully accepted my uncle Frank's invitation to share his house at 2 St Leonard's Terrace, Chelsea. It was a large house with a spacious nursery and night nursery on the top floor. Communication between nursery and kitchen was maintained by means of a speaking-tube through which my newly enlisted nanny regularly complained to the cook about the unpunctuality and unsuitability of the nursery meals. My uncle Frank, an elderly bachelor of fixed habits, was a good water-colourist and had a number of young artist friends, most of whom were now on active service. Consequently, he felt lonely and irritable and depended much on my mother's company. However, when, after a few months, he proposed marriage to her, she thought it time to move on and rented a small flat in Lower Sloane Street. This flat was not only conveniently near St Leonard's Terrace but my nanny could continue to meet her cronies pushing their prams in Burton Court or the garden of the Royal Chelsea Hospital. I can only remember one item of their gossip: this was the awesome revelation that, even in the coldest winter months, the infant Peter Scott had been exposed in his pram, dressed only in a cotton shirt and shorts, in order to harden him so that he might follow in his father's footsteps as an Antarctic explorer. However, I dare say that this recollection dates from a later period when we had moved to a slightly larger flat in the quaintly named St Loo Mansions. Although the neighbouring Chelsea Old Church was destroyed by bombs during the Second World War, St Loo Mansions still stands, a solid ugly memorial to late Victorian residential development.

By the autumn of 1917 the Zeppelin raids were becoming more regular. In that year my future wife was born in neighbouring Tite Street during the heaviest of these air-raids and she spent the first hours of her life shut, for safety, in a chest of drawers. After three years of war in the trenches many of my mother's friends had lost their husbands and London had become a sad place apart from the frenetic gaiety of officers home on short leave from the Western Front. Accordingly, she decided to move to Eastbourne where the sea air would be good for my health and where she could be near her step-mother's hospital.

Our tiny rented house at 3 Matlock Road was on the western edge of the town and beyond us lay open country leading up to Beachy Head. It was within walking distance of the pier and of De Walden Court, my grandmother's hospital. This was an imposing building and I remember the deep litter which was spread on the street in front of it to deaden the sound of the horses' hooves. I also remember my grandmother's brougham (she never owned a motor car). As a special treat, we made occasional excursions to Pevensey Bay which I enjoyed so long as I could sit on the box with the coachman. However, if on account of bad weather I was made to sit inside the carriage with my back to the horses, I expected to be sick at any moment. My mother went daily to the hospital where she helped answer letters and inquiries. I was not allowed in the wards but I had free run of the gardens. On sunny days these gardens were thronged with convalescent soldiers dressed in their distinctive blue uniforms, white shirts and red ties. I used to see them lolling on the garden seats, 'smoking fags and spinning yarns'. Many of them were Australians and, far from their own wives and families, they made a great fuss of me. I loved to hear them recounting, in gruesome detail, their ghastly adventures while they gorged me with chocolate from their Red Cross parcels. As a special treat some would show me the stumps of their amputated limbs. There were regular entertainments and sing-songs at the hospital which I greatly enjoyed but there were few opportunities to meet other children of my own age apart from a fortnightly dancing class which I detested. The only friend that I remember from those days is Eddie Shackleton whose father, Sir Ernest Shackleton, the famous Antarctic explorer, had recently returned to England having made an epic rescue attempt, sailing 800 miles to South Georgia in an open boat. Eddie was several years older than me and had a model tank which I greatly coveted but was not allowed to play with. I remember that on Armistice Day, 11 November 1918, we were both allowed to stay up to watch the fireworks which celebrated the end of the Great War.

When the war ended and the De Walden hospital was closed down, there was no reason for us to remain in Eastbourne. I was now nearly five years old and, in choosing Camberley for our new home, my mother acted solely in my interest. She did not particularly like soldiers and the military life did not appeal to her. However, she thought that at Camberley she would find officers attending the Staff College or who were serving as instructors at Sandhurst who would have known my father, and whose families might provide the friends which, as an only child, I so urgently needed. Moreover, at Camberley there was reputed to be an excellent kindergarten.

'Corries', Waverley Drive was the sort of four-bedroomed house rented by officers attending the Staff College. Its small garden backed on to open heath-land which provided a wonderful adventure playground for me and my friends. Our neighbours were army families for the most part and there were frequent cricket matches and other entertainments for small boys and the sort of hearty social life which my mother found uncongenial but endured for my sake. We were relatively badly off and had no motor car and my mother took me everywhere riding pillion on the carrier of her bicycle. For me it was a golden time, evoked even today by the smell of warm bracken and sun-baked pine needles and the gloomy banks of ponticum rhododendrons where we small boys used to have our hide-outs.

That summer, for the first time, we had a succession of visitors, including several of my mother's Scottish cousins who had recently been demobilized and had nowhere to live. I remember their grave young faces and sometimes caught a faraway look of melancholy which I could not understand. I had yet to learn the truth of the claim that you can tell how much real fighting an infantryman has done by looking at his eyes. As if trying to recapture their own innocence, those young men joined with great zest in our games and we small boys accepted them without question as battle-scarred members of our own tribe.

After a short stay, they disappeared, often leaving me a large tip. I dare say they thought of me as, in my own way, another war casualty.

Among the visitors who stayed with us at 'Corries' was my mother's first cousin, Frank Cramer-Roberts. Frank had joined the Egyptian Irrigation Service in 1906. On the outbreak of war, although having been partially blinded in one eye while playing football at Rugby, he obtained a commission in the West Kent Yeomanry and had taken part in the Gallipoli landings. He loved horses and when his regiment was finally 'dismounted' and sent to the Western Front, he transferred to a field squadron of Royal Engineers, serving with the Cavalry Division during the Palestine Campaign and later in Salonika. Demobilized in August 1919 and having nowhere else to go, he spent several weeks with us at Camberley while waiting to return to the Middle East where he had been appointed Inspector of Irrigation at Atbara in the Sudan.

Atbara was classified as a 'hardship post' with an entitlement to annual home leave and early next summer Frank stayed with us again. One morning my mother told me that Frank had asked her to marry him and that she had accepted. It seemed to me the most natural thing in the world; he had already secured my affection by buying me my first bicycle and I was delighted at the prospect of having a step-father.

Frank and my mother were married quietly in London in July 1920. I was spared the ordeal of being a page, and to compensate me for not accompanying them on their honeymoon I was taken by my nanny to *Chu-chin-chow*, a popular musical then running at His Majesty's Theatre, Haymarket. Shortly after my parents returned from their honeymoon, my step-father's leave came to an end and he went back to the Sudan, leaving my mother and me to go, as usual, to Studland for our summer holiday.

My mother's eldest sister, May, was ten years older than her. Aged nineteen when her father had remarried in 1896, my aunt May had found it unbearable to have a step-mother of her own generation and had left home to study art at the Slade. In London she had shared rooms with Jean (Jattie) Welch, the daughter of a prosperous Scottish wine exporter living in Bordeaux. Together they had rented five acres of land at Studland where they built a wooden bungalow. It was a magical spot on the edge of the moor overlooking Poole Harbour and Studland Bay. Both had considerable talent, May as a landscape painter and Jattie Welch as a portraitist, but their careers were cut short by the outbreak of war in 1914 when both joined up as VAD nurses in Millicent, Duchess of Sutherland's Hospital at Etaples. It was not long before they found themselves dealing with horribly mutilated men at casualty clearing stations sometimes only a few hundred yards behind the front line, and at the armistice they had returned to Studland too shocked by their recent experiences to resume their painting careers.

Both loved children and, in August, nephews and nieces descended on them in force either camping out in the Studio and its dependencies or living with their parents in rented lodgings in the village. I had become reconciled to my mother being addressed as Mrs Cramer-Roberts instead of Mrs Wilkinson and now that Frank had returned to the Sudan, I had her once again entirely to myself. It was a spade and bucket existence with 'sand in the sandwiches, wasps in the tea'; a time of water-wings and sunburned bodies, for we bathed naked; and tempestuous family rows. However, it was too good to last and, as September approached, I became aware of plans being made for my aunt Helen, whom I particularly disliked, and her two small boys to come and live in our house at Camberley, and of my mother's intention to leave me in her charge while she joined Frank in the Sudan. It was a prospect which filled me with foreboding but I did not realize that my intense relationship with my mother was about to be broken for good. On the day of her departure she took me early to school on the back of her bicycle. With tears streaming down her face, she said goodbye to me and I, taking refuge in the locker room, wept my heart out. But not for long for other children were arriving and it would have been shameful to have been found in tears. I never wept for my mother again.

It was a horrible winter but I cannot believe that my aunt Helen was actually as cruel and insensitive as I remember. Anyhow, my mother came home again in April in time for my seventh birthday. Frank followed two months later, arriving with a Singer two-seater motor car. It had a dickie in which I travelled when we set out for Studland on our summer holidays. Before leaving, my mother had confided in me that she was expecting a baby and my half-sister, Benita, was born at Camberley on 17 September 1921.

We had no telephone in the house and I remember my step-father going to fetch the doctor in the middle of the night. However, I took no further interest in the proceedings for, while waiting for my sister's arrival, it was decided that the doctor should remove my adenoids and tonsils. He performed this operation on the kitchen table and, to this day, I can remember the smell of the chloroform and the taste of the cotton-wool, baked brown in our oven for sterilization, which was used to stop my bleeding. A few weeks later Frank returned to Cairo, the house at Camberley was packed up and, with Benita and our nurse, we moved into furnished lodgings at Studland. The following January, now aged seven and three-quarters, I was packed off to my first boarding school.

CHAPTER 2

School

DURING their brief stay at Winchester before my father had embarked for France, my parents had put my name down for the College; and my prospective housemaster, asked to recommend a preparatory school, had suggested Winton House, a local boarding school with a good academic record. Aged seven, I was too young to go to Winton House but the headmaster, a certain Mr Johns, in explaining the situation, told my mother that his brother-in-law and his sister had started a small pre-preparatory boarding school next door to Winton House. Eastacre, as it was called, sounded exactly what she was looking for.

Since I was no longer emotionally dependent on my mother, going away to boarding school for the first time was, for me, a less traumatic experience than for most boys of my age. On the other hand, I sensed that my mother was unusually upset when we arrived at Winchester station on that cold January afternoon. I did not know and she did not tell me that it was on this same platform, carrying me in her arms, that she had said goodbye to my father seven years ago almost to the day. However, she could not have done better in her choice of my new headmaster, Mr Marsham. He was a retired Indian civil servant; the sort of Englishman, already a threatened species, who 'never lied, never cheated' and, perhaps wearing a Free Forester tie, had administered innumerable natives in some vast tract of Empire with more sympathy and justice than they were ever to know again. He was, for me, an ideal father figure. There were only thirty boys in the school aged between six and nine; and most of their fathers had either been killed in the Great War or were serving overseas in one or other of the Services. Our formal education was entrusted to three extremely competent ladies while Mr Marsham himself taught us to ride, shoot, box and play cricket with a straight bat, all of which were considered to be essential skills for prep-school boys of my generation.

Even the best preparatory schools leave horrible memories but my time at Eastacre was as happy as it could have been in the circumstances; and as uneventful except for an accident which seriously affected my health for the next fifty years. I describe this incident merely as an example of the casual medical treatment afforded to schoolboys in the 1920s.

During fielding practice one morning I and another boy ran for the same catch. He was smaller than me and the top of his head collided with my right eye-socket. I was temporarily concussed and put to bed. By the time the doctor arrived, my eye was completely closed over and I had a splitting headache. He diagnosed a simple black eye. I was told to stop making a fuss and go down to lunch. Obediently I struggled through the first course but, when it came to the pudding, I fainted and was put back to bed. Typically, Mr Marsham himself came up to the dormitory to apologize for making me come down to lunch; he said he had had no idea how badly I was hurt. Even so, I had to do lessons the next day and the following week, it being the end of term, I travelled home by train by myself to Swanage where I was picked up by Mr King, the carrier, and driven over the hill to Studland in his wagonette. Nothing more was done about my eye which remained completely closed for the next four months. Fifty years later when I was Ambassador in Vienna and suffering from persistent asthma and recurrent sinusitis, I consulted the leading ENT specialist. Having examined the X-rays, the latter asked whether the extensive damage to the right side of my face was due to a war wound. He went on to say that my eye socket had been fractured in three places, my septum displaced and my antrum seriously damaged. It took an operation lasting four hours to sort me out but, happily, I have been free from sinusitis ever since.

I was due to go to Winton House in the autumn of 1923 and my mother came home that summer in order to outfit me and see me safely in. However, during my last term at Eastacre, she had lunch with Mr Marsham and his wife during which Mrs Marsham said, with a sigh, that I was growing into such a good-looking little boy she rather wished that I wasn't going to Winton House though she was sure that her brother would be kind to me. My mother, who had, presumably, no previous acquaintance with prep-school pederasty, nevertheless took the hint. After consulting the family lawyer, she immediately withdrew my name from Winton House although she was obliged to forfeit a term's fees paid in advance. In all this, she showed extraordinary perspicacity. Many years later I read in J. R. Ackerley's memoirs that, when he had been a pupil there, Winton House had had a very evil reputation.

It had been a narrow shave but my mother was now faced with the problem of finding, at very short notice, another school willing to take me without, of course, revealing the reason for my withdrawal from Winton House. Against his better judgement, for he thought me too old at nine and a half, Mr Ronald Vickers of Scaitcliffe, Englefield Green, finally accepted me as a favour to my uncle Claud whom he used to meet out shooting. Scaitcliffe was acknowledged to be one of the best preparatory schools in the country even by Gabbitas & Thring, the educational agents, who included it in their list of recommended schools on the back page of the *Eton College Chronicle*. There were only fifty boys, aged between eight and thirteen, but they were left in no doubt that they were expected to achieve some distinction either by winning Eton scholarships, playing cricket at Lord's or in some eminent position in later life. I have before me the school photograph taken in the summer of 1927. It includes three future ambassadors; Humphrey Searle, the composer; Richard Sharples, who was to be assassinated in 1973 when Governor of Bermuda; Julian Tennyson, grandson of the poet, who after winning poetry prizes at Eton and at Cambridge was killed in action; so was his brother Penrose, an equally promising poet who had left Scaitcliffe the previous year; happily the third brother, Hallam, survived to become a notable radio and television commentator. In the front row, in short trousers like all of us, is seated Paddy Butler, later Lord Dunboyne, who became a High Court judge and also David MacIndoe, the future Vice-Provost of Eton. Finally, there were my own particular friends, the two Tatham-Warter brothers: John who was to be killed in the Western Desert while serving with his regiment, the Queens Bays; and Digby who won the DSO at Arnhem and was to be immortalized in the film *A Bridge Too Far*, carrying a ragged umbrella to protect him from the mortar shells while rallying his company of the Airborne Regiment. Amid such eaglets, I had an undistinguished school career. Nor did Mr Vickers conceal his disappointment when my mother, on the advice of her Edinburgh physician who thought Winchester unhealthy, decided to send me to Rugby instead. It was only my pleading which dissuaded her from choosing an even more bracing establishment in Scotland which, as I was later to learn, had been the Edinburgh physician's first choice.

In those days, most prep schools had special links with one or other public school; and Rugby was not a school for which Mr Vickers prepared his boys. Consequently, I did rather worse in my common entrance exam than I might otherwise have done. Of no less concern, when I went to Rugby in September 1927, there were no former Scaitcliffe boys to befriend me as there would have been at Eton or Winchester.

For my future boarding house my mother had chosen School Field on account of its connection with Rupert Brooke, at that time her favourite poet ('Ring out you bugles over the rich dead ...'), whose father had formerly been its housemaster. My own housemaster, Canon E. F. Bonhote, a bachelor clergyman, was in no way the sort of dashing father figure I was seeking, though, as I was later to discover, he had temporarily resigned his Holy Orders in order to fight in the trenches as a private soldier. I had no difficulty in adjusting to public school life but, as Mr Vickers had predicted, I found few kindred spirits at Rugby and made no lasting friends there. If at times I felt something of a misfit, this was probably due to my background as an only child. It may be that my general sense of insecurity affected my school work but, in any case, after receiving outstandingly good reports for my first two terms, I gave up trying and thereafter lived under a continuous threat of superannuation.

Nor did I find Rugby particularly salubrious for, on the last day of my first term, I contracted pneumonia as a direct consequence of a sadistic punishment inflicted on me by a master I detested; the dislike was mutual. He was a parson and had been a former Australian Test cricketer. I had to spend most of my first Christmas holidays in the school sanatorium. Happily, owing to the failure of the school to communicate with my mother, who was in Egypt, she was unaware of the seriousness of my condition until I was well out of danger. Not the least important of my legacies from Rugby has been a tendency to asthma and a weak chest.

Not only my bad school reports but my general attitude distressed my mother and irritated my step-father, both of whom had made a considerable financial sacrifice to send me to a first-class school. The truth was that, like many boys of my age, in order to compensate for my sense of inadequacy, I had become a horrid little snob. During the holidays from Scaitcliffe I had stayed several times with the Tatham-Warters at Buckland St Mary or with other friends who had nice country houses and often rather dashing parents. It had turned my head. By contrast, most Rugby boys were the sons of professional people – lawyers, doctors, civil servants – or had fathers who were 'something in the City' and, by comparison with my Scaitcliffe friends, I found them dreary. There were, of course, also plenty of rich boys with country houses and the rest of it, but most of them seemed to be the sons of Midlands industrialists who had a made a good thing out of the war and had certainly never heard a shot fired in anger. Although they themselves were as poor as church mice, my Wilkinson relations looked down on war profiteers and *nouveaux riches*; and so did I. That I should have found as many sons of war profiteers had I gone to Eton or any other public school did not occur to me but, neither at Eastacre nor at Scaitcliffe, had I met boys of this sort and I was unprepared for them, although envious of their material possessions.

In the 1920s Rugby was flushed with evangelical socialism and R. H. Tawney was the cult-hero. Pacifism and disarmament were all the rage and there was a strong prejudice against the military ethic which I had been brought up to believe in. This attitude was encouraged by some of the younger masters who drew their political opinions, undigested, from the *New Statesman*. There were exceptions and my first house tutor, Mr J. T. Christie, a Wykehamist who had served briefly with a Guards regiment, might have been the role-model I was looking for; but, unfortunately, he left after my first term to become the headmaster of Westminster. If I thought some of the masters too 'progressive', I found the majority of the boys smug and suburban. Here again there were exceptions. From the day he arrived, Philip Toynbee disregarded all school rules which he considered oppressive or unnecessary. Although I sometimes had the thankless duty of chastising Philip for his many transgressions, I never ceased to admire his libertarian principles nor the insouciance with which he accepted what must have been almost a record number of beatings as the price of liberty. He, at least, was no slave-heart. Though nowhere near as bloody-minded as Philip, I too had a modest reputation for insubordination. Many years later when asked by some idiotic television interviewer when I first became 'seriously interested in resistance', I had no hesitation in replying, 'at my public school'.

Quite by chance, I learned that one of the boys in my house had an uncle who owned a stable at Hillmorton, a village about two miles from Rugby, where he kept a dozen or more valuable horses for sale to members of the Pytchley and Warwickshire hunts. Mr Darby was a kindly man who seemed quite glad to have an extra stable-boy to exercise his horses and, during my last year, whenever I could escape from compulsory football, I bicycled out to Hillmorton. In frosty weather it meant merely jogging round the manège but, even so, it was a marvellous relaxation from school life. Sometimes, however, I was able to go for a short ride. On one occasion, while jumping into a lane, I nearly came on top of one of the masters, Mr Chatwin, who was taking a solitary walk. Fortunately, he chose not to see me although I was conspicuous in my school uniform, for he should certainly have reported me and I would have been severely punished since I was out of bounds and activities such as riding were strictly forbidden. As Tony Quayle recalls in his memoirs, Mr Chatwin was unfortunate in his choice of given names. Returning from OTC field days, the town echoed to the refrain of 'John Brown's Body', played by the school band, with the words, sung lustily by all ranks: Greville Augustus Francis Mason Chatwin. I found him a rather unapproachable bachelor who prepared boys for the School Certificate but I owe him one incalculable debt for he introduced me to the English Metaphysical poets.

One other incident sticks in my memory. One hot summer afternoon I and Duggie Stewart, who subsequently, while serving in the Royal Scots Greys, rode for England in the Olympic games, were idly throwing stones in the house yard when one of them went through the window of the study belonging to the head of house. It was pure accident that it was his window that we broke, but a great deal was made of the incident.

Our housemaster, perhaps unwisely, decided that as a punishment we should be 'beaten in Hall' by the head boy, Harry B. This was a punishment usually reserved, as a last resort, for obstreperous Lower boys and delinquent fags. To inflict it on boys of seventeen was a calculated insult. So Duggie and I resolved to 'ham it up'. As required of small boys, we waited obediently outside the door until summoned to receive our punishment. We then behaved with a mock humility which entirely unnerved poor Harry B., who consequently caned us very inexpertly despite the encouragement and advice we offered between the strokes. Having insisted on shaking hands with our executioner, we emerged from Hall to be greeted with cheers and congratulations. Though gratified by this demonstration, I nevertheless felt embarrassed, for poor Harry had only been carrying out instructions and we had already given him a hard time. Predictably, Canon Bonhote took a dim view of this ovation and, after prayers that evening, he went around the room scolding each member of the house individually. This extraordinary performance was later re-enacted in the dormitories amid scenes of great hilarity. For my part, I have always regretted that, basking in undeserved popularity, I did not have the decency to apologize to poor Harry who was deeply wounded by the affair and, shortly after-wards, left Rugby for good. His subsequent career did not fulfil its early promise; he joined the Colonial Office and finished up as an under-secretary in the Ministry of Education.

Much to my surprise, when I returned from the summer holidays, I found that although only in the Upper Fifth, I had been made a so-called 'Sixth Power'. This gave me prefectorial status and entitled me to three small fags to do my bidding; one of these, my favourite, later became a distinguished Canadian Ambassador. Evidently the authorities considered that I was too dangerous to be left as a loose cannon. However, I did not have long to enjoy the fruits of office for, as soon as I had passed my entrance exam for Corpus Christi College, Cambridge, my parents very sensibly took me away.

CHAPTER 3

Holidays with
my Aunts

No account of my school days would be complete without some description of my holiday arrangements. The discipline of a Victorian schoolroom, to which I was subjected by my Wilkinson aunts, contrasted vividly, but not always unfavourably, with the *vie de bohème* I enjoyed with my aunt May in Dorsetshire. Once I knew what was expected of me, I adapted easily to either regime and learned to comply and not to kick against the pricks. However, my experiences brought home to me the truth of Goethe's assertion that you have to choose between order and freedom; you cannot have both. I have yet to make up my mind which I prefer.

Shortly before he died, the old General, my grandfather, now aged well over ninety, moved his family from Thorpe to Longcross, a small village on the edge of Chobham Common, where he rented a yellow-washed Regency house. It had seven or eight bedrooms and stood in about five acres of paddock and garden which included, surprisingly, three grass tennis courts. The modest establishment consisted of a cook and a house parlour-maid; a gardener and a garden boy who also cleaned the boots and the knives; and to begin with there was a manservant whom I dimly remember who valeted my grandfather and my uncle Claud and acted as a sort of butler.

By the time I first came to Longcross for my holidays when I was nine years old my grandfather had been dead for several years and I was left in no doubt that the household revolved around my uncle Claud. During the Great War he had been a captain in the Grenadier Guards and had now returned to the Stock Exchange, travelling up to London every day from Virginia Water. I saw very little of him for I was always in bed by the time he returned from the City and he spent his weekends shooting or playing golf. At mealtimes I found him a formidable figure who discouraged conversation. Despite this, he seemed

to have a surprising number of friends and spent his winter holidays at
St Moritz, figure-skating; in June he went trout fishing in Hampshire;
and his summer holidays he spent shooting chamois in Austria. My
mother used to say that, with the possible exception of my uncle Frank,
he was the most selfish man that she had ever known. Nevertheless,
once a term he used to collect me from Scaitcliffe and bring me to have
Sunday lunch at Longcross which was only six miles away, and when
I was about twelve he began to take some interest in me, took me to
the Boat Race where, in the crowd, I could see nothing and later that
holidays to Portsmouth to see HMS *Victory*. He also took Aunt Eleanor
and me to the Guards' point-to-point at Hawthorn Hill. Unfortunately,
the following year he lost a lot of money speculating in oil and died of
a brain haemorrhage during my second term at Rugby, leaving my
aunts very badly off. I inherited his ivory hairbrushes and his gold
watch, both of which I still have today, but his Mannlicher rifle and his
Purdey shotguns were sold to pay his debts.

When I returned for the Easter holidays after my uncle's death, I no
longer had to be in bed by half-past six so that the bath water was hot
again by the time he wanted to dress for dinner. Henceforth my lights-
out was calculated by dividing my age by two. Until I was seventeen
I was not allowed to come down to dinner and my supper consisted of
a large bowl of bread and milk which I ate in bed since it was often
too cold in my bedroom to sit at a table. One or other of my aunts
always said prayers with me and tucked me up.

While staying at Longcross I was rarely asked out to tea or to
children's parties, so having to go to bed early did not interfere greatly
with my social life. However, when I was nearly sixteen Aunt Eleanor
took me skiing in Switzerland and I was dismayed to find that she had
arranged for me to have children's high tea at half-past five when the
other members of the party, some much younger than me, all stayed up
for dinner. I felt very desolate on the first evening when Aunt Eleanor
took me down to the dining room and handed me over to the *maître
d'hôtel*. In my grey school sweater and shorts, the latter took me for one
of a party of prep-school boys who were similarly dressed and sat me
at their table. To my surprise we had a delicious tea consisting mainly
of left-overs from dinner the previous night and I soon made friends
with the young boys from Eagle House who afterwards asked me to
play racing demon with them until bedtime. From then on I spent every
evening with them and with their young headmaster, Mr Parmiter, and
greatly preferred their company to that of the adolescents in my own
party whose idea of *après ski* was to sit in the bar swapping dirty stories

and jeering at the middle-aged Swiss trying to tango to the hotel dance band. Aunt Eleanor greatly approved of my new friends and was overheard remarking to Mr Parmiter how healthy and British we looked in our shorts and grey sweaters compared to the scruffy teenagers lolling about in the bar in their ski clothes.

In those days hot baths in Swiss hotels were not included in the board and lodging and were an expensive extra. For economy I shared my bath with two boys, both younger than me, and found it hard to bear that while they were dressing for dinner next door, I was having to get ready for bed. Every evening looking, I thought, very sophisticated in their new dinner jackets they would sit on my bed while, in my striped Viyella pyjamas, I was having my nursery supper of milk and biscuits. Besides describing in mouth-watering detail the feast that they were about to have downstairs, they regaled me with stories of the wilder shores of sex which they had certainly never visited and of which my knowledge was rudimentary or non-existent. These lurid accounts were punctuated with stern warnings about the dangers of self-abuse, a delight which I had only recently discovered and which I kept a deadly secret. Admittedly my comparative innocence made me fair game; but they were heartless boys who were obviously enjoying them-selves at my expense, and I was usually glad when, punctually at a quarter to eight, Aunt Eleanor appeared to say goodnight and 'settle me down'. Kneeling beside my bed, I would say my prayers: 'God bless mother and Frank and Benita; and Uncle Frank, Aunt Edith, Aunt Eleanor and Auntie May; lead me not into temptation and make me a good boy. Amen.' For social reasons Hetty, the family cook who looked after me at Longcross and to whom I was devoted, was not included in this litany. Nevertheless, beset as I was with the problems of puberty, my final supplication was both genuine and heartfelt.

Though sometimes unimaginative, as on this occasion, my Wilkinson aunts never meant to be unkind and were devoted to me. However, childless and in their late fifties these two spinsters were ill-equipped to deal with the day-to-day exigencies of an active schoolboy. This task fell to Hetty, the family cook. Hetty had begun her domestic service as a nursery-maid in a big house in the West Country and she knew how to deal with boys. For eight years she ruled my life at Longcross; got me up in the morning; bathed and put me to bed at night; saw to my clothes and decided what I was to wear; applied *Pomade Divine* to my bruises and iodine to my grazed knees. She also took a keen interest in my bowel movements, dosing me liberally with Syrup of Figs at the least sign of constipation. Best of all she liked to bath me and continued to do so, much to the amusement of my mother, who decided not to interfere, until long after I had gone to Rugby. No boy, Hetty used to grumble, could be trusted to wash himself properly. She attached great importance to personal cleanliness and, with the rigour of a Guards' sergeant major, would inspect my fingernails, my ears, my neck and my knees, before taking me downstairs to have tea with my aunts in the drawing room.

Poor Hetty had a serious disability: she was profoundly deaf. She had an ear-trumpet into which one bellowed without any certainty that the message was getting through and important communications had to be conveyed by writing on a school slate. So far as I was concerned, her deafness made protest or argument of any kind impossible. I simply had to do what she said or risk being sent to bed for disobedience. Over the years her attitude became increasingly authoritarian, or so I thought as I grew older, but I loved her dearly and cannot conceive what my time at Longcross would have been without her. Hetty rose daily at 5 a.m. to light the kitchen range and heat the water which was carried up to my aunts' bedrooms by the housemaid in polished brass cans. For boys of my age, cold baths every morning were obligatory and Hetty saw to it that I had mine although, in the Christmas holidays, she sometimes allowed a trickle of hot water to temper the shock. By the time I got back to my room, she had laid out my clothes for the day and vanished to the kitchen in order to cook breakfast. Besides bathing me and putting me to bed, Hetty had nightly to cook a three-course dinner for my uncle and aunts. She had half a day off on Sundays when I had to put myself to bed at half-past six and the housemaid brought me up my supper of bread and milk. Hetty had a fortnight's annual holiday and I think her wages with full board and lodging were forty pounds a year. I do not recall her ever being ill and she looked after my aunts until 1947 when they gave up Longcross and she retired to an old people's home in Cheltenham.

It was left to Hetty to decide what I was to wear and my clothing was unfashionable to say the least. At sixteen I still wore grey sweaters and shorts which were ordered regularly from Billings and Edmonds, the school outfitter, and sent down to Longcross on approval. I liked these clothes, which were both comfortable and practical. However, for tea in the drawing room with my aunts, I was expected to change under Hetty's supervision into a dark green jersey with knitted shorts to match and short white socks. These jerseys were knitted by Hetty by gas-light during the dark winter evenings and she used to present me with a new outfit every birthday. I would have given almost anything not to have had to wear these hateful garments, particularly on my birthday, but my aunts insisted on it for fear of hurting Hetty's feelings; my feelings apparently did not count and, as usual, I had to make the best of it. Nevertheless, Aunt Eleanor must have sensed my embarrassment for when older boys came to tea I was sometimes granted a dispensation.

For church on Sunday, instead of a sweater, I wore a grey flannel jacket to match my shorts. Aunt Eleanor, who was a church warden, made me wear an Eton collar so that, if needed, I could don a surplice and reinforce the choir or pump the organ. After Sunday lunch and my afternoon rest, I changed into my green outfit and set off for Sunday school. This I considered a monstrous imposition. When my uncle Claud had been alive he used to take me with him on Sunday afternoons to watch him playing golf or squash or even on long silent walks on Chobham Common. However, after his death, when I was thirteen, my aunts did not know what to do with me on Sunday afternoons and the vicar suggested that it would set a good example to the village if I attended Sunday school. On the first occasion Hetty insisted that I wore my Sunday suit; I knew this to be a mistake but there was no arguing. After school one of the other boys seized my straw hat and threw it into a tree from which it had to be retrieved by the sexton with a ladder, and when I got home I found that the boy sitting behind me had scrawled 'SHIT' in ink on my Eton collar which greatly distressed my aunt. From then on I wore my horrible green jersey suits and got on well enough with my classmates, who obviously regarded me as a freak. However, I did not set a good example and harassed the elderly governess who taught us scripture with indelicate questions. In consequence I often spent most of the afternoon standing in the corner in disgrace. Looking back, it seems pathetic that aged fifteen I was the terror of the Longcross Sunday school but, at the time, I felt victimized and rebellious and harboured most unChristian thoughts. After I had been confirmed by Archbishop Temple, my aunt and the vicar agreed that if I accompanied her to early communion I might be excused having to go to Sunday school.

For party clothes, I had a white sailor-suit, bought for my uncle Frank's wedding, which Hetty washed and starched though I had long since lost the hat with HMS *Victory* on its ribbon. I also had a page's outfit which I had worn at my aunt Edith's wedding and which consisted of dark green velvet shorts which buttoned on to a white shirt. All these garments had come from Rowe's of Bond Street, the leading children's outfitter of the day, and were almost impossible to grow out of so ingenious were the tucks, extra seams and turn-ups which could be let out almost infinitely. I preferred the sailor-suit, which at least had long trousers, but both my aunts and Hetty liked me best in my velvet shorts. 'Short trousers stop boys having big ideas' was one of Hetty's favourite maxims. Having to wear these horrible clothes cast a blight over any children's dance to which I was invited and I felt ridiculously self-conscious. In fact, the young Etonians in their well-cut dinner jackets paid little attention to me and were far too self-absorbed to notice my juvenile appearance. However, I lived in dread of meeting another Rugby boy but, though I had some narrow shaves, I never did. Dressed in my velvet shorts I dared not ask a girl to dance unless compelled to do so by some meddling grown-up. But in my sailor-suit I felt more confident and even spoke to the boys in dinner jackets, some of whom I found almost as shy of girls as I was. I sometimes noticed that grown-ups looked kindly at me and some even engaged me in conversation when I was standing alone. I used to hope that they would not try to force their children to be nice to me, as it nearly always ended in mutual embarrassment.

Looking back, my time at Longcross seems in many respects to have been a 'time-warp', and in reading accounts of Victorian childhoods I have often been struck by their resemblance to my own. However, any 'repressions' which I might have suffered were more than off-set by the complete freedom which I enjoyed when staying with my aunt May in Dorset and even more by my parents' cosmopolitan lifestyle of which my Wilkinson aunts so heartily disapproved. In any case I rarely spent more than a fortnight of my Christmas and Easter holidays at Longcross, which was not long enough to get me down.

At Studland my aunt May and her friend Jattie Welch had adopted what might now be called an 'alternative lifestyle'. On their return from France in 1919 they had added a number of small bedrooms to the Studio which they had built before the war. Water had still to be pumped by hand and there was an earth closet at the bottom of the garden but they had acquired numerous chickens, some goats, some rabbits and a donkey and, with their large garden now mainly turned over to vegetables, they were nearly self-supporting. The cooking was 'country French' and delicious and my aunt Jattie had inherited a fine cellar of claret from her father, who had been a wine-shipper in Bordeaux. The donkey, William, when harnessed to a coster's cart, provided the main means of locomotion and every morning at six o'clock he woke the household by poking his nose through the open bow window and braying. Though he usually rose to a crisis, William could at times be unco-operative and refuse to budge. In an emergency and as a last resort it was permitted to light a newspaper between his hind legs which usually galvanized him into motion. This was not a practice that was encouraged and the daily trip to the beach pulling a cart piled high with picnic things, bathing clothes and children too small to walk the distance, was usually accomplished without such drastic measures.

In the summer months the Studio used to be filled to overflowing with children of all ages but in the Christmas and Easter holidays I was usually the only child. Provided that I went to church on Sundays, turned up for meals and had an occasional bath, nobody seemed to mind very much what I did. However, I was not left entirely to my own devices, for my aunts were heavily involved in the village and there were always errands to be run as well as domestic chores to be done such as pumping the water, feeding the animals or milking the goats, a job I particularly disliked. My wardrobe was limited but I wore what I liked, there were no children's dances and bedtime was no problem. More often than not I stayed up late into the night listening to the grown-ups arguing about art and social politics. Whenever there was something they did not wish me to hear, such as the pioneer work of their friend Marie Stopes, they lapsed into French which was my aunt Jattie's native language.

There was a small community of artists at Studland, and friends of my aunts who had studied with them at the Slade before the war under Professor Tonks came to stay at the Studio from time to time. Consequently, much of the conversation was about art and about the new Cubist movement in particular. Nevertheless, neither May nor Jattie was in a mood to resume serious painting after their harrowing experiences in Flanders during the Great War. Instead they devoted themselves to the village which, in those days, before the building of the toll road across the moor, was virtually isolated. Mr Lovelace, the carrier, drove his horse and wagonette twice a week to Swanage which was about an hour distant and brought out any guests who had travelled down from London by train as well as groceries and other provisions; and there was a village shop which sold basic necessities. However, until the mid-1920s there was no taxi service and village life proceeded at a walking pace.

It took up to five hours to fetch the nearest doctor and my aunts' nursing skills were often in demand. In these emergencies I usually accompanied them at all hours of the day and night, even if it meant crossing the moor by lantern-light. My first task was to help catch and harness William. Then, having arrived at the scene, I had always to get a fire going, find the well and ensure that there was an ample supply of clean, boiling water for sterilizing instruments. These responsibilities made me feel grown-up and I enjoyed the excitement.

As soon as I had learned to swim I was allowed to take a rowing boat out by myself and explore the Old Harry rocks. I knew most of the boatmen and fishermen by name and they kept an eye on me. I was too big to ride William but, infuriated by his waywardness, my aunt Jattie had bought a New Forest pony which she harnessed to a governess cart and which I was allowed to ride. I also went for long solitary walks across the moor when the weather was fine. When it was wet I curled up by the stove and read any books I could lay hands on. There was a wide selection ranging from Edgar Wallace to Wyndham Lewis and Roger Fry and my aunts encouraged me to read them all. In the 1920s Cecil Sharp was all the rage and my aunt May introduced folk singing and folk dancing in the Women's Institute. Surprisingly unself-conscious in my cricket flannels, I found myself 'gathering peascods' in the village hall and setting to gigantic Dorset farmers' wives who were often remarkably nimble on their feet. As we danced we sang, 'If all the world was paper and all the sea was ink, and all the trees were bread and cheese, what would we have to drink?' I pondered this question as, hot and sweaty from my exertion but no longer shy, I walked home from the village hall in the clear and frosty moonlight. It was a far cry from the battlefields of Flanders. Nevertheless, in this quiet corner of Dorset, I was witnessing the sort of rural socialism which so many had dreamed of and some had died for in the Great War. I was infected by Aunt May's enthusiasm and shared her optimism that Jerusalem might yet be built in England's green and pleasant land.

About the time I went to Rugby, this idyll came abruptly to an end. A toll road had been built across the moor with a car ferry linking Studland with Sandbanks. There followed an influx of day-trippers and charabancs and the village lost its attraction for the poets and artists, most of whom migrated to the valley lying between Swanage and Corfe Castle. Here my aunt May found a derelict barn which she converted into a studio, while her friend Jattie Welch built a substantial house next door. Theirs was no longer an alternative lifestyle and I regretted their *embourgeoisement*. Nevertheless, they were still as generous and warm-hearted as ever. The winters at Langton Matravers were harsher than at Studland but I grew to love the roaring gales and the great seas smashing against the rocks at Dancing Ledge and Chapman's Pool. I used to go for long cross-country runs along the cliff-tops and, being now a romantic adolescent, the blustering wind and driving rain often suited my mood.

Freed from her involvement in village life, my aunt May started painting again and on a brief holiday with Paul Nash made one or two preliminary sketches for oil paintings, which she never completed. However, she exhibited watercolours at the Royal Academy Summer Exhibition in 1932 and 1933. Although she did not often discuss this with me, her main interest now lay in psychoanalysis and she became a disciple of Jung. She made several visits to Kussnacht to sit at the master's feet though without, I think, establishing her identity to her own satisfaction. She died of cancer in 1944 while I was behind the lines in Yugoslavia, and I remember deciphering the signal with a feeling of great sadness. Aunt May was, by far, the most important influence during my formative years; yet despite her intense humanity and her deeply-felt pacifism – for she knew the reality of war – she never tried to dissuade me from following my father into the army, though I know she deplored my choice. The motto which she inscribed over the door of the Barn was 'SEMPER AGENS, SEMPER QUIETUS'. Yet I felt that, unlike my aunt Eleanor, Aunt May never found the peace that she was seeking. There was always too much still to be done.

CHAPTER 4

Holidays with
my Parents

CONSIDERING everything, I saw quite a lot of my mother during my schooldays. My step-father was entitled to two months' home leave every other year, and in the alternate years, I went out to visit my parents in Alexandria. The excitement of these summer holidays more than made up for the disadvantage of having parents who lived abroad for the rest of the year. Besides, sometimes my mother came home for part of the Easter holidays as well. One Easter, she collected me from a family in Normandy where I was trying to learn French and took me off for a week in Paris. She herself spent most of the time with dress-makers as she was to be presented at Court that summer and needed what she insisted on calling a *robe de style* for the occasion. Under pressure, however, she took me to the *Folies Bergère* which I found sadly disappointing; also, to a performance of *Tannhäuser* at the Opéra. That evening was spoiled for me by her insistence on humming the better-known arias *sotto voce* but audibly, to my embarrassment and the annoyance of our neighbours. Also, I was wearing an Eton collar with a 'saw-edge' which was lacerating my neck. However, I remember (or am I dreaming it?) the elderly gentlemen promenading during the *entr'actes*, immaculate in their white tie and tails, wearing, of all things, bowler hats. For me, the highlight of our visit was a performance at the Madeleine of a revue starring Sacha Guitry and Yvonne Printemps. It had an elegance which I had never previously encountered and which I can only compare to the first post-war performance of *Cosi fan tutte* in Vienna in 1945.

For my last Easter holidays at Scaitcliffe, I went to meet my parents at Florence. Aged twelve, it was the first time I had travelled on the Continent entirely alone. I was given a packet of sandwiches for my lunch, but nobody thought to inquire whether I had any money for the rest of the journey. Thos. Cook had made a muddle and the foreign currency my mother had ordered had not been delivered to me before I left. All I had on me was the balance of my school pocket-money, amounting to seven shillings and sixpence. I changed five shillings of this on the cross-channel steamer to pay for the taxi across Paris and spent the remaining half-crown on breakfast in the Wagon restaurant while travelling through Switzerland. I was so bewitched by the sight of the mountains and lakes that I had no time to feel hungry. At Milan, where I had to change trains, I was met by a smiling courier with a bundle of banknotes. My financial stability now assured, I bought a huge ham roll on which I subsisted for the next six hours until I was met by my parents.

Next morning I was woken very early by the church bells and, opening my shutters, saw Florence for the first time stretched out before me in all its magic, rosy and gold in the morning light. I have often been to Florence since but have never been able to recapture that first enchanted moment. Armed with E. V. Lucas's *A Wanderer in Florence*, we spent our days like any other tourists. I was too young to understand the *cinquecento* paintings, but I fell in love with the bustle of the streets and the quiet of the churches and have remained so ever since. I had been given a Zeiss Ikonta camera with which I photographed everything in sight; one of these photographs winning me a prize in a children's competition organized by the *Morning Post*. After ten days' sight-seeing, my parents hired a car and we drove to Assisi, Perugia and Siena (where I was to spent four months during the Second World War). Then, after five days in Venice, we put up at a hotel on Lake Garda, in sight of d'Annunzio's preposterous villa, protruding from the hillside in the shape of the bows of a destroyer. From Gardone Riviera, my step-father had to return to Egypt, leaving me to look after my mother who had caught a chill in Venice and was now running a high tempera-ture. Against the advice of the Italian doctor, who unwisely called her hysterical, my mother insisted on returning to England. We had a horrible journey, sitting up all night in the second-class and, by the time we got to Paris, she was feeling very ill indeed. However, she bravely continued the journey and, after leaving her in a nursing home in London, I collected my school trunk and returned to Scaitcliffe. For a boy of barely thirteen, it had been quite an adventure. However, these two holidays were exceptional and I usually spent my Easter quietly either in Dorset or at Longcross.

My holidays in Egypt were nearly as exciting and a more regular feature. It was wonderful to leave Victoria on a rainy August morning, to have supper at the Gare de Lyon, and to wake up with the train racketing through the sunny vineyards of Provence. At Marseilles, after a wild taxi ride to the docks, we boarded ship. I had read *The Count of Monte Cristo* and thought it thrilling when we came up from lunch to recognize the Château d'If on our starboard bow. The rest of the six-day voyage was equally romantic. After sailing between Corsica and Sardinia we passed under the lee of Stromboli, my first sight of an active volcano. In the Straits of Messina, between Sicily and Italy, we made a stately S-turn to avoid the perils of Scylla and Charybdis. On the following day we sighted Crete, rich with legends of the Minotaur, where, in May 1941, I was to witness the German airborne invasion. In those days, Latin and Greek took up a major part of a preparatory school curriculum, but although for me this passage down the Mediterranean put flesh on the dry bones of the *Aeneid*, it did nothing for my Latin verses which were so nearly to sink me in my Common Entrance.

None of us children slept much the last night and we were on deck at dawn to watch the ship gliding inside the breakwater at Port Said. Sadly, on my first visit, when I was ten years old, I had no chance to see the carpet-sellers displaying 'antique' prayer mats made in Axminster or to watch the gully gully men making their pitch on deck and plucking baby chicks from the pockets of unsuspecting Australians; for I was travelling with the wife of a senior customs official and our ship had hardly dropped anchor before a sleek green launch was nosing its way through the bum-boats to come alongside with faultless boat-drill and take us off. Soon, to the envy of the other children who had to await passport and customs formalities, we were speeding our way across the harbour. After luncheon, we were taken to the station in a large Buick with two burly Egyptian policemen in the front seat, behind which was slung a Lee-Enfield rifle ready for the passengers' use in an emergency. The Scaitcliffe playing-fields seemed very far away.

To begin with, our train ran parallel to the Suez Canal, and I was fascinated by the sight of great ships proceeding at walking pace or moored to the bank to let others pass. Our white shirts and shorts were grey with the dust and sand which came through every crevice, even in the dining-car. At Zagazig, where we changed trains, I saw a convict manacled to an armed policeman. No one took any notice of him and he looked so forlorn that I was suddenly overcome with immense compassion. After we had crossed the Nile, the country became more fertile. The fields of Indian corn were criss-crossed with irrigation canals; patient oxen turned water-wheels and diminutive donkeys with enormous loads trotted along the bank. Our escort could not forbear telling

us that the scene had scarcely changed since biblical times, but she
failed to break the spell.

The joy of our arrival at Sidi Gabr station is indescribable and there
followed two of the most blissful hours I can remember: the rapturous
greetings, the cold shower to wash off the journey's dust, the gala
supper and, finally, bed cocooned in a mosquito net and cool in a pair
of silk pyjamas which had belonged to my father. I knew that, at last,
I had come home.

For an English boy used to grey skies and holidays at the mercy of
the weather, the Mediterranean climate was miraculous: the sun shone
every day and the sea was so warm that one could bathe indefinitely.
The weeks passed in a succession of beach parties, sailing picnics and
other entertainments and our parents vied with each other in their
efforts to make up for the holidays which they had missed. My step-
father owned a sailing dinghy and there were races twice a week at the
Yacht Club; he also had two ponies and, in those days, it was possible
to ride all the way to Sidi Bishr and beyond, where the beach was
empty except for a cluster of beach huts belonging to members of the
British community. At the Sporting Club there was polo and racing at
weekends and, if you liked it, tennis and cricket; which I did not. Then,
without warning, in mid-September the idyll ended as suddenly as it
had begun; trunks were packed and farewells said for another nine
months. I cannot remember how often I said goodbye to my mother on
Sidi Gabr station but the last time was in the middle of the Second
World War; for nearly twenty years, it was a recurrent feature in my
life. Morale was low as far as Zagazig where we changed trains but
picked up after supper in the dining-car. On arrival at Port Said, we
went straight on board and to bed and, by the time we woke up next
morning, we were already at sea.

As on the voyage out, the ship was crowded with children and I
should have felt sorry for the passengers who had paid full fare. When
I inadvertently squirted an elderly gentleman with a water pistol, I was
sent before the Captain. This was an unnerving experience, but having
threatened to 'put me in the brig' if I misbehaved again, he took me up
to the bridge and, for a full minute, let me steer the ship.

Escorts across France were hard to find on the journey home, and
when I was ten I had to travel 'long sea' via Gibraltar and the Bay of
Biscay. However, later on, I was allowed to travel across France with an
older boy; later still I was the older boy myself. From sixteen onwards,
I generally travelled by the Lloyd Triestino line which sailed direct to
Alexandria and saved three days. This meant embarking at Venice,

Trieste or Brindisi. I particularly liked Venice where I used to be rowed out to the ship in a gondola.

I do not think that anybody who did not experience them can imagine the delight of those summer holidays in Egypt between the wars. However, I was to find Alexandria as a young *lycéen* not nearly as much fun. When my mother took me away from Rugby, Canon Bonhote had recommended sending me to a crammer's establishment at Bonn to learn German. However, my step-father pointed out that I would certainly spend my time in the nightclubs in Cologne which was still occupied by the British Army, and that I would do better to come out to Egypt and learn French. Accordingly, I was told to buy a third-class passage to Port Said and, after Christmas at Longcross, I embarked on a P & O cargo ship bound for Australia with a full complement of emigrants.

I could not see any likely fellow passenger on the grubby train that I boarded at Liverpool Street that January afternoon. At Tilbury I was lucky enough to find an ancient taxi on to which I loaded my trunk, and we set out to look out for my ship. The docks, lit by flickering gas-lamps, were almost deserted and a sea fog was swirling in from the river; it was a scene which Joseph Conrad might have described. It took some time to discover my ship and first impressions were not reassuring. I shared my cabin with two young Australians in their mid-twenties whose personal habits I found uncouth. As instructed by my mother, I slept with my money in a money-belt and kept my luggage locked. By the time we reached the Bay of Biscay, my cabin companions were very sick indeed. I was not and had to look after them so we became mates. There was plenty of food of the boarding-house variety which I washed down with tea since I did not have enough money to get regularly drunk on beer like the others. I doubt whether my pristine Old Rugbeian tie, of which I was so proud, was recognized by my fellow travellers. Although we became quite friendly, I was thankful to say goodbye to them when we reached Port Said.

Two days after my arrival, having discarded my Old Rugbeian tie and suitably attired in blue shorts and a blue-and-white striped jersey, I was taken by my mother to be interviewed by the Proviseur of the Lycée Français d'Alexandrie. It had been established by the Mission Laïque and my mother had chosen it in preference to the College where she feared I might think the Catholic discipline oppressive, though I might have made more suitable friends there. My interview was short; I recited the *Stances de Polyeucte* which was the only piece of classical

French that I knew by heart and the Proviseur took me to the second form and left me to my fate. I never saw him again. Most of my form-mates were Levantine Jews, but there was also a small group of French boys who kept to themselves, a sprinkling of Greeks and Egyptians and two cheerful Turks with whom I immediately made friends. Their average age was fifteen. I managed to keep up with the lessons with some difficulty but I was overwhelmed by the amount of homework which we were set. I stayed the better part of two terms at the Lycée and acquired a fair smattering of schoolboy French. My mother then arranged for me to have private lessons with a voluble Frenchwoman from Versailles, married to a Greek naval lieutenant whom she considered her social inferior. Mme Pakudaki came every day and introduced me to the history and literature of the *Grand Siècle* with such success that, when I went to Cambridge, I gained, much to the surprise of my supervisor, a respectable second class in Part I of my Tripos without having attended a single lecture.

On weekdays I was not allowed to go out in the evening unless I had finished my homework; which meant never. However, at weekends there were no constraints and I attended a succession of fabulous dances given by the Anglo-Greek cotton magnates with a show of opulence which quite outclassed most of the debutante parties I was later to attend in London. However, in my innocence, I found myself critical of this sophisticated, selfish and pleasure-loving society, so brilliantly des-cribed by Lawrence Durrell in his *Alexandria Quartet*. I had a bad start; at my first dance I knew nobody and had a horrible evening although I bravely pretended to enjoy it. I was, therefore, thankful when a young woman offered to drive me home for, under Egyptian law, at seventeen I was still too young to have a driving licence. After a short distance, she stopped the car on a piece of wasteland, leaving me in no doubt of what she expected of me. Boarding-school life at Rugby and holidays with my aunts had not prepared me for this unexpected development; I said goodnight and walked the rest of the way home. My diffidence clearly disconcerted my seductress and I was only later to discover that she was a notorious nymphomaniac who later succeeded in comprom-ising an unfortunate naval commander. I thought it better not to tell my mother of this adventure lest she should think me too young for grown-up parties.

In springtime when the desert is brilliant with flowers, my parents liked to go camping. Together with some English, American and Dutch friends, they had rented a disused carpet factory built in the Italianate style on the edge of the desert at Bourg el Arab, some three or four hours' drive from Alexandria. Here they formed a desert club where they could leave their tents and heavy kit. In those days before the Cairo–Alexandria road was built, the desert began at the Mex Gate, and there was only a rough desert track which had to be negotiated carefully with a full car. After spending the night at Bourg el Arab to collect our kit, we used to make expeditions into the desert within a radius of about 100 miles and I became quite an experienced desert driver. In the summer, when the weather was too hot for excursions into the desert, we used to pitch our camp on the beach at Sidi Abdel Rachman and spend the weekend bathing. Who could have foretold that that lovely curving bay with its silver sand and blue-green sea was destined, ten years later, to become the northern flank of the Battle of Alamein.

With the beginning of the summer holidays and the arrival of my schoolboy friends from England, there was the usual round of teenage entertainments in which I participated for the last time. However, these beach picnics and treasure hunts no longer had the magic of earlier years. My sister Cecile, seventeen years younger than me, had been born the previous spring and my mother was too taken up with nursery matters to have much time to spare for Benita and me. In any case, I was no longer a schoolboy and she felt no need to make up for missed holidays.

In mid-September when the time came once again to say goodbye at Sidi Gabr station, I felt that both my parents were thankful no longer to have to deal with a tiresome eighteen-year-old. As for me, the delights of Cambridge beckoned and I was on my way.

CHAPTER 5

Cambridge

I HAD not particularly wanted to prolong my education by going to a university; or to put my mother to this extra expense, for at Sandhurst as a King's Cadet – that is, the son of an officer killed in action – I could have been educated for nothing. However, my mother insisted that I should go to Cambridge even though my step-father's contract with the Egyptian government had not been renewed and money was very short. Not for the first time she did what was best for me at considerable personal sacrifice. Cambridge undoubtedly changed my life, though not perhaps in the direction she intended for she hoped that at a university I would lose my interest in a military career.

Instead of King's College, of which two of my great-uncles had been Fellows, she chose Corpus Christi where her cousin, Terence Sanders, a former Cambridge rowing blue, had recently become a Fellow. Moreover, Canon Bonhote had assured her that at Corpus I would be required to work hard and would be less likely to make expensive friends than if I were at Trinity or Magdalene which had been her first choice. On both counts I managed to disappoint them. I chose the easy option of doing Part I of the Modern & Mediaeval Language Tripos in two years instead of in one. This was short-sighted for it meant that, unless I were to stay up for a fourth year, I had only one year instead of two for Part II. In these circumstances, I judged that I could not possibly complete my modern language Tripos and opted for Military Studies which, like estate management, was known throughout the university to be a last resort for dunderheads. For me the main drawback was that, in my last year, I no longer had the freedom to go to lectures as I chose (which meant virtually never) but, like a schoolboy, was compelled to attend every class. Given my previous record, this was probably no bad thing and, narrowly failing to get a first class, I nevertheless passed top of the University Candidates and was awarded an Army Council scholarship on first appointment. I do not propose to dwell on my time at Cambridge, which was all too typical of its kind. I joined the Cavalry Squadron and the Pitt Club and affected a style of living which I was not used to and could ill afford. However, after three years, I emerged with much worldly wisdom, half a dozen life-long friends, an ability to play poker within my means and an elementary knowledge of the points of a horse. These attainments, so expensively acquired, came in more useful when I joined my regiment than the modern and medieval French and German which I studied with so little enthusiasm during my first and second years. Although it was the view held by the College authorities and by my step-father, it would be wrong to say that my time at Cambridge was entirely wasted.

In the previous century my uncle Frank had been a Royal Fusilier, the regiment which I, too, hoped to join. During my first year at Corpus the Colonel of the Regiment, General Sir Reginald Pinney, an old friend and contemporary of my uncle's, invited me to lunch at the Wellington Club and then insisted on introducing me personally to his tailor, his boot-maker, and his breeches-maker. I took this as an almost unprecedented act of confidence, which perhaps it was, though I later learned that my uncle also patronized these establishments so the financial risk was comparatively small. On the strength of General Pinney's introduction, I ordered my first expensive blue suit at Pulford's in St James's Street which proved a very wise investment. A few days later, I received a charming letter from the General saying that he had put me on his 'list' and inviting me to stay at Racedown, his house in Dorsetshire. He also promised to arrange for me to be attached, the following summer, to the 2nd Battalion Royal Fusiliers at Pembroke Dock.

In your second year at Cambridge you were allowed a motor car and life became even more hectic than before. However, my German being nowhere near as good as my French, I felt obliged to spend part of the winter vac. in 1933 in Freiburg-im-Breisgau. I stayed with a certain Freifrau von Kornberg who was living in extremes of genteel poverty with her elderly unmarried daughter who was to coach me in German and who had given up her own bedroom to accommodate me. In the short time I knew her, I grew very fond of Baroness Kornberg. This frail old lady whose husband had been killed in the Great War was both charming and proud, assuring me that her husband's title, being 'Reichsunmittelbar' and received from Charlemagne, was, therefore, impeccable. I was, I fear, a sad disappointment on every count. She had hoped for a rich and titled young Englishman of the sort who stayed with her friend, Countess Romberg, while studying for the Foreign Office exam and who paid handsomely for their board and German lessons. Instead she found that I was almost as poor as she was, though she was far too well-bred to show her disappointment. In her freezing sitting room, for she could not afford to heat the stove until the evening, we sometimes crouched over her antiquated wireless while she recounted how the first time that she had heard the piece of music we were listening to, had been in the company of some vanished princeling whose world, like hers, had crashed with the defeat of Germany in 1918. I found such reminiscences far more instructive than the arid history lessons delivered by her daughter. On one occasion Baroness Kornberg arranged a tea party for me to meet people of my own age. They were children of her friends and relations and I found them very agreeable and easy to get on with. Among them were two young officers in the Reiter SS, with elegant black uniforms and well-cut riding boots. They joined with the others in jokes about Hitler, and Baroness Kornberg later explained that belonging to the Reiter SS was the next best thing to being a cavalry officer. She added that, terrible as it was to have a corporal as Reichskanzler, Hitler's policies had, at least, saved millions of young Germans, like her young friends, from unemployment and despair. My other encounters with young Nazis were in youth hostels on the Feldberg where, like me, cheerful groups of Hitler *Jugend* used to spend the night. Our conversation was mostly about skiing but I found I had far more in common with them than with the spotty Levantine schoolboys at my French Lycée. Unduly conscious of the apparent injustices of the Treaty of Versailles, I was attracted to the Hitler movement which seemed to bring a sense of order and purpose to these young people which was absent from the lives of my English friends and contemporaries. My family had had previous connections with Germany. My great-uncle Charles had been Dr Keate's favourite pupil at Eton and later, as a junior master and Keate's curate, he had had to accompany the headmaster when he had personally flogged 200 boys in one night after the Eton Rebellion in 1832. Legend has it that my great-uncle had mixed up the lists so that the Doctor started by flogging the confirmation candidates. Be that as it may, when asked by Queen Victoria to recommend an Anglican domestic chaplain for the King of Hanover, Keate had suggested my great-uncle, who spent the rest of his life at the Hanoverian Court. Because of this, my father, before being sent to an army crammer for the Sandhurst exam, had received his secondary education at a *Gymnasium* at Heidelberg where he had remained until he was sixteen. Nevertheless, my aunts, desolated by his death, had no friendly feelings for the Germans, and let me know they thought my sympathy for the Huns was misplaced.

Attachment that summer to the 2nd Battalion, Royal Fusiliers at Pembroke Dock proved a less intimidating experience than I had expected, though I made a bad start. Arriving on the eve of the Eton and Harrow match, at dinner that night I expressed surprise that anyone had gone to Harrow when they might just as easily have gone to Eton. Nobody demurred. It was only later that I discovered that all but one of those 'dining-in' that night had been at Harrow. I can only think that they agreed with me. Fortunately the majority of the officers of the battalion had been at either Oxford or Cambridge and were more indulgent than they might have been had they come from Sandhurst. I was immensely impressed by the smartness and sheer efficiency in which the business of the battalion was conducted; nothing short of perfection was accepted. Inside the mess, relations were as informal as you could have wished, but on parade there was no nonsense. As an attached officer, I was exempt from the punishments inflicted on other subalterns who made mistakes and, in any case, I tried my utmost to make a good impression for I had set my heart on being accepted. I had excellent mentors; my company commander, who had won the Military Cross in the Great War, had been educated at Harrow and Trinity, Cambridge, and spoke excellent French, German and Spanish; while my platoon commander, who had won the Sword of Honour at Sandhurst, was the son of the new Colonel of the Regiment, an outstanding athlete and by far the most efficient subaltern in the battalion. Platoon and company training were in full swing when I arrived and the daily excursions into the lush Pembrokeshire countryside and the occasional nights spent in the open under the stars were pure delight. Even church parade, wearing my father's sword, was a pleasure, such was my youthful enthusiasm. In that summer of 1934, in a military backwater like Pembroke Dock, there was a pre-1914 atmosphere about our training programme. Horse-drawn limbers galloped purposefully up the dusty Pembrokeshire lanes while we marched and counter-marched, occasionally running in short bursts up some hill to attack an imaginary enemy. Instead of appalling me, this military make-believe appealed strongly to my sense of fantasy and I imagined stout Germans in Pickelhaube emerging from their positions with their hands up shouting 'kamarad'. On the only afternoon that I was acting orderly officer, there was a fire directly in front of the deserted officers' mess. Fortunately, the situation was immediately taken under control by an extremely competent sergeant major who, while appearing to look to me for orders, took matters very firmly into his own hands; organizing the chain of buckets so effectively that I was later, somewhat wryly, congratulated on my performance by the adjutant.

I got through my six weeks without disgracing myself and returned to Cambridge in a martial mood. This was just as well since I was about to abandon my Arts curriculum for the more mundane military studies. Nevertheless, after my attachment, I felt a greater sense of purpose than I had previously and, admittedly under compulsion, worked far harder than I had at my modern and medieval languages. However, I failed to cover the syllabus as I spent half the Easter term in bed with glandular fever and, consequently, did not obtain a first class as I had hoped.

Our Director of Studies had very sensibly arranged for our exams to be held at the beginning of the summer term and we were consequently able to enjoy our final weeks at Cambridge in utter idleness and dissipation. After the May Week balls where I and my friends, like many others, behaved in a manner unbecoming to officers and gentlemen, we left for camp with the Cavalry Squadron at Shorncliffe. We were attached to the 15/20th Hussars who were models of efficiency and who were shocked by our stable management. I confess that I was very envious of my friends, nearly all of whom were joining cavalry regiments. However, the cavalry and, for that matter, the Diplomatic Service required a private income which was quite beyond my parents' means and I knew I was far better off in a good infantry regiment. Before we finally dispersed, Michael Grissell, who was joining the 10th Hussars, and Paul Makins, who was destined for the Welsh Guards, gave about six of us a splendid lunch at Boodle's as a fitting conclusion to our military studies.

I spent that last summer vacation with my parents in Egypt, travelling out as cheaply as I could as a deck passenger in a Lloyd Triestino cargo ship via the Dalmatian coast, Athens and Rhodes. In a multi-cultural society like Alexandria, people were more conscious of the worsening international situation than we were in England. Adolf Hitler had yet to remilitarize the Rhineland but Mussolini was already flexing his muscles. Our house was opposite the summer residence of the Italian Ambassador. While sitting at dinner on our terrace, my parents and I used to watch a procession of self-important little men hurrying up and down the Ambassador's steps, greeting each other with ridiculous fascist salutes, conferring and gesticulating and behaving in an excited way. Seen from a distance, it was rather like a silent Marx Brothers' film and hard to take seriously. More sinister were the ship-loads of Italian soldiers on their way to Abyssinia which I saw when embarking at Port Said for my journey home. My recent experiences in Germany, in Italy and now in Egypt, not to mention the activities of the peace movement which I had encountered at Cambridge, all convinced me that, unless the Great Powers changed direction, war was inevitable. The prospect did not worry me for, in September 1935, I had been gazetted as a 2nd Lieutenant in the Royal Fusiliers.

CHAPTER 6

Regimental Life,
1935–37

M Y motives for joining the army were mixed. Certainly there was
an element of family tradition, for my grandfather and two of his
brothers had been generals and my father and my uncle Frank had
both been regular soldiers. However, a more compelling reason was
that in 1935 Britain was only just recovering from the great depression
and jobs were very hard to find. My Rugby headmaster, Dr W. W.
Vaughan, had told my mother, in my hearing, that I had not the slightest
chance of entering the Diplomatic Service; I had no vocation for the
Church like my great-uncle Charles, the King of Hanover's domestic
chaplain; nor was I attracted to the law like my great-uncle Hindley, a
fellow of Eton and of King's College, Cambridge, and reputed, in his
time, to have been the cleverest boy in the school except for W. E.
Gladstone, the future Prime Minister. Apart from my uncle Claud who
had been an unsuccessful stockbroker, I had no family connections with
the City. Perhaps the deciding factor was that it seemed to me futile to
start any civilian career which, in a few years' time, was bound to be
interrupted by the European war which I believed to be inevitable. I
cannot pretend that I ever saw myself as a fighting man; and although
G. A. Henty had been one of my favourite authors as a boy, I harboured
no heroic fantasies. On the contrary, at Cambridge I had read *All Quiet
on the Western Front* both in German and in English and, during a short
course on French literature at the Sorbonne in 1933, my professor had
urged me to read Louis-Ferdinand Céline's *Voyage au bout de la nuit*. Both
books, coming on top of my reading of Siegfried Sassoon and Robert
Graves and the literature of the Great War which I devoured, had left
me in no doubt about the horrors of modern warfare. While I found
this prospect terrifying, I seemed certain to have to face it sooner or
later whatever I decided to do, and meanwhile the prospect of peacetime
soldiering appealed to me. In my regiment I was assured of congenial

companions; the work was far from taxing and mainly in the open air; and there was ample opportunity for foreign travel and for the field sports which I could not otherwise afford. Moreover, the regiment provided the sort of family background which I needed as a rootless young man with no home in England and no close relations of my own age. On balance, I reckoned that I was likely to have more fun as a soldier than as a civilian. To my surprise, this view was shared by my tutor, Kenneth Pickthorn, though he warned me that soldiering was a job for boys and that I would sicken of it by the time I was thirty. All these thoughts were in my mind during the 250-mile drive to Pembroke Dock.

I had chosen to arrive in the middle of the afternoon when I knew that the mess would be deserted. Notwithstanding my attachment to the battalion during the previous summer, I felt all the apprehensions of a new boy. However, my morale was temporarily lifted, for on the writing table on which I inscribed my visiting cards – one to the Lieutenant Colonel cmdg and one to the officers of the 2nd Battalion Royal Fusiliers – I noticed a silver calendar and saw that it had been presented to the officers of the 4th Battalion Royal Fusiliers by Captain O. C. Wilkinson, East Yorkshire Regiment. Whether this link with my father was the act of a thoughtful mess sergeant or sheer serendipity, I do not know; nor do I remember ever seeing the calendar again. However, at the time I took it as a good augury and a sign of my father's approval.

Besides myself, the young entry consisted of Tommy Chamberlayne who had been at Cambridge with me and whom I already knew; Roger Zambra from the regiment's Supplementary Reserve; and George Hodgson and Ian Hope Johnstone from Sandhurst. Together we spent our first six weeks dressed in denim overalls, being drilled until we nearly dropped by a ruthless, but always respectful, colour sergeant. Irritated by the two Sandhurst boys who pretended that they knew all the drill already, he saw to it that I and Tommy were first and second regardless of merit when the time came for us to be 'passed off the square' by the adjutant.

Tommy and I were posted to Christopher Kingsford-Lethbridge's machine-gun company which, though we found it irksome at the time, was fortunate for us for he was one of the company commanders who took his soldiering seriously. Educated at Wellington and Oxford himself, he had no illusions about university candidates and chased us mercilessly. I did not particularly relish commanding a machine-gun platoon and developed a strong dislike for the Vickers machine-gun Mk 2 with which we were armed and which was a relic of the Great War. Nevertheless, it had its compensations, for machine-gun platoon commanders were entitled to a horse. Moreover, during the summer we camped for a fortnight on Salisbury Plain to practise our field firing which was a welcome change from Pembroke Dock and an excuse for a weekend in London.

During the winter months, which were devoted to 'individual training', company officers usually worked only in the mornings except when orderly officer, which came round about once a fortnight. Young officers were encouraged (actually compelled) to hunt at least once a fortnight and many afternoons were spent schooling the light-draught horses to negotiate the Pembrokeshire banks. Tommy Chamberlayne had brought his own horse, a good-looking chestnut, and he thereby acquired merit in the eyes of senior officers, but the rest of us were dependent on the thirty-odd horses, comprising officers' chargers and light-draught, all of them chosen as potential hunters, which made up the battalion's establishment. These were allotted to those of us who had no horses of our own and we paid fifteen shillings a month for them as well as a contribution towards their extra forage. We also paid ten shillings a month for our grooms during the hunting season. In the close Pembrokeshire countryside we got on very nearly as well on our 'fifteen-bobbers' as Tommy did on his valuable hunter, which was unused to the Pembrokeshire banks.

Besides the married officers' wives on whom new arrivals were required to call at the earliest opportunity, having ascertained beforehand that they would be 'at home', we were given the names of the local gentry on whom it was worth our while to call. Many of these Pembrokeshire families were odd, some were very odd indeed, but they were extremely hospitable and we were never short of invitations to dine or shoot or, in the summer, to play tennis or fish. It was taken for granted that most of them had daughters of marriageable age but I am afraid that none of us rose to the occasion. In return we asked their fathers to dine in the mess. These invitations were popular for we had an excellent French chef and our dinners were greatly superior to the average country-house fare. They were also expensive and the cost weighed heavily on some of the younger members of the mess, whose Army pay of ten shillings a day covered only the bare necessities of life. For the rest we depended upon whatever private income our parents allowed us. The Royal Fusiliers was a moderately expensive regiment and there were guidelines set by the Colonel of Regiment as to parental contributions. Some of us had considerably more than the recommended minimum but others, including me, managed on less. However, this disparity of wealth was not very noticeable except when it came to motor cars or horses. My mother allowed me one hundred and eighty pounds a year (which, in modern terms, would be something in excess of five thousand pounds). This was somewhat below the minimum recommended allowance but I also had my Army Council scholarship. This was worth fifty pounds a year for five years and by the time it expired I was already a major and financially secure.

The battalion had no motor transport so a private car was essential. Moreover, young officers were expected to have a wide variety of sporting equipment. Here I was fortunate for I had my father's 12-bore shotgun and two of his Sowter saddles. I also had my uncle Claud's split-cane trout rods and his golf clubs. From my Cambridge days I had squash and tennis rackets and, more important, black hunting boots and brown cavalry field boots. Fitting out a young officer was expensive. The army outfit allowance barely covered the cost of two suits of service dress and a regimental greatcoat. Mess kit, blue patrols, riding breeches and a host of other essentials all had to be paid for by one's parents. Moreover, all were of regulation pattern and could be obtained only at the most expensive tailors and outfitters and these items were inspected by the adjutant of the depot to ensure that they fitted properly. In my case the inspection was carried out by Walter White Thomson and was hilarious though none the less rigorous since not for nothing was the Royal Fusiliers known as the 'Shining Seventh'. Unexpectedly, my uncle Frank produced seventy pounds towards the cost of my uniform (the equivalent of more than two thousand pounds at present-day values) which paid, among other things, for a tweed knicker-bocker suit for shooting and a black hunting coat, for one was not permitted to go out in 'ratcatcher' as I had as an undergraduate. My father's tailor wrote to me to say that he still had his scarlet full-dress tunic. To my surprise, I found that this fitted me perfectly and only needed the regimental facings changed. I wore this in 1936 when I attended a levee at St James's Palace 'on first appointment' and felt proud to be wearing it and my father's sword, engraved with his crest, when making my ceremonial bow to His Majesty King Edward VIII who, I remember, looked remarkably bored by the whole proceedings. Anyhow, it was fun walking down Pall Mall in a bearskin hat.

On the whole I enjoyed all this dressing up in the same way that I enjoyed the Edwardian extravagance of the regimental silver with which the groaning dining-room table was loaded on Band Nights. It was as completely unrelated to the mud and blood of the Flanders trenches as it was to the hunger-marches of contemporary England or, for that matter, to Hitler's reoccupation of the Rhineland or to the Spanish Civil War, and I was fascinated by the *surréalisme* of the situation which was so peculiarly British. This peculiarity also fascinated Captain Ulrich von Salviati, the German officer who was attached to the battalion for three months in 1937. Twenty years later, when I was the Political Counsellor at the British Embassy in Bonn, I invited Salviati to lunch. He told me that in 1944 he had commanded a regiment at Monte Cassino where two battalions of the Royal Fusiliers were engaged and he had found it impossible to reconcile the latter's dogged professionalism with the indolence and extravagance which he remembered from his attachment to the 2nd Battalion before the war. It only went to show, he ruefully admitted, how difficult it had been for the German Army to understand the nonchalance of the pre-war British officer whom they had so greatly underrated.

In the army reorganization of 1936, the Royal Fusiliers was one of those chosen to be converted from an infantry to a machine-gun and anti-tank gun regiment. It was not a prospect which was viewed with much enthusiasm and, in the autumn of that year, the battalion moved from Pembroke Dock to Shorncliffe where our horses were taken from us and we were issued with 15-hundredweight trucks and 'motorized'. Though I was not in any sense a horsey man, this transformation marked the end of my honeymoon with regimental soldiering. At Pembroke Dock we had lived in a world of our own, apparently little affected by the Great War or by the depression or, indeed, by anything which happened outside this 'little England beyond Wales'. It was a way of life which I had found extremely agreeable, where outside pressures were minimal and where I had plenty of time and opportunity to follow my own pursuits. At Shorncliffe I was confronted with the horror of garrison life from which there seemed to be no escape. I was kept extremely busy for I was one of the few officers who had attended both machine-gun and anti-tank gun courses but I took little pleasure in my work as I disliked the Vickers 2-pound anti-tank gun almost as much as the Vickers Mk 2 machine-gun. Even a day's hunting offered no escape. The field consisted mainly of members of the garrison and their wives and families. Fortunately, sailing was not in those days a 'recognized' army sport. George Hodgson and I bought a small sailing dinghy which we kept and raced at the Royal Cinque Ports Yacht Club at Dover which was not patronized by the Shorncliffe Garrison. When it came to small boat sailing, Dover Harbour was not a patch on Milford Haven but at least one got away from the army.

While fox hunting with the East Kent Hounds was far less fun than

with the South Pembrokeshire, there were compensations in the shape
of several point-to-point meetings within reasonable distance of Shorncliffe in which we were encouraged to take part. I was a complete
beginner and was usually thankful if I got round the course safely,
though, on one memorable occasion at Brabourne, most of the other
horses in front of me having fallen, I found that I had come in third.
My first ride was at the Ashford Valley meeting at Charing and I well
remember getting my horse out of its box in a slippery siding at Charing
station, a siding which has now become a housing estate. In 1963 my
wife and I bought a house with a windmill on the top of Charing Hill
and I have used Charing station regularly for the last thirty years and
each time I remember this frosty morning in 1937 when my world was
still young.

   That year I had taken my 'hunting leave' at Garmisch-Partenkirchen
in Bavaria. There was a cheap hotel, run on youth hostel lines, called
the Kreuzeckhaus halfway up the Zugspitz much patronized by students
from Munich. Here I fell in with a very congenial party of British
expatriates who had been expelled from Shanghai by the Japanese and
were making their way back to England by easy stages. The party
consisted of Edward Ward who had been the Reuter's representative in
Shanghai and was later destined to become one of the best-known war
correspondents in the Western Desert and later still the 7th Viscount
Bangor; Maisie Middleton who was in due course to become his second
wife; and Rupert Bibby, a scion of a wealthy Liverpool shipping family.
All this I discovered later but when I first met them they had a three-
bunked room next door to mine and all were flat broke. While waiting
for his next remittance Rupert had been living for the last two days on
dry bread rolls and tea water. They were the perfect antidote to garrison
life at Shornecliffe and, in their company, I realized with something of
a shock how stuffy and conventional I had become during the short
time I had been in the army. It was kind of them to let me tag along,
for I was considerably younger and a great deal less sophisticated than
they were. However, besides being broke they were obviously rather
bored with each other's company and enjoyed pulling my leg and trying
to shock me. During that winter leave I had plenty of time to consider
my position and the fortnight spent with 'Tweaks' Ward and his friends
brought home to me how right my mother had been in trying to
persuade me that there were certainly more amusing and probably more
rewarding ways of spending my life or, for that matter, losing it than as
a regimental officer in a line regiment. However, as the war clouds
gathered, so the choice narrowed as far as I was concerned.

The previous autumn my application for three months' approved language leave to study German, followed by attachment to a German regiment, had been turned down by my colonel on the reasonable ground, which I accepted, that for the time being I was needed in the battalion as a machine-gun and anti-tank gun instructor. However, I continued working for my German interpretership exam. I had already taken my French exam in which I had gained 93 per cent and a first class and if I could not obtain official sponsorship I proposed to take my German exam in the same way, though in this case I would forfeit any chance of the attachment to a German regiment on which I had set my heart. The *101 Gebirgsjaegerregiment* was giving its recruits elementary ski-training on the practice slopes in front of the Kreuzeckhaus and I made friends with two German lieutenants who were in charge. They not only allowed me to watch but invited me to visit their barracks at Mittenwald, an invitation I was unfortunately unable to accept as my leave was running out. I also witnessed a motor cycle rally in Garmisch and, talking to one of the participants, I learned that although it was being organized ostensibly by a civilian club, they were in fact all army reservists and were carrying out a military exercise testing the use of motor cycles and side-cars in severe winter conditions. Encouraged by my colonel who had formerly been a military attaché, I wrote short reports on both these subjects which he forwarded to 'higher authority', though I cannot believe that either was of the slightest interest. For my compulsory 'winter study' I wrote an essay suggesting that Germany's rearmament under Hitler might yet prove a useful bulwark against communist Russia. This theme was commended by my brigade commander and forwarded to Division. I have sometimes wondered whether this juvenile effusion still exists, carefully preserved in some MI5 file as evidence of my pro-Nazi sympathies.

When my next hunting leave came round, I planned to spend part of it skiing in Italy and, afterwards, to pay a quick visit to my parents in Egypt. Before setting out, I made up my mind to see whether I could get a job at the War Office. This was extremely irregular and I risked being severely punished for short-circuiting the usual channels. However, I presented myself to Major Jervois, the Head of the French Section, MI3a and, to my delight, he said he would employ me as a language officer when I returned from leave. It was, therefore, with a light heart that I set off to Italy. Sestriere proved more expensive than Germany and altogether less satisfactory from my point of view. Consequently, after ten days of skiing I took a deck passage in a cargo ship sailing from Naples to Alexandria via Athens and Rhodes.

I returned travelling from Alexandria to Brindisi third-class, but in comparative comfort, in the *Vittorio*, the flagship of the Lloyd Triestino line. I shared a cabin with a very presentable young Frenchman of my own age who seemed unduly reticent about his business in the Middle East. However, he introduced me to the Duchesa della Villarosa, a chic Italian of uncertain age who was travelling in the first-class. We spent most of the voyage in her company drinking champagne provided by her friends who, surprisingly, did not seem to resent us. Disembarking at Brindisi, I spent two days in Rome and a further two days in Florence, returning to London in time to take up my new job at the War Office on 1 March. My French friend I was to meet in similarly equivocal circumstances in Paris during the winter of 1939, once again finding him extremely reticent about his precise employment.

When I joined MI3a it consisted of the GSO2, Major Jervois; his GSO3, a senior gunner captain called Buzz d'Aubuz with whom I shared a room; and me. To begin with I spent much of my time reading through the sporting pages of French newspapers noting the towns at which military units played 'at home' football matches so as to fix their locations. I also had to search the pages of *Le Journal Officiel* for notices of land about to be requisitioned by the military authorities, in the hope that this might indicate future development of the Maginot Line, about which we seemed to be singularly ill-informed. I also translated a long paper received from the French about a Soviet parachute exercise which I found extremely interesting as a study of airborne tactics. When I confessed to a school certificate knowledge of Spanish and the ability to read Italian as well as German, I was given virtual charge of the Spanish Civil War. I felt very important. Each morning I arrived at 10 a.m., had a two-hour break for lunch and left the office punctually at 5 p.m. in ample time to attend one of the many cocktail parties to which young men were invited during the 'deb' season. I could not afford a flat of my own and, for reasons of economy, lived at the RAMC mess at Millbank. This, in itself, was a remarkable experience and, having watched a senior army surgeon with a hangover making three attempts at an incision in his fried egg, I decided that in future I would, if possible, rely on Sister Agnes and civilian surgery. However, the mess provided me with a cheap bed and breakfast and a soldier-servant.

Nineteen thirty-eight was the summer of the Czech crisis when Hitler's arrogant claim for the return of the Sudetenland threatened to involve us all in a European war. There was a call for two volunteers to learn Czech. I put in my name at once and, to my delight, I was selected. I expected that there would be fierce opposition from my battalion for I had already been away for five months. However, my new commanding officer was my old company commander who had himself been military attaché in Budapest and had progressive views about the need for young officers to speak foreign languages. He therefore raised no objections and it was arranged that I should start an intensive course at the School of Slavonic and East European Studies at Torrington Square as soon as I had finished my three months' duty in MI3a.

By now the 'deb' season was in full swing and I was finding it increasingly difficult to keep awake during my working hours. Not only was I going to dances almost every night, but Buzz d'Aubuz expected me to turn out at 8 a.m. every morning in order to ride in Rotten Row on one of the troop horses which officers working at the War Office were able to borrow from the Household Cavalry at Knightsbridge Barracks. Jodhpur breeches were not permitted and I had to be properly turned out in black butcher boots and spurs and a bowler hat. This imposed a considerable strain when I had only stripped off my white tie and tails a mere four hours previously. As the season progressed, I learned to leave the dances shortly after supper. This got me to bed at a reasonable hour but was bad luck on my partners. It also infuriated their mothers who reckoned that, having given me an expensive dinner, the least I could do was to dance with their daughters until dawn. But personable young men were in fairly short supply and I was more or less able to make my own terms. Fortunately, now that I was facing the intricacies of Czech grammar and could no longer afford to let my attention wander, the 'deb' season came to an abrupt close.

The other officer selected for the Czech language course was Captain Alan Brown, Royal Tank Corps. Alan was several years older than me and a dedicated professional soldier who had won the Military Cross while serving on the North-west Frontier. To begin with he was rather suspicious of my university habits and was irritated by my laid-back attitude and my ability to learn languages much more easily than he did. However, we soon got to know one another and, during the next eighteen months, we had some amusing and sometimes exciting adventures together.

The plan was that we were to undergo six weeks' intensive instruction in the Czech language at London University and this was to be followed by nine months with the British Legation in Prague and, possibly, a short attachment to a Czech regiment before returning to England to take the interpretership examination. Our tutor at the School of Slavonic and East European Studies was Dr René Wellek, later to become a

Professor of English Romantic Literature in the United States. He made us work very hard for two hours every morning and gave us a massive amount of prep for the following day. In the afternoon I often drove my car to Richmond Park to do my homework, not returning until it was time to change in order to go out in the evening. Besides going for long walks while learning my Czech vocabulary, I was still riding every morning in the Row. My weekends I spent in the country staying with friends or with my aunts. While the war clouds were gathering in central Europe, I was rapidly forgetting my anti-tank and machine-gunnery, determined as I was to make the most of this Epicurean interlude.

CHAPTER 7

Czechoslovakia,
1938–39

E VEN as late as August 1938, the British Ambassador in Berlin, Sir
Nevile Henderson, remained convinced that Hitler was bluffing and
did not intend to invade Czechoslovakia. Nevertheless, most of the
intelligence reaching London indicated that the Führer was determined
to use force. Faced with the prospect of war, French morale was steadily
collapsing and the British Cabinet agreed unanimously that the Prime
Minister should seek a personal meeting with Hitler in a last attempt to
save the peace.

By the time that Alan Brown and I were ready to leave for Prague
in late August the situation had deteriorated so much that it was
considered inadvisable for British officers to travel across Germany;
instead it was decided to send us via Yugoslavia and Hungary. Alan and
I were delighted at the prospect. We caught the boat-train from Victoria
on 25 August; a few hours earlier Mr Chamberlain had taken off from
Croydon on his first visit to Hitler at Bad Godesberg.

The luxury of the Simplon–Orient Express was a revelation. I knew
the route well as far as Trieste and the familiar landmarks brought back
happy memories of school holidays. Beyond Trieste, the railway climbed
steeply to the Yugoslav frontier at Postojna. It was a stretch of line
which I was to cross and recross in the winter of 1943 while with Tito's
Partisans but on this occasion it struck me as dark and sinister. At
Subotica we changed trains for Budapest and my first impression of
Yugoslavia consisted of an altercation which I had with an over-zealous
sentry who tried to prevent me taking a photograph, which I still have,
of the romantic names displayed on our *wagon-lit*: Paris, Lausanne,
Milano, Trieste, Zagreb, Bucuresti. They were place-names to stir the
imagination of any boy-adventurer and I was destined to visit most of
them at one time or another during the war years to come.

The Budapest train was less luxurious than the Simplon–Orient

Express and the journey was almost as dusty as that from Port Said to Alexandria. However, it was no less romantic. Instead of the patient little donkeys trotting along the banks of the canals, there were herds of horses galloping alongside the train. The Carlton Hotel, where we put up, was on the banks of the Danube and Alan impressed me with his sophistication by immediately sending for the valet to sponge and press his clothes before we crossed the river to report to the Legation. Here we were told that the frontier between Hungary and Slovakia had been closed and that we were to remain in Budapest until further notice.

We spent that last fateful week of September 1938 in agreeable idleness, bathing in the Gellert Bath with its famous artificial waves and lunching and dining in open-air cafés on the banks of the Danube. However, war continued to cast its shadow. Besides a Browning .38 pistol and my sword, I had in my luggage a 12-bore shotgun. These weapons had been impounded by the Hungarian customs on my arrival at Budapest and, to retrieve them, I had to call at the Hungarian War Ministry. Here I was received by a supercilious major with a monocle who could easily have doubled for Conrad Veidt. He informed me icily that, should war be declared, I and my colleague would be interned for the duration since we had no diplomatic status. However, not everybody shared his complacency. Later I overheard the conversation of a young German and his girlfriend sitting behind us in a café. He was extolling Hitler's speech at the Sportpalast and welcoming the prospect of war. His girlfriend was not so sure and I heard her remark, 'Aber vergiss nicht, Liebchen, dass England nie ein Krieg verloren hat.' ('Don't forget, darling, that England has never lost a war.')

Alan and I took the Hungarian major's warning seriously, and since there seemed no immediate prospect of continuing our journey to Prague, we telegraphed daily to the War Office asking to be recalled. Finally, on 29 August we received orders to return to London. Remembering that, when twelve years old, I had had to cross Europe without any money, I had cabled my bank to send me fifty pounds. This arrived just before we left Budapest. Even so, our return journey was far less comfortable than our journey out. The train to Subotica was crowded with refugees from central Europe; the majority of them Jewish families of every description. On arrival at Subotica, we found that there was no chance of a sleeping berth but we had a first-class compartment to ourselves and spent a comfortable night. No news of the international situation was available in Yugoslavia, but when we reached Trieste I was able to buy a newspaper and found the reports of Hitler's latest discussions with Mr Chamberlain far from reassuring. We had no doubt that should war overtake us in Italy, as army officers we were most likely to be interned even if Italy remained neutral for the time being. At Milan, however, there were rumours that a Four Power Agreement had been reached at Munich and these rumours were confirmed when we arrived at the Swiss frontier. At dinner, we shared our table with Lady Drogheda and a portly Albanian diplomat in a pink shirt whose diplomatic passport, which he had spread out to show to the Italian authorities, covered the entire table top. We celebrated our escape with champagne and the night passed very quickly.

Our reception by the War Office was far from cordial. We reported to the Head of MI1(X), Lieutenant Colonel Gerald Templer, who intimated that we had panicked unnecessarily. This we found unjust; particularly so when he added that the Finance Branch had ruled that, since we had now expended our travel allowance, there could no longer be any question of sending us to Prague. However, Alan Brown, who was more experienced than me, had sized up Gerald Templer and produced what proved to be an effective time-bomb. He lit the fuse by innocently asking whether General Staff policy was always dictated by the Finance Branch. This seemingly innocuous inquiry triggered an immediate explosion: 'No, by God, it's not.' Reaching for the telephone, Colonel Templer instructed that immediate arrangements should be made for our journey to Prague at the earliest opportunity.

This time, we were told, there would be no difficulty about travelling across Germany, and on arrival at Eger (previously known as Cheb) we should find a Czech train which would take us direct to Prague. This briefing, like so much military intelligence at that time, proved inaccurate in almost every particular. As predicted, our journey across Germany was uneventful but, at Eger, when we asked about the next train to Prague, we were greeted with incredulity. Were we not aware, the booking clerk asked, that we were now in a military zone and that all civilian traffic had been suspended. As it was now late, he suggested that we should return the following morning and discuss our problem with the German transport officer. Accordingly, we left our luggage at the station and went in search of somewhere to sleep.

It did not take us long to discover that all the spare accommodation in the town had been requisitioned by the army, and we were both beginning to despair when we chanced upon a seedy hotel in a back street which offered us a double room. The window frame had been shattered and there was a gaping hole in the ceiling which seemed likely to have been caused by a burst of machine-gun fire. Nevertheless, the sheets seemed clean so we sent the hotel porter to collect our luggage and went out to look for some supper.

The whole town was seething with soldiers; all restaurants and cafés were packed and a good time was clearly being had by all. I noticed that the soldiers were still wearing their regimental flashes and Alan and I set about memorizing these identifications, entering them in due course in my diary encrypted as a timetable of trains from Egham to Waterloo. We noted at least thirty different units and it was past midnight before we got to bed. Early next morning we presented ourselves to the RTO at Eger station who proved friendly and helpful when we explained our predicament. He said that the new Czech frontier lay some 50 kilometres to the east of Eger and that it was forbidden to cross the military zone. However, a troop train was leaving later that morning for Komotau (formerly known as Chomotov) and he promised to find us places on it. Komotau was not only much nearer the new Czech frontier, but it was also the German Military Headquarters which would, he was sure, facilitate our journey.

We reached Komotau without incident except that, at one point, we came to a halt opposite a long train travelling in the other direction transporting what seemed to be a battalion of light tanks. These were certainly not made of cardboard as was rumoured in the British press, and Alan made a small sketch of the suspension which had features which interested him. We set our sights on a comfortable-looking hotel in the main square which was flying a large swastika flanked by French and Italian flags. Assuming that the French and Italian flags were flying in honour of the Munich Agreement, I sent for the manager and upbraided him for not displaying a British flag as well. A Union Jack was eventually found which, happily, proved to be almost as large as the Nazi swastika, so honour was satisfied. Having secured this advantage, I demanded two single rooms and, after a hasty consultation with a German corporal, these were provided. It was now lunchtime. In the corner of the dining room sat the German general and three or four staff officers. Alan and I presented ourselves as stiffly as we could after what we imagined to be the German manner. I explained our business and presented an imposing looking *laissez-passer* which we had obtained from the German Embassy in London. This impressed the general, who received us affably, promised to issue the necessary instructions for our onward journey and told us to call on the town-major the following morning. The general was as good as his word and a staff car was provided to take us as far as the forward company covering the new frontier with the Czech Republic. Here we hit a snag; we were told that a German military vehicle would not be allowed to take us over to the Czech lines and that to attempt to cross no-man's-land even in a civilian vehicle was a risky business, for the Czechs were very jumpy and trigger-happy. Nevertheless, after some delay two elderly taxis were procured into which we transferred our luggage and ourselves.

We were just about to set off when a young man appeared. He was scruffily dressed but unmistakably English and he introduced himself. He said that he had been on a walking holiday photographing birds in the Sudetenland and had been overtaken by events. He now wanted to get to Prague where he was to stay with his uncle, the passport control officer at the British Legation. Knowing something about what passport control officers did in their spare time, I sensed the delicacy of his position and told him that he might travel in the second taxi with our luggage, and, if necessary, we would pretend that he was our servant. At this he seemed greatly relieved. I was to meet him three years later at Suda Bay during the German invasion of Crete. He was then in uniform with an Intelligence Corps badge. An air-raid was in progress and it was no time to exchange more than a casual greeting but I gathered that he was then working for SOE. What he was doing in the Sudetenland in October 1938 is, perhaps, best left to the imagination.

A thousand yards of no-man's-land separated the two frontlines and, on the advice of the German company commander, Alan and I proceeded on foot, followed at a respectful distance by the two taxis containing our luggage and 'our servant' Alan, who spoke no German, had become rather resentful that, until now, I had been forced to be our spokesman. We had, therefore, agreed that when we reached the Czech lines he should have the opportunity to air his Czech. Alan's Czech was even worse than mine and, after his first sentence, the sentry who challenged us shook his head sadly and said, 'Do you by any chance speak German?' From then on, everything went easily and, by the evening, we were safely in Prague.

With its incomparable baroque buildings, Prague is one of the most beautiful cities in Europe; nevertheless, at the best of times its inhabitants lacked the elegance of Vienna or Budapest, and in the aftermath of the Munich Agreement there was everywhere a pervasive air of gloom. There was no resident military attaché at the British Legation but the air attaché, Hugh Macdonald, had arranged for two of his friends to have us to stay until we found our feet. It was an uneasy arrangement. There was strict currency control at this time and Czech citizens were forbidden to transfer funds to the West. Although the matter was never mentioned, both Alan and I had an uncomfortable feeling that our hosts had hoped we would repay their hospitality in pounds sterling lodged in a London bank, for we suspected that both families were partially Jewish. However, at this stage neither of us wished to be involved in illegal currency dealing. Besides, both families were obviously very rich and we felt too shy to broach the subject. I had imagined that I would find a family who would take me in as a paying guest and provide me with Czech conversation. Arrangements of this sort were common in Germany or Austria, but in Prague they were unknown. Indeed, very few households seemed to have a spare bedroom; moreover, since neither of us had a motor car, we needed to live in the centre of the city. In the end we gave up the search for a family and rented an apartment on the Vodičkova Ulice overlooking the Václavské Namĕsti, and arranged to pay the Jewish owner in sterling in London. We also took on the owner's housekeeper to look after us.

My original host still had some property in the Sudetenland and, having obtained permission from the Germans to visit it, he invited me to accompany him. Possibly he thought that having a British officer with him was a wise precaution. Surprisingly, his farm had not been expropriated and his courageous farm manager had stayed on to run it. Fearing lest our Prague number-plates might attract trouble, we avoided the towns and kept to the by-roads. At one stage on our drive home, my host remarked to me, 'This village is at least one hundred per cent Czech.' No sooner had he said it than a stone came hurtling through the windscreen. My host had prudently chosen to drive his wife's Tatra instead of his new Jaguar which was his pride and joy, and the damage was easily repaired. Nevertheless, the family seemed relieved when we returned safely.

On another occasion, Alan's host invited us to shoot with him in southern Bohemia. The other guests included the German and Swiss military attachés. It was my first experience of the alarming way in which partridges and hares are shot in many parts of central Europe. The guns form a large circle with a diameter of about 2,000 yards and then close in. When within range of the guns on the other side of the perimeter, the keeper blows his horn and, after this signal, the guns are supposed to shoot only at game that has broken back. However, on this occasion, the more adventurous guns continued to shoot into the circle until I could literally see the whites of their eyes. Among these was the Swiss attaché, one of whose pellets ricocheted against my stocking. For a moment I considered returning his fire but, fortunately, did not do so, for I had forgotten that my borrowed gun was a one-over-one which contained, in its second barrel, a solid ball for use if we should put up a wild boar. After a bibulous dinner, the local village girls were brought in to entertain us. By now the German attaché was both drunk and maudlin; he sat one of the plumper village girls on his knee and, somehow including me in his embrace, sang mournfully, 'I'll be loving you, always'. Notwithstanding the recent Munich Agreement, I did not feel that the international situation justified me in reciprocating his sentiments.

Alan and I worked hard at our Czech during the day and in the evening repaired to a bar where we could drink and meet our Czech friends. At a party given in our honour by the Czech military attaché before we left London, I had been introduced to Colonel Kadajnka, the leader of the Czech equestrian team competing at Olympia. He invited me to come out with the so-called Prague Hunt. 'Only the dogs are Aryan', commented one of my new friends. They met weekly at the cavalry barracks at Stara Boleslav, about twenty miles from Prague, where they organized a drag hunt which, so far as I was concerned, all too often degenerated into an international steeplechase. However, Colonel Kadajnka, though remarking that I could not ride for toffee, lent me a very good young horse and I enjoyed myself. After the hunt, we repaired to the local pub where we drank tea and cognac and ate delicious ham sandwiches until it was time to return to Prague. When the ground became too hard to hunt, the White Hussars, who were stationed in Prague, let me borrow one of their troop horses one or two evenings a week to ride in their indoor riding school. In this way, I kept reasonably fit despite spending most of the day at my Czech lessons, and most of my evenings drinking.

Early in January, we took a week's leave to ski in Slovakia. In Bohemia and Moravia the farms were as neat and tidy as in Germany. Slovakia, however, was far more akin to Eastern Europe. We took the night train from Prague, sitting up in the second-class. Next day, we were the only passengers to get off the train at Liptovsky Sv. Jan where we had been assured we would find a sleigh to take us to our hotel at Certovice. However, the station yard was deserted and the village still asleep, so we put on our rucksacks and shouldered our skis and set off on the five-mile walk to our hotel. We had been advised to choose the Low rather than the High Tatra mountains where the skiing was more precipitous. At Certovice the skiing was easy and the snow several metres deep but there were no facilities like ski-lifts and, in order to have a run home in the afternoon, we had to spend the morning climbing on skins. There were one or two Slovak couples staying at the hotel and a young Czech film actress. There was also a large St Bernard dog with whom the film actress used to fool about in the snow on all fours. On one occasion she excited the St Bernard to such an extent that it tried to mount her. I was laughing so much at her embarrassment that I lost my balance and fell, wrenching my knee. Although I had it put in plaster as soon as I returned to Prague, it never entirely recovered and I had recurring trouble with it throughout the war. It served me right for my lack of chivalry.

January and February in Prague are horrible months; there is a perpetual grey overcast, the streets are covered in dirty snow and slush and a piercing north-east wind knocks you breathless. We stayed indoors and got on with our Czech. I found both the Czech and the German editions of Erich Kastner's *Emil and the Detectives* and learned much of the Czech version by heart. This gave me a useful colloquial, if somewhat juvenile, vocabulary. It was a humdrum existence but we managed not to get on each other's nerves. After work we usually repaired to the Est Bar, the fashionable nightclub underneath the Esplanade Hotel. Here we met our Czech friends and drank away the evening. Among the girls at the Est Bar was one known as Mickey Mouse. Although she was almost certainly in the pay of either or both German and Czech intelligence services, she was not unduly inquisitive about our activities and we became good friends. We were to meet again in a bar in Bucharest in September 1939, where Colin Gubbins, Alan and I were celebrating our escape from Poland which we had hoped to keep secret from the Germans. On such chance encounters are one's fortunes made.

With the first signs of spring, we obtained permission to rent a house in the country, about 30 miles south of Prague where we hoped we should be able to work undisturbed before returning to England for our exam. Our Czech friends promised to drive out to see us at weekends and I had rented a small car which I hoped to use for expeditions in search of trout fishing.

At the beginning of March we set off once again for Slovakia for a final week's skiing before the snows melted. This time, we chose an isolated ski-hut on the summit of Dumbier, the highest point in the Low Tatra mountains. To reach it, we had not only to walk up the valley for about five miles but we also had a three-hour climb on skis. The valley was the same one that we had walked up at Christmas but, instead of a damp fog which blanketed everything but our immediate surroundings and a frozen road underfoot, this time the sky was clear and the road was criss-crossed with rivulets of melting snow. After the frowsty railway carriage in which we had sat up all night, the mountain air was intoxicating.

At Christmas we had climbed up to the Dumbier hut from Certovice and, with the wind howling outside, had found it a warm and comfortable place in which to eat our sandwiches and prepare for the run home. I had not realized how primitive were the facilities it offered. We had a slit of a room with two bunk beds, a stool and a table with a basin and a jug of cold water. For our clothes there were two hooks on the back of the door. Faced with this austerity, I think that Alan was as tempted as I was to move down to the comfortable hotel at the head of the valley where we had stayed during our previous visit. However, emerging on to the terrace and seeing the virgin ski-slopes stretching in every direction into the far distance, I at least was ready to put up with any discomfort in order to enjoy this incomparable terrain. Besides ourselves, there was a mixed party of Slovak students and a solitary middle-aged German who bore all the marks of a reserve officer. He did not join in the singing and dancing in the evening and we viewed each other with mutual suspicion, though there was no reason to suppose that he was any more nefariously engaged than we were. The skiing was tough and it was hard work climbing on skins in the virgin snow. Nevertheless, we used to cover about 15 miles a day, usually without seeing another soul.

At the end of our week's leave, we decided to ski down the north side of the mountain and pick up our train on the mainline at Ružemberok. It was only about 25 miles as the crow flies but, with our heavy rucksacks, turning was difficult and we did not dare to ski very fast in the deep snow. It was late afternoon by the time we reached our destination and we were surprised to find that many of the houses and shops were shuttered and the railway station deserted.

We had seen no newspapers for a week nor had we listened to the Slovak radio which was difficult for us to understand. We were consequently unaware of the dramatic developments that were taking place. Under Thomas Masaryk and President Beněs the Czechs had succeeded in dominating the ethnic minorities, the Sudeten Germans, the Slovaks and the sub-Carpathian Ruthenians which comprised the Republic of Czechoslovakia under the Treaty of St Germain. Hitler's strategic plans involved the neutralization of Czechoslovakia and, having successfully annexed the Sudetenland, his next project was to detach Slovakia from Bohemia and Moravia, the so-called Czech Lands. During the first week in March, the Germans encouraged Slovak irredentists known as the Hlinka Guards to stage demonstrations in favour of Slovak independence. These demonstrations received a certain amount of popular support in the main towns and, fearing that a Slovak declaration of independence was imminent, the Czech government had reacted strongly, arresting the Slovak leader, Sidor, in Prague. They had also ordered the Czech police to occupy the Slovak government offices in Bratislava, the capital of Slovakia, and arrest a number of leading Slovaks on the grounds that they were members of the Hlinka Guards. The Czech President, Hacha, next proceeded to dismiss the Slovak government. All this had taken place unbeknown to us during the week we were skiing on Dumbier.

We had about an hour to wait for our train and, by now, it was growing dark and a keen east wind had sprung up which was blowing the snow off the station roof. We heard some desultory shooting. None of it was at us but it explained the shuttered windows and the locked station buildings. Otherwise the town itself seemed unnaturally quiet. With the waiting room locked up and no prospect of a meal or a hot drink, our main preoccupation was to keep warm and we were thankful when, right on time, the Prague express drew into the station and we found an empty compartment in which we could spend the night.

At the Legation there was mild surprise that, having so recently returned from Slovakia, we had so little to report. However, by now there was no longer any doubt that the crisis was being orchestrated by the German government and that the action had shifted to Berlin where the Slovak leaders were being put under extreme pressure to invite Hitler to 'protect' Slovakia and proclaim its independence.

Considering that as early as the beginning of March there were intelligence reports that Hitler was massing troops on the Czech front, it seems extraordinary that the air attaché had not warned us that an invasion was imminent or made any attempt to stop us leaving Prague. On 13 March Alan collected the car which I had hired and drove our belongings down to the country. I remained in Prague as I had arranged to have a minor operation on my jaw. I had taken a room at the Wilson Station Hotel on account of its convenience although we knew that the manager was a Nazi sympathizer. After my operation, I returned to the hotel and went to bed ignorant of the fact that the Czech President had been summoned to Berlin where he was being bullied into accepting a German protectorate of the Czech Lands. In the small hours of the morning of 15 March, going down the corridor to the lavatory, I was dimly aware through a haze of pain-killers that, instead of the row of shoes waiting to be cleaned outside the bedroom doors, there was a row of black jackboots. However, the significance of this escaped me; but not for long. Shortly after 6 a.m., I was rung up and told to report to the Legation at once. Although my face was the size of a football, I dressed and found a taxi. I caught the air attaché on his way to a meeting with the Minister. He seemed surprised to learn that Alan was not in Prague and told me to get hold of him at once as the Germans had already crossed the Czech frontier. He arrived with my car and our luggage shortly after 9 a.m. By now, there were numerous German bomber aircraft flying low overhead, and the air attaché told Alan and me to go out on to the terrace of the Legation, which overlooked the city, and identify them. After about twenty minutes, we were interrupted by a message from the Minister, Mr Basil Newton, who was being posted to Baghdad, to the effect that he wished one of us to go to the station to measure the sleeping compartment and see whether he could take his skis with him with his personal luggage. This was too much for Alan who sent back a very curt message that, for the time being, we were otherwise engaged. By now the German motorized infantry were arriving and, partly to keep out of Mr Newton's reach, we sallied forth in search, once again, of unit identifications.

It was miserable weather; wet snow was falling and the sky was heavily overcast. The civilians who watched the proceedings on their way to work looked utterly defeated and gazed blankly as the troop carriers went by with the Germans, in smart uniforms and without greatcoats despite the freezing weather, sitting upright with their rifles between their knees. Some of the older people were in tears and the children on their way to school looked on goggle-eyed but there was no sign of any hostile demonstration; everyone seemed completely cowed. It was one of the saddest sights I can ever remember.

While Alan noted down numbers and unit identifications, I took photographs with my Leica of any equipment that was passing. To my surprise, nobody made any effort to restrain me. Indeed, later that afternoon, German soldiers actually posed for me. They seemed entirely impervious to the misery and despair which their arrival was occasioning and entirely convinced of the justice of their cause. Even more pathetic than the people lining the streets were the refugees who were now crowding into the Legation courtyard in a desperate bid for visas for the United Kingdom. Most of them were Jewish but there was a sprinkling of German Social Democrats from the Sudetenland. Among the latter was Wenzel Jaksch who was later to work with us in SOE; though in danger of his life he was entirely composed. There was also Eric Gedye, the *Daily Telegraph* correspondent and author of *Fallen Bastions*. He too was a marked man with a price on his head but he was waiting in the passage entirely unconcerned while means were discussed of smuggling him out of the country. There was another well-known journalist, who was in no danger whatever, but lacked Gedye's composure. However, he was a rare exception, for most people behaved with the utmost dignity and a small group of English women led by Miss Wanender and Miss Anty, representing refugee organizations, set a wonderful example of calm efficiency.

When we returned to our hotel, we were met by the manager in a high state of excitement. He said that his hotel had been taken over by the SS, which was all too apparent from the black uniforms now thronging the vestibule, and that an officer wished to see us immediately. We were shown into an office at the end of a corridor where jackbooted SS were rushing to and fro in a frenzy of activity. We were interrogated by an officer aged about thirty dressed in SS uniform and presumably a member of the *Sicherheitsdienst*. He asked us our business in no very friendly way, demanded to see our passports, said that it was clearly impossible for us to remain in the hotel and that we must leave at once. This was obvious, but I replied in what Alan later described as 'the right sort of German' that this demand was outrageous and that we had no intention of leaving our rooms until alternative accommodation had been found for us. Which it was, about two hours later, but of very inferior quality since all the better hotels had been requisitioned.

The Excelsior Hotel, we were told, had been taken over as the headquarters of the Gestapo. However, that evening, we had no difficulty in getting into the Est Bar as usual, where the band was still playing and business seemed to be normal, though there was a general atmosphere of gloom. Three or four of the tables were occupied by German officers in either army or SS uniforms. We sat at the bar and by providing the girls with champagne, which the Germans could not afford, persuaded them to refuse the latter's invitations to dance. Not that many needed much persuading, for the Germans had little to offer. However, it was a sad occasion when we said goodbye to the band and to our friends at the bar and retired to our hotel room which we strongly suspected of being bug-infested.

When we arrived at the Legation next morning, we learned that we had been recalled to London and that we should arrange to leave as soon as possible. Meanwhile, there was plenty for us still to do at the Legation. The previous afternoon, one of our friends, a British engineer working in a Czech arms factory, had deposited with the air attaché a prototype of a gun-barrel which he claimed would greatly accelerate the muzzle-velocity of a bullet and which, he was certain, would be of interest to the War Office if he could get it back to England. The air attaché asked whether we could take it back with us in our luggage. I would have agreed but Alan, who was older and wiser than me, replied that he would only do so if given an order in writing since we had to cross Germany and it seemed an unnecessarily risky thing to do. The air attaché demurred at this and told us, instead, to cut the barrel in half so that it would fit into a normal diplomatic bag. This was a ridiculous suggestion for it would have been impossible to reconstitute the dynamics of the barrel but we bought a hacksaw and a variety of blades and set about it. Since the barrel was of hardened steel, it took the better part of the day to cut it through. Later that evening, we attended a very bibulous farewell party given for us by our Czech friends.

The next morning, these same friends suffering, as we were, from shocking hangovers, gathered on the platform at the Wilson station to see us off. They had brought a large bottle of Slivovic which we passed from hand to hand and mouth to mouth until it was drained. Only one or two of these friends survived the war and then only to fall victims to the communist purge in 1948. I never saw any of them again.

On arrival in Paris, we reported to the Embassy and spent the morning describing our experiences, for we were the first to bear first-hand news of Prague. Since no one offered to give us lunch, we repaired to La Crêmaillère, which has remained to this day one my favourite Paris restaurants, where we had a very expensive meal. It had been an exciting morning being the centre of attention and it was in a mood of high euphoria that we caught the afternoon boat-train for Calais.

Our reception at the War Office was far more cordial than it had been when we had returned from Budapest the previous October. Having reported to Gerald Templer, we spent the morning with the German Section checking identifications and describing the equipment we had seen. For a romantic like me who had not yet reached his twenty-fifth birthday, all this attention was heady stuff and confirmed my determination never to return to the anonymity of regimental soldiering if it could be avoided.

CHAPTER 8

Summer Interlude, 1939

GERALD Templer was still Head of MI1(X) and he told us that we were to return to London University to finish our Czech course. I was delighted at the prospect, notwithstanding a feeling that I was fiddling while Rome burned. This time I decided to stay at the Royal Fusiliers depot at Hounslow which was more friendly than the RAMC mess at Millbank and, as before, we had lessons until lunchtime and in the afternoons I did much of my homework while taking long solitary walks in Richmond Park. I had to spend most weekends at Longcross revising for my exam; but it was while staying with friends that I first met Theresa Villiers. In the absence of her mother, Lady Hunsdon, she invited our house party to dine at Briggens before the Puckeridge Hunt ball. Although she did not know me, I was the only member of my party wearing a pink coat so she put me next to her at dinner. We subsequently spent much of the evening together 'sitting out' in the police cells under Hertford Town Hall where the dance was being held. Here, inappropriately, we chose to discuss fox hunting and Handel, two subjects about which, I soon found, she knew very much more than I did. Many years later, she was to tell me that, on getting home that evening, she had told one of her friends that she had had a good time. 'Surely not with that conceited soldier?' her friend had scornfully replied. Fortunately for me, however, Theresa was not so easily put off and, six years later, we were married in Rome.

So as not to lose touch entirely with the army, I used to lunch regularly at the Army and Navy Club where there was a cheap buffet much patronized by officers working in the War Office. On one such occasion in early May, a middle-aged man sat down next to me and engaged me in conversation. I knew him by sight for he looked more lively and intelligent than most of the other members; and his clothes were better cut. He introduced himself as Colin Gubbins and we were soon talking about Czechoslovakia where he had been one of the officers sent out to supervise the Czech withdrawal from the Sudetenland after the Munich Agreement. After lunch, we had coffee together and he said how much he wished that there was an easy way of learning German and I recommended a recently published textbook, *The Basis and Essentials of German*, which I had found particularly helpful in preparing for my German interpretership. Gubbins said that he would like very much to meet Alan Brown and, two days later, we both received an invitation to lunch with him. The address he gave us was a mews off the Marylebone Road which proved to be the back entrance of one of the large Regency houses facing Regent's Park. (The house, I subsequently learned, belonged to Edward Beddington Behrens.) My curiosity was aroused when, on emerging from the back stairs, I found myself faced with what looked like, and proved to be, Epstein's head of Paul Robeson and, hanging above it, a magnificent *explosion de couleur* which, on closer examination, proved to be a sunset painted by Kokoschka. We were shown into the elegant drawing room overlooking Regent's Park. Besides Colin Gubbins, there were two other men, one of whom was Percy Legard, a captain in the Inniskilling Dragoon Guards, whom I had met with one of my cousins, and the other was a subaltern in the Hussars who had just completed a course in Serbo-Croat. We had a delicious cold lunch, washed down with Chevalier Montrachet, and finishing up with *fraises des bois*. It was only when we were having coffee and brandy that Colin Gubbins explained why he had invited us. He said that it now seemed highly probable that, if war broke out, large areas of Eastern Europe would be overrun by the Germans and that, in that event, there would be scope for guerrilla activity behind the German lines. He went on to say that he was a member of the secret branch of the War Office which was making preparations for this eventuality and that he was selecting serving officers and civilians for training in guerrilla warfare for possible employment of this sort. He stressed that, at this stage, all this was very secret and very tentative but asked us to let him know whether we were interested in this sort of work.

Alan, who was a dedicated tank officer, was not particularly attracted by the proposal but it seemed to me that any job which involved cold luncheons washed down with Chevalier Montrachet and finishing up with *fraises des bois* merited careful consideration. On this point Alan agreed and, without imagining that anything very much would come of it, we both let our names go forward.

We took our exam at the end of June and I did reasonably well, securing a first-class interpretership and an award of seventy pounds. While I had been away, the battalion had moved from Shorncliffe to Dover where we occupied the Shaft Barracks on the west side of the town, facing Dover Castle. Returning to regimental life was quite a shock. I found myself in command of the Headquarters Company and, on the first Sunday after my return, the adjutant with calculated malice put me in charge of Church Parade, knowing that I should be hard put to it to remember the drill. Though I felt far from confident when I stepped on to the parade ground to 'take over' the battalion, all went well.

A mere ten days after my return to Dover I received a secret letter from Gubbins telling me that I had been selected for a weekend course on guerrilla warfare beginning almost immediately and requiring me to apply for four days' leave to attend it without revealing the reason for my application. Since I had only just returned to the battalion, I did not expect my request for leave to be treated very sympathetically. However, I was mistaken and, without asking me any embarrassing questions, the adjutant, Claud Rome, let me go.

We were a very mixed bag who assembled at Caxton Hall, Westminster, at what became known as the first MI(R) training course. I was relieved to find that Alan Brown was also there for, at first sight, it did not appear that there were many kindred spirits. We were all wearing plain clothes so it was difficult to say which of us were serving officers and which civilians. Colin Gubbins gave a good but somewhat superficial lecture on the principles of guerrilla warfare and we had lectures on elementary demolition and radio communication. Having worked with my step-father, who was an engineer, I knew something about demolition but the idea of using the ionosphere and the 'skip-gap' to ensure radio security was entirely new to me and I enjoyed the two lectures given by the head signal officer of MI6. For the first time I met Lieutenant Colonel Jo Holland, the head of MI(R) and also his personal assistant, Joan Bright, with whom, some fifty years later, I was to write a biography of Colin Gubbins. I cannot say that I learned very much from the course and remember remarking to Alan Brown that we might have been more profitably employed spending a weekend re-reading T. E. Lawrence's *Seven Pillars of Wisdom*. Nevertheless, I was gratified to find that I had been 'selected' for special employment of this sort and wondered what the future held. Though I could envisage being a guerrilla in Slovakia, I did not relish such a prospect in the Czech Lands.

The battalion did not start serious training until after the August break. That spring we had had the first intake of conscripts and, although now more nearly up to strength and better equipped than when I had left Shorncliffe, there was a smaller proportion of trained soldiers in the battalion than previously. This put a great strain on the NCOs and, to some extent, on the officers. Meanwhile, the international situation was worsening almost by the hour and, by all accounts, it was no longer a question of whether Hitler would invade Poland but when. Even so, our sham fights remained reminiscent of the Franco-Prussian War and while the unhappy conscripts were still learning how to form threes (a recent innovation) while giving a smart salute, Hitler's Panzer units were already taking up their positions along the Polish frontier.

Senior company commanders who had fought in the Great War seemed particularly reluctant to say what it felt like to go into action, though this was really what concerned me most of all. Their attitude reminded me of a married woman who conceals the realities of childbirth from a young bride. Everything was left to my imagination and, steeped in the writings of Wilfred Owen and Siegfried Sassoon, I did not feel as self-confident as I pretended.

Amid all the confusion of the weeks leading up to the outbreak of war, one event stands out very clear in my memory. This was Jake Astor's coming-of-age ball at Hever Castle. It was a magnificent occasion and I remember particularly the arrival of Mr Churchill who had driven over from Chartwell. He was not, at the time, a member of the government, but as the war clouds darkened, more and more people were tending to look to him for leadership. When he entered the ballroom that evening at Hever, the dancing stopped and all the guests applauded. I was not the only person with sombre thoughts while watching the reflection of the fireworks in the lake. I found it hard to relate this glittering evening to the Czech tragedy which I had so recently left behind and the present opulence seemed to me more like Balthazar's feast than the Waterloo Ball. In any case, I was sure that I would never see the like again.

In the late afternoon of 22 August, I was at the head of the column, marching back from a battalion exercise. We were in sight of Dover Castle when a motor cycle dispatch rider drew up and gave me a message from the adjutant marked 'Secret' which ran as follows:

To Lt. P. A. Wilkinson from Adjutant. Report to Room 124 War Office at 10.00 hrs Wednesday 23rd August 1939.

Take necessary kit to proceed to Continent *under active service conditions.*

Pistol, steel helmet, mob container on respirator, etc. etc. Take mufti suits and blue patrols. This is SECRET. You will not inform any unauthorized person of these orders.

ACK to Orderly Room this evening. Hand over HQ Cmy to Lt. G. F. H. Archer.

(Sgd.) F. D. Rome – Captain.

That evening, I packed up my few personal possessions as best I could and arranged for them to be put into store; then, without saying goodbye to anyone, I caught the last train to London.

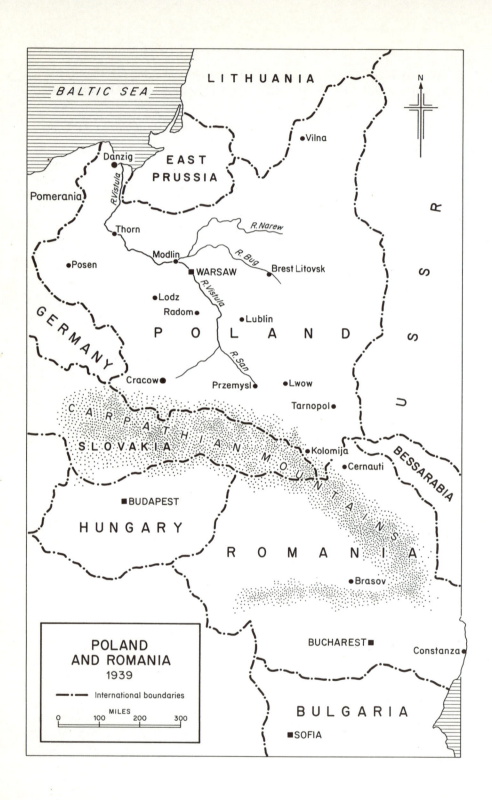

LITHUANIA

BALTIC SEA

•Vilna

N

Danzig
•

EAST
PRUSSIA

R. Vistula

Pomerania

Thorn

R. Narew

Modlin

R. Bug

•Posen

WARSAW

Brest Litovsk
•

R. Vistula

GERMANY

•Lodz

Radom•

•Lublin

P O L A N D

R. San

Cracow•

Przemysl•

•Lwow

U

S

S

R

Tarnopol•

C A R P A T H I A N

Kolomija•

•Cernauti

BESSARABIA

SLOVAKIA

M O U N T A I N S

•BUDAPEST

HUNGARY

R O M A N I A

•Brasov

BUCHAREST■

•Constanza

**POLAND
AND ROMANIA
1939**

—·—·— International boundaries

MILES
0   100   200   300

BULGARIA

■SOFIA

CHAPTER 9

Poland, 1939

I SPENT the night at the Charing Cross Hotel. When I met Alan Brown on the steps of the War Office, neither of us had the slightest idea of what was in store. In Gerald Templer's room, where we fore-gathered, there were about a dozen people including Gubbins, Holland and Joan Bright, Holland's assistant. Conversation was mainly about the Molotov–Ribbentrop Pact which had just been made public, and which seemed to seal Poland's fate for good. It was therefore a slight shock when Holland told us that we were to leave immediately for Warsaw as the MI(R) component of No. 4 Military Mission. He added that Lieutenant Colonel Gubbins had been appointed GSO1 of the mission and would be in charge of our party. Gubbins then explained that it was now too late for us to travel across Germany and that the Foreign Office feared that if we were to fly via Sweden our arrival in Stockholm, bound for Poland, might be considered provocative by the Germans. While alternative arrangements were being made, we were sent away and told to keep in touch.

I made some last-minute purchases in the Army and Navy Stores including, on my step-father's recommendation, a pair of hunting wire-cutters and a liquid prismatic compass; I then travelled to Longcross to spend the night and say goodbye to my aunts. There followed orders and counter-orders, all too reminiscent of our departure for Czecho-slovakia the previous August. Finally, on 25 August, I received a telegram instructing me to report that evening to Victoria station with all my kit. Here I learned that the Polish and Romanian missions were bound for Egypt and were to wait there until war was declared. We were to travel out inconspicuously with the 500 officers and officials serving in the Middle East and India who were hurriedly being recalled from home leave.

Our special train left at 8 p.m. The scene at Victoria was chaotic and the concourse echoed with the commanding accents of the Maidan

67

peculiar to Indian Army officers and their memsahibs. In these surroundings the MI(R) party looked far from inconspicuous. There were
about twenty of us in all and I remember Colin Gubbins clutching a
diplomatic bag, but wearing a decidedly undiplomatic green pork-pie
hat while Tommy Davies, in a Brigade of Guard's tie, stood disapproving
and aloof amid all this heartiness; nor could 'Boy' Lloyd-Johnes be
mistaken for a polo-playing subaltern; in his grey pin-stripe suit and
seedy bowler hat, he looked more like an absconding financier. Only
the Royal Signals NCOs, who were to handle our radio communications,
in their sports coats, grey flannel trousers and trilby hats looked unmistakably what they were.

The scene at Newhaven was no less chaotic for there were no porters
and we had to man-handle not only our own kit but the thirty large
packing cases of radio equipment which accompanied us. There was no
opportunity for elevated thoughts on leaving England for the last time
before we cast off. I spent a comfortable night on a settee in the ladies'
saloon where, since there were no ladies on board, I was undisturbed.
I have no recollection of landing at Dieppe but I remember that our
journey across France was hot and uncomfortable. Many of the stations
we passed through, their windows already obscured with blue paint as
an air-raid precaution, were thronged with reservists recalled to the
colours. At Villeneuve we waited for five hours while the troop trains
rattled past bound for the Maginot Line, their trucks containing considerably more than the regulation eight horses or forty men.

Although we had a special train, the journey across France took
thirty-six hours and we did not arrive at Marseilles until early on the
morning of 27 August. Here we were met by motor buses and transferred
to HMS *Shropshire*, a County class cruiser, which was waiting for us
with steam up. *Shropshire* cast-off as soon as the last man was aboard.
This was Major Hugh Curteis, Highland Light Infantry, of the Polish
Mission who arrived by taxi having dallied in the town to buy sufficient
wine for the voyage which he rightly surmised would be 'dry'. Everyone
slept on deck but, for added security, the MI(R) party was allotted one
of the ship's boats in which to stow their personal kit and the secret
papers we kept under officer guard. To avoid the Italians, our course
was set close to the North African coast and, after a brief stop at Malta,
we reached Alexandria early on the morning of 31st August.

Gubbins was taken off in an official car to naval headquarters and,
at my suggestion, the rest of us made our way to the Hotel Cecil. At
the British Consulate we obtained civilian passports. Unfortunately, these
were issued in consecutive numbers which destroyed any pretence that

we were a casual party of tourists. After this, I was told that I could have the rest of the day to visit my family. My mother had been surprised when I had telephoned her after we first landed. She had immediately driven into town and was waiting outside the Hotel Cecil when we returned from the Consulate. Our old Hudson saloon was filthy and covered in dust from the previous weekend in the desert and I felt as self-conscious about it as a small boy being taken out by his parents from his prep school. My mother had a picnic lunch on board and Alan and I spent a happy afternoon surf-riding at Sidi Bishr.

Meanwhile, orders had arrived from the War Office that we were to leave for Warsaw at once. Gubbins managed to charter an Imperial Airways' flying-boat and had obtained two other Short-Sunderlands from the Royal Air Force – the eyes of the fleet, as one naval officer sadly commented – and we were to set off for Greece on the first leg of our journey at dawn the next morning. Since I knew my way about Alexandria, it fell to me to collect the wireless gear and our personal kit from Mustafa Barracks and escort it down to the Imperial Airways jetty. The picquet officer of the Coldstream Guards gave me a whisky and soda while the kit was being loaded up and I then directed the two trucks to No. 1 gate. We drove along the Corniche, past the Etablissement de Bains at Chatby, where we used to swim when I was a schoolboy at my Lycée, past the Pavilion Bleu, a nightclub of doubtful reputation and much patronized by British officers but which my parents had put out of bounds to me, much to my chagrin; and so into the native quarter itself with its hissing kerosene lamps, its cacophonous music and, above all, the rich smell of Indian corn grilling on charcoal braziers. I had time to feel sentimental that these should be the last sights, sounds and smells of home that I should take with me to the war.

We were twenty minutes late and the Royal Air Force officer in charge was in an extremely evil temper. There was difficulty in finding the tackle to hoist our main radio transmitter aboard the aircraft and it was 2 a.m. before all was stowed to the pilots' satisfaction. The three flying-boats took off at first light in a flurry of spray, circled once round Ras-el-Tin Palace and headed out to sea. Soon Alexandria was no more than a smudgy strip on the horizon. The RAF pilot, who had been so tiresome the previous evening, had not recovered his temper and saw to it that our flight was as bumpy as possible. This was sheer malice on his part for the passengers in the Imperial Airways' flying-boat reported that they had had an entirely smooth flight. After a fleeting view of the Acropolis, we touched down in Piraeus harbour. The first news that greeted us was that German troops had crossed the Polish frontier early that morning. In this event, the three flying-boats had orders to return to Alexandria instead of flying us on to Constanza, so they dumped us on the quay while they took off on their return flight to Egypt. Gubbins borrowed an Imperial Airways' car and set off for Athens but he found the British Legation in a complete state of flap and in no position to offer him any assistance. In desperation he turned to the Polish minister who promptly requisitioned two Lockheed aircraft belonging to LOT, the Polish airline, which happened to be staging in Athens and instructed them to fly us to Warsaw. The rest of us found taxis to take us into Athens and, after an early lunch at the Hotel Grande Bretagne, set out for Tatoi airfield. Here, despite the protests of the Greek police, we drove straight on to the tarmac, helped the Polish crew load our personal luggage – we had had to abandon the radio gear – and climbed aboard. The two pilots took off immediately, ignoring the instructions of the control tower to return at once to enable us to complete the formalities. Flying over the pass of Thermopylai with Mount Olympus to port, I persuaded myself that this was a classic, even an heroic, road to war, and noted as much in a purple passage in my diary. But I had had a good lunch and no sleep at all the previous night and I soon dozed off. Salonika, where we landed to refuel, had already been put partially on a war-footing; some barbed-wire barricades had been placed at both ends of the runway, and slit-trenches dug round the perimeter. However, these obstacles presented no problems to the Polish pilots and, after the shortest of stops, we were airborne again and reached Bucharest about 6 p.m. Geoffrey Macnab, the military attaché, was on the tarmac to meet us. He had been my brigade major at Shorncliffe and his wife was a cousin of my step-father. They had both visited Alan and me when we were in Prague for, though resident in Bucharest, Geoffrey had also been accredited to the Czechs. He took Gubbins off to stay at his villa and the rest of us put up at the Athenee Palace Hotel. We had a free evening and Alan and I ventured forth for what we thought might be the last decent meal we should have for some time to come. Sitting in the open air at the Jardin des Melodies we ate well; iced borsch followed by cold sturgeon, stuffed with beluga caviar, followed by fresh *fraises des bois*. We seemed already to have travelled a long way.

There was no reliable information available at Bucharest about the progress of the war, but most of the rumours seemed to agree that German Panzer divisions had broken through the Poles' front-line defences, and that all the aerodromes around Warsaw had been bombed and put out of action. Gubbins decided to defer a decision about whether we should try to fly direct to Warsaw until we came down at Cernauti to refuel. By then, it was hoped that a situation report would have been received about the state of the Warsaw airfields. We took off shortly after breakfast, only to return twenty minutes later because the Legation wished us to take a confidential bag containing war instructions to the British Consul at Cernauti, where we eventually touched down about midday. Gubbins decided that it was impossible to attempt to fly to Warsaw, and indeed there was some information suggesting that, had we done so, German fighters intended to intercept us. Our Consul, who had only recently arrived, was at a complete loss about how to get us to Poland. However, the Polish Consul General rose to the occasion. After giving us all an enormous lunch, he chartered four taxis, into which we were bundled, and we set out in the most glorious of autumn afternoons for the Polish frontier. The richness of the Moldavian countryside, later to be incorporated in the Soviet Union, is almost indescribable. Our progress was slow, often interrupted by the farm carts bringing in the last of the harvest, while the balconies of the houses in the villages we drove through were heavy with ripening maize cobs. The peasants waved and the children shouted as we drove past for we were clearly persons of importance. I was intoxicated, as much by the delicious local wine which we had had at luncheon as by the richness of the scene, its golden colour and its aura of happiness and contentment so soon to be destroyed.

Once we had crossed the river Dniestr, which was the Polish–Romanian frontier in those days, the scene changed abruptly. At Kolomija station, which was heavily blacked out, there were groups of conscripts recalled to the colours waiting for the next train. We learned that the daily passenger train to Lwow had already left, but that within an hour or two a goods train was expected. An ancient first-class passenger coach, dating from the days of the Austro-Hungarian Empire, was found in a siding, its compartments inlaid with veneer and its red plush seats redolent of stale cigar smoke. This coach was attached to the rear of the goods train and we trundled along the single track railway from Kolomija to Lwow never dreaming that, in less than a fortnight, this single track railway would be the only life-line between Poland and the outside world.

We arrived at Lwow early next morning. Here we were met by a dapper Polish officer in breeches and boots who put us in a motor bus and took us to an hotel. After a short pause to clean up and have some breakfast, we were taken on a tour of the town. It had been only lightly bombed during the previous twenty-four hours but the damage included a wrecked school, a church and a hospital. There were many inquiries as to when the Royal Air Force would retaliate by bombing the Ruhr. This was an awkward question for the British and French governments had reached no decision about bombing Germany, and anyway we were not yet at war. But we felt guilty and were thankful to set off for Warsaw.

Stopping at Lublin to stretch our legs, we heard the tail end of Mr Chamberlain's announcement in the House of Commons that we were at war with Germany. This seemed the moment to change into uniform and, by the time we emerged again, the news had spread and a small crowd had assembled in front of the hotel. They cheered and clapped and presented us with flowers; and a bearded giant of a farmer embraced Hugh Curteis and kissed him on both cheeks. One cynical member of our party remarked that the crowd probably mistook us for Romanians. However, we continued our journey with easier consciences. We reached Warsaw as dusk was falling and drove to the Embassy where Gubbins reported to Major General Adrian Carton de Wiart VC, the Head of the British Mission. Several fires were burning in the outskirts of the city but there were few signs of bomb damage in the streets through which we drove. Nevertheless, heavy air-raids were expected and those whose presence in central Warsaw was not considered essential (which included me) were dispatched to a suburb called Constantin where we spent the next three nights.

In Warsaw itself, life seemed to be going on very much as usual. No one paid much attention to the frequent air-raid warnings and, in fact, there was very little enemy air activity to be seen; occasional aircraft came over in twos and threes and dropped their bombs, mostly in the outskirts, and ambulances and fire engines rushed past to the scene of these incidents but, for the most part, people went about their business or sat in the autumn sunshine drinking coffee and earnestly discussing the situation. The newspapers were issuing new editions every half-hour but there was little reliable news of the extent of the German advance, even at the Ministry of War. Nevertheless, anyone doubting the serious-ness of the situation had only to look at the procession of dusty motor cars, mostly driven by women, crammed with personal possessions and with pale, wide-eyed children looking out of the windows. A few cars bore bullet marks and many had mattresses strapped to the roof as a vain protection against the German dive-bombers. Alan Brown had been roped in as a staff captain and, in the first set of orders, I found myself designated as the liaison officer covering the 'western front'. Since the Germans were already encircling Warsaw, this seemed a job without much future. However, before I had time to reflect on this, the news came that the Polish general staff had left the capital for an unknown destination and that the Mission would shortly follow suit. In Alan's marching orders I occupied a less glamorous role, being put in charge of two Polish army trucks and a requisitioned 5-ton diesel lorry carrying the Mission's heavy baggage. When I protested next day at having been given such a menial job, Alan had replied disarmingly that, at this stage in the campaign, the most important thing of all was not to lose one's personal kit and that I was the only captain on whom he knew he could rely.

My immediate task was to get what appeared to be a mountain of assorted baggage in the Embassy courtyard loaded on to the three vehicles. In the final stages, the loading was personally supervised by General Carton and, at one moment, his voice could be heard loud and clear above the anti-aircraft fire, 'Mon Dieu, les ressorts! Where is that fellow Buggins?' The Ambassador's butler was standing on the steps of the Embassy wringing his hands. He disclaimed any knowledge of the ownership of a case of very decent-looking hock which seemed to have been abandoned; so I hoisted this on board my truck in case of future need. Tutored by Hugh Curteis, I was learning fast how to be a soldier. I was told that our destination was Lukow, a township about 60 miles east of Warsaw which I was shown on a map of which no copies were available. I did my best to memorize the route, which was not difficult once we were clear of Warsaw; and I decided that my immediate object was to get our little convoy across the river Vistula before the main bridge was destroyed. I could, of course, speak no Polish, but one of the truck drivers spoke a little German and I was able to use him as an interpreter. To begin with the traffic streaming out of Warsaw was very heavy but as darkness fell, it dwindled – perhaps there was a curfew – and soon our small convey had the road virtually to itself. Even so, driving conditions were difficult since the trucks' headlamps had been covered with opaque blue paint which gave practically no light whatever. However, the night was bright with stars, some of which, low on the horizon, the Polish drivers maintained were German parachutists. After we had been going for about an hour and a half, one of the trucks ran out of fuel. I blamed myself for having accepted the assurances of the drivers that their tanks were full instead of inspecting them personally. For the time being we were stranded; but, while I was discussing with the German-speaking driver what to do, a car drew up driven by Captain Perkins, a locally recruited member of the Mission whom I had only met the previous day. 'Perks', as he was universally known, was one of those chosen few for whom no problem is insoluble. Within twenty minutes he was back with a 5-litre can of petrol which he had coaxed out of a nearby cavalry barracks and we were on our way; but not for long. Shortly after we had turned off the main road and headed south for Lukow, one of the army trucks had a puncture. No spare wheels were carried and there was nothing for it but to take the inner tube out and repair it. This operation we carried out by the light of the blacked out headlamps and the Polish drivers were replacing the wheel when the general arrived. I made the sort of glottal noise which is universally recognized as calling troops to 'attention', saluted smartly and reported. The incongruity of the situation evidently amused the general for Gubbins told me later that he had inquired who I was and what I was doing. After uttering some words of encouragement in Polish to the army drivers, he left us to our fate.

Dawn was breaking by the time we got to Lukow, a long straggly township of mainly single-storey houses. The members of the Mission had spent an uncomfortable night without their kit in a school which had been chosen as Mission Headquarters. I, at least, had my own bedding roll in which I curled up and went to sleep. In searching for his personal belongings, the military attaché, Lieutenant Colonel Roly Sword of the IV Hussars, had come across the case of hock which I had 'liberated' and claimed it as having come from his own cellar. I disputed his right of ownership maintaining that, since he admitted he had abandoned it, it was at least public property. We compromised by opening a bottle there and then. It had become nicely chilled in the open truck and drunk accompanied by a plate of home-cured ham it made a memorable breakfast. Early next morning Gubbins sent for me and said that he was setting out immediately for Brzesc nad Bugiem – better known as Brest Litovsk – which was the new location of the Polish general staff. Since the conversations were likely to be in French, he wanted someone to accompany him to take notes. Thus began our very close association which was to last until the end of the war.

Before the realignment of Europe after the Great War, Brest Litovsk had been a frontier town on the border between Poland and Russia. It had a magnificent railway station where passengers changed from the European network to the broad-gauge Russian railway system. It also had a red-brick eighteenth-century Vauban fortress, built on classic lines, where Germany had made peace with Russia in 1917 and in which, between the wars, the many political prisoners of the Pilsudski regime had been incarcerated. Among the facilities at Brzesc station was a barber's shop. I opted for a shave which I thought would be refreshing, but Gubbins advised me to have a haircut instead. You can always shave yourself, he said, but goodness knows when we'll get another decent haircut.

We had some difficulty in gaining admission but once inside the fortress Gubbins called on the deputy chief of staff and the directors of operations and intelligence. The news from the front was scanty but what there was sounded extremely bad. We had a quick lunch in the officers' mess with General Rajski, an Air Force officer responsible for war production, who told us that almost all Poland's munition factories had been either overrun or destroyed. It was the same gloomy story wherever we went. He also said that eighty per cent of the Air Force had been attacked on the ground and put out of action. At every turn, Gubbins was asked when the Royal Air Force was going to bomb Germany to ease pressure on the Poles.

Our visit lasted until mid-afternoon and, on the way back, our driver asked whether he might make a short detour to Siedlce where he believed that his wife and children were now living after their evacuation from Warsaw. Gubbins readily agreed and both he and I tried to catch up with our sleep as we drove westwards into the hot September sun. The country was flat and the roads which were dead straight were macadamized but not tarred; as we sped along we left clouds of swirling white dust. The metalled centre of the road was narrow, barely allowing two cars to pass but on each side there was a wide strip of laterite on which there was a procession of horses being driven westward to the battle; a touching sight was the young foals trotting eagerly to the war alongside their mothers. As we passed under the railway bridge on the outskirts of Siedlce, I noticed a peasant woman with a headscarf carrying a bucket and making her way across a field to where a mare and her foal stood peacefully cropping the grass. Behind them stood a one-storeyed white farmhouse and a barn. It was something that Breughel might have painted, a scene that time had forgotten.

Our driver left us in the main street and went in search of his family. Almost immediately, the air-raid alarm sounded. Gubbins and I took shelter from falling fragments of anti-aircraft shells in a porch where we were shortly joined by Colonel de Choisis from the French Mission. A column of horse-drawn Red Cross ambulances had been passing when the alarm had sounded and they now halted, apparently uncertain about what to do. At that moment, two German aircraft dived out of the sun, dropping a string of bombs along the main street where the column of ambulances stood. The chaos was made worse by the frightened horses, some of whom bolted down the main street, trailing traces and, in one case, intestines behind them. There was nothing much that we could do; the townspeople were already rescuing the patients in the shattered ambulances and rounding up some of the horses; other horses lay wounded or dead. The scene was a shambles and, turning to the French colonel, Gubbins remarked that wounded horses always seemed an additional horror. When I nodded in agreement, the French colonel said kindly, 'But you, Captain, were surely not old enough to have fought in the war.' In the company of these two older men, I did not feel as upset by the scene as I might have, had I been alone. Anyhow, there was no time for reflection for our driver now reappeared saying that his family had taken to the woods when the air-raid started and he could not find them. The poor fellow had been a white Russian officer who had lost his first family in the Revolution; had started again with a new family in Warsaw, and now they too seemed likely to have gone for ever. Indeed, he never saw them again, for six weeks later he was drowned when the troop-ship in which he was travelling to England was sunk by a U-boat in the Bay of Biscay.

The railway bridge under which we had passed twenty minutes previously had received a near miss and the road was a mass of tangled signal wires and cables. For the first and only time in the war, I was glad of the hunting wire-cutters which my step-father had insisted that I should buy. Gubbins was amused to find that I had been so provident, but in twenty minutes we had cut our way through. Glancing back from my work, I saw that the farmhouse which had seemed so peaceful was now in flames; the mare and the peasant woman lay dead, the latter with her skirts blown over her head leaving her bare thighs obscenely exposed. Only the foal remained alive, quietly cropping the grass. On our return to Lukow, we found that the German bombers had been there too. The house in which Mrs Shelley, the Polish wife of the passport control officer, had been billeted, the only substantial building in the street, had received a direct hit and she was buried under tons of masonry. Members of the Mission were still vainly trying to extricate her but it was clearly a forlorn hope. Mrs Shelley was the first and only fatal casualty suffered by the Mission during the campaign.

Gubbins and I set out for Brzesc again early next morning before it was light. I was driving and, in the blackout, nearly ran into a large bomb crater on the outskirts of the town. This woke me up and we reached Brzesc without further incident. We spent the morning vainly trying to get reliable information about the state of the battle but the civilian telephone system on which the General Staff depended for communication with the front had broken down and there was nothing but wild rumours. In our absence the Mission moved from Lukow to

Vlodawa, about 30 miles south of Brzesc, where General Carton had arranged for his headquarters to be billeted on his friend Count Zamoyski at Adampol. Gubbins and I reached Adampol in the early afternoon and found the Mission already established in the stables. Our office in the saddle room was redolent of familiar English smells like Propert's saddle soap and Neatsfoot oil and we felt very much at home. Adampol, a large country house, was overflowing with refugees. Nevertheless, the Zamoyskis offered meals and baths to members of the Mission whom they treated as though they were weekend guests. It was a real home from home; even the dogs were addressed in English.

I spent the rest of that afternoon in the woods writing up the War Diary and trying to catch up with my sleep. As soon as it was dark, Gubbins and I set out again for Brzesc. During the drive back that morning, I had dozed off for a second at the wheel and we had nearly run off the road. This time, Gubbins insisted that we take a Polish driver and he himself soon fell asleep in the back of the car while I kept watch. Halfway to Brzesc I saw in the moonlight a small group of men with rifles standing beside the road. Fearing that they might be German parachutists, I woke Gubbins up and told the driver to accelerate. As the car approached at speed the men scattered but we were both relieved when we rounded the next bend without having been pursued by a volley of rifle shots. The news at general headquarters was even more gloomy than it had been that morning and the staff officers we met were showing evident signs of strain and fatigue. We ran the head of the operations staff to ground in a corner of a large hall in the heart of the fortress which was thronged with officers of all descriptions. He and his deputy had just finished a meal and their operational maps were spread out on the table, unfortunately just out of our sight, amid half-empty bottles and dirty glasses. We had barely sat down when there was a general commotion and everyone stood up as a small group of senior officers entered the hall. Among them I recognized General Stachiewicz, the Chief of Staff, and Marshal Smigly-Rydz, the Polish Commander-in-Chief, though the latter appeared shorter and less flamboyant than the photographs I had seen of him in the English press. Holding up his hand for silence, he made a short announcement then turned smartly on his heel and left the hall. After his departure there was a moment's stunned silence followed by a hubbub of conversation in which Gubbins and my presence seemed to be entirely forgotten. It was some minutes before we learned that Marshal Smigly-Rydz had announced that the Germans had already encircled Warsaw; he had just told the divisions in front of Warsaw to stand and fight it out but he had ordered the rest of the army to withdraw behind the line of the river Vistula and the river San. This withdrawal meant the surrender of almost half the country and the news seemed to be greeted almost with disbelief. As soon as we decently could, Gubbins and I slipped away in order to return to Adampoi and report, and we spent the rest of the night drafting signals informing London of this dramatic development.

I spent the next day at Adampol writing up the War Diary, and attempting to make sense of the German and Polish orders of battle in a long signal to the War Office. Meanwhile, General Carton, accompanied by Gubbins and Sword, set out for Brzesc to see the Marshal and find out at first hand what his plans were. They returned with the news that the Polish general staff was leaving Brzesc, once again for an undisclosed location. General Carton's first inclination was to transfer the Mission to the house where he himself had been living on Prince Charles Radziwill's estate. The Pripet marshes, he maintained, would be inaccessible to the German armour and we should be able to hold out almost indefinitely; he implied to the last man and the last round. Gubbins took a somewhat less heroic view of the Mission's role which he considered to be primarily to keep contact with the Polish general staff. Although the latter had left Brzesc for an unknown destination, they were obviously tied to the Stanislawow–Cernauti single track railway which now provided Poland's only rail link with the outside world; and so were we. Reluctantly, the general accepted this practical advice though he mourned the abandonment of his personal possessions and, in particular, the loss of his precious Purdey shotguns. For some reason I do not recall, General Carton was not with us when we left Adampol very early on the morning of 10 September and Gubbins, Alan Brown and I travelled in great comfort in the general's Hudson, an open roadster capable of well over 100 mph. After we had crossed the river Bug the flat plain gave place to low hills with fields and little white villages and, as we neared Lwow, the countryside became progressively more Austrian in character. Lwow itself was in the process of being bombed by two Junkers 88s which later flew very low over us firing a burst or two and forcing us to stop and take cover. Lwow itself was a charming old Austrian town with a number of distinguished buildings dating from the days when Galicia was the north-eastern province of the Dual Monarchy and Lwow, then known as Lemberg, its capital. Since our first visit it had been regularly bombed and there was considerably more damage, particularly around the railway station.

Our immediate destination was Tarnopol, which the general had picked as being most likely to provide accommodation for his Mission

Headquarters. We arrived there in the late afternoon and first impressions were favourable. It was a great relief to be in a town which had not, so far, been bombed, where people seemed to be going about their everyday business unconscious of the war. Gubbins and I called on the Mayor who fortunately spoke a little German. He promised an office for the Mission but said the town was crowded with refugees and he had no living accommodation to offer. However, Hugh Curteis reported that he had found a country house about ten miles distant. Only half of it was habitable as the remainder had been sacked by the Bolsheviks in the 1920s and had never been repaired. The housekeeper made us welcome, saying that the owner, a Polish countess who lived in Warsaw, very rarely visited her estate. The only place ruled out of bounds was the one and only water closet which, owing to the limited capacity of the plumbing was, we were assured, always reserved for the exclusive use of the countess. In the library I found a beautiful contemporary edition of the Goethe–Schiller letters in a tooled leather binding which I was sorely tempted to 'liberate'. I have always regretted that I did not do so, for a fortnight later the place was overrun by the Red Army and it would scarcely have been missed.

I spent the next day, 13 September, in Tarnopol. Gubbins and Group Captain Davidson, the air attaché, drove back to Lwow to see General Sosnkowski while I remained at Tarnopol to write up the War Diary and order of battle and deal with the backlog of signals from the War Office. Sosnkowski was not available as he had flown up to the southern front over the heads of the advancing Germans. However, it was late by the time Gubbins and Davidson returned and all three of us decided to spend the night in the office. The following day we were up at 3 a.m. and set out for Krzemenice, a small town about 30 miles north of Tarnopol, to which the British Embassy had been evacuated. They had been bombed the previous day and, to the amusement of his junior staff, a bomb landing in a midden had drenched the Ambassador in manure. While Gubbins was conferring with the Ambassador, whom he urged to move south without delay, I helped Robin Hankey, the Head of Chancery who, with many imprecations, was burning the Embassy's confidential papers including a naval cipher book which seemed designed to be incombustible. (Robin, later Lord, Hankey was my first departmental head when I joined the Foreign Office in 1948.) Krzemenice was full of rumours and the French Mission reported that the head of the nearest German armoured column was now only 15 miles away. This seemed improbable and Gubbins and I set off in the direction of Plock to try to find out where the Germans were and to trace the general staff. Driving through Mlynow, Gubbins caught sight of Smolenski, the director of intelligence. The big house at Mlynow was in ruins, having been burnt down by the Bolsheviks in 1920. However, we followed Smolenski to a small dower house in the grounds where we found him sharing a room with Colonel Jacklicz, the chief of operations. The latter and his deputy were asleep under their greatcoats on truckle-beds, having just ordered a 200-mile retreat. Otherwise, the place was deserted except for two orderlies who were packing up their personal kit. It was a scene worthy of Stendhal. Colonel Smolenski confirmed that although the German column had halted briefly to refuel, it had now resumed its advance and the Polish general staff had been obliged to relocate in Kolomija. He added grimly that this was the end of the line.

Next day, we left Strusow. General Carton did so very reluctantly for it meant abandoning for good all prospect of returning to his beloved Pripet marshes. After the general had left, Gubbins and I stayed behind for a further night to deal with some signals and clear up the office before setting out for Kosow, our next destination, which was a mountain resort on the Romanian frontier. I was driving and we shortly overtook Captain Horok, General Stachiewicz's ADC and two majors from the general staff, all three of whom seemed utterly exhausted. However, when we stopped for a breakfast of scrambled eggs at a farmhouse, one of them produced a bottle of brandy and, with gallows humour, they joked about what they would do now that all was lost and ruin stared them in the face. Despite everything, it was a cheerful meal. Captain Horok had confirmed that we should find General Stachiewicz at Kolomija, so we stopped there on our way and Gubbins had a long conversation with the general. According to the latter, after advancing from Przemysl the main body of the German 14th Army had turned northwards and Lwow was now virtually surrounded. The Chief of Staff said that he had no reserves left, but with local defence units he hoped to be able to hold for the time being a narrow bridgehead along the Romanian frontier centred on the Stanislawow–Cernauti railway. He inquired urgently when the British and French proposed to attack the Germans to relieve the pressure or, at least, to bomb the Ruhr. He said that in the long-term everything depended on the Western Allies taking the offensive and in the short-term on General Dembinski's ability to hold the Germans on the river Stryzj. However, he maintained that the situation was by no means hopeless. It was hard to share Stachiewicz's optimism and, while driving on to Kosow, Gubbins took stock of the situation. The Poles had lost a third of their army which was cut off in the Danzig corridor in the first week of the campaign.

The Army of Poznan which had been told to stand and fight it out in front of Warsaw and which was to continue its desperate resistance for another fortnight was, nevertheless, entirely encircled by the German pincer movement and had lost at least nine infantry divisions and three cavalry brigades. Meanwhile, it seemed as though General Rundstedt had now embarked on an even wider pincer movement designed to cut off those troops which Marshal Smigly-Rydz had ordered to withdraw behind the river Vistula and the river San. Nevertheless, although doubly encircled, outmanoeuvred and out-gunned and now entirely without air support, the Polish Army was still grimly fighting on and the Germans had not yet had time to consolidate their victory. General Stachiewicz's latest plan of forming a narrow bridgehead along the Romanian frontier was virtually hopeless without air support even if the main Polish armies succeeded in breaking out from their encirclement, which seemed extremely improbable. However, the immediate threat to this bridgehead came from General List's 14th Army which was advancing along the northern side of the Carpathian mountains and had halted at the river Styrzj.

On 16 September, General Carton and Gubbins saw the Chief of Staff again, and the latter described in more detail his plan for holding a line from the river Styrzj to the river Dniestr which, he said, was the most advanced possible until the arrival of reinforcements. He repeated his plea for action by the Royal Air Force and mentioned that he had difficulty in maintaining communications with General Dembinski's headquarters due to lack of radio equipment. Colin Gubbins immediately offered one of the mobile sets which we had brought out from England and for which we had so far found no use. Early the following morning Gubbins, Hugh Curteis and I set off for the Styrzj front to deliver the radio equipment to General Dembinski. Once again, it was a brilliantly sunny day and we drove along the northern foothills of the Carpathians enchanted with the scenery. We found the general confident of being able to hold his position for the time being. He said that the sector was quiet and that, earlier that morning, his troops had driven the Germans out of one of the forward positions. He also reported that General Sosnkowski had counter-attacked elements of the German 14th Army surrounding Lwow, capturing over a hundred tanks. While the radio gear was being unpacked and tested, Gubbins asked whether we could visit the front. There was not much to see. There were some desultory exchanges of fire across the river, the railway bridge had been demolished and in the distance we could see the flaming oil-wells which had been set on fire by the retreating Poles. When we got back to Dembinski's headquarters, the general mentioned almost casually that news had been received that Soviet troops had crossed the Polish frontier near Wilno earlier that morning.

Leaving Hugh Curteis at Dembinski's headquarters to act as a liaison officer, Gubbins and I started back via Stanislawow where we had a puncture. The news of the Soviet invasion had put Gubbins in a reflective mood and we discussed what we should do if we were intercepted. He said he was all in favour of making a dash for it as the prospect of a lengthy internment in a Soviet prison was too horrible to contemplate. It was late afternoon by the time we reached Kolomija for what was to be a final call on General Stachiewicz. We found him sitting by himself in an almost deserted headquarters. He confirmed the news that Soviet troops had crossed the frontier and said he had given orders that they were not to be resisted. He added with some bitterness that last evening, for the first time, he had believed that his plans *allaient se réaliser*. Then this morning had come news of this treacherous stab in the back. Gubbins waited in silence until he had finished and then made a moving little speech in French in which he expressed his sympathy for the Polish predicament and his admiration for the courage with which the army had fought against overwhelming odds. He promised that Britain would fight on until Poland was once more free and its territory restored. After this we shook hands and took our leave.

When we got back to Kosow we learned that the Russians were already in Kolomija where we had, so recently, said goodbye to General Stachiewicz and I wondered what had become of him. Shortly after our return, Prince Paul Sapieha, General Carton's personal liaison officer with Smigly-Rydz, arrived with a message from the marshal to say that the Polish government had surrendered and were crossing into Romania that night. General Carton, who had viewed the German advance with equanimity, became a new man now that we looked like being overrun by the Russians and was itching to be off. The advance party had already left and the rest of us sat down for a final supper – the last meal we were to have on Polish soil. Having been reared on G. A. Henty and the *Boys' Own Paper*, I felt badly about abandoning Hugh Curteis. I enlisted Dickie Wright, one of the Polish language officers, and we volunteered to go back and collect him but Gubbins would not hear of it.*

---

* Curteis, who was a natural survivor, escaped into Hungary and in 1940 was to escape once again from the Germans, having been wounded and taken prisoner in France. In 1950 I met him in Berlin when he gave me a drink and said that Gubbins had told him of my offer to go back for him which he appreciated. Sadly, he was killed shortly afterwards rock-climbing with his son in France.

We finally left Kosow at 9.30 p.m. The rear party consisted of about a dozen people including the general, Gubbins and Sword, the military attaché. I led the way in the blackout with Captain Dabrowski, the Polish liaison officer. The going was easy for the first few miles but when we reached the main highway, the scene became chaotic. During our regress across Poland, we had become fairly inured to the sight of refugees, mostly women, children and old people, fleeing in front of the advancing Germans. This time, the stream of refugees included uniformed personnel of all ranks in military vehicles of every description desperately making their way towards the Romanian frontier. The rout of a defeated army is an awesome sight. Many of the troops seemed in a state of utter shock; hollow-eyed and blank-faced, they did not seem to care what became of them. They took orders from anyone and Gubbins and I soon found ourselves directing the traffic which edged forward at walking pace in a continuous stream. It was a moonless night and only our car headlamps, coated out with blue paint, illuminated the scene. After we had been going for upwards of an hour, the column came to a full stop and Gubbins and I went forward to investigate. We found half a dozen large army trucks slewed across the road with the exhausted drivers slumped over their steering-wheels. While I was trying to coax one of them into life, I heard Gubbins shout, 'Look out, Peter, he's going to shoot!' Turning, I saw a Polish officer pointing a pistol at me. 'Who are you,' he cried, 'giving orders to Poles? What are you doing in Poland?' Before I had time to explain, the traffic started moving again and the officer put away his pistol. But the question remained unanswerable and, walking back to our car, Gubbins remarked bitterly, 'What *are* we doing here? What help have we been able to give the Poles?'

Before reaching the Romanian frontier most of us had changed into civilian clothes but, somewhat to our dismay, General Carton had insisted on leaving Poland in uniform. Fortunately it began to drizzle and he was persuaded to put on a raincoat and remove his general's hat. However, he was in a truculent mood and at the first Romanian checkpoint he remarked loudly to everyone within earshot, 'There are only three sorts of Romanians: they are either pimps, pederasts, or violinists and bloody few are violinists.' He then repeated this observation in French for the benefit of the sentry who saluted in blank incomprehension and waved us through. There had been a long delay at Kuty on the bridge over the river Dniestr which marked the Romanian frontier where a very drunk Polish officer was trying to separate the military traffic from the civilians. However, by 12.45 we were all safely across. We decided to split up and travel separately from now on. Leaving Roly Sword to look after the general, Gubbins and I set off for Cernauti. The road was now free of pedestrians and horse-drawn carts and we made reasonably good time. The Romanian authorities were making desperate attempts to round up the military refugees but they were overwhelmed by the sheer numbers and, although there were one or two tense moments, we had no serious difficulty in getting through. At Cernauti we were met by Geoffrey Macnab who had driven up from Bucharest to meet us. He had been unable, in the short time available, to obtain a safe conduct for members of the Mission, but he had brought an ample fund of Romanian money and, in a country where liberty has its price, he was confident of being able to see us through.

We spent the morning at Cernauti sorting out our kit and getting our passports regularized. The Romanian official, on being told that we were a party of tourists who had been overtaken by the war, remarked on the coincidence that so many of our passports had been issued in Alexandria and bore consecutive serial numbers. However, Geoffrey saw to it that he did not press the point. I stayed behind at Cernauti with Methven, the embassy archivist, Harris Burland and Davidson, the air attaché, in a vain attempt to obtain a *laissez-passer* legitimating our radio equipment, and I finally left Cernauti with Davidson at about 6 p.m. It was now pouring with rain and growing dark and the heavy traffic had scored deep ruts in the country roads which were covered in mud. We took two-hour stints at the wheel and drove as fast as we dared using side roads wherever possible to avoid the Romanian check-points and the worst of the traffic. We reached Piatra Neamt at about 11 p.m. where we had a puncture and decided to spend the night there. It was an unfortunate choice, for the town had been chosen by President Mozicki and Marshal Smigly-Rydz for their first night in exile and the only hotel was fully booked. However, a friendly German *Volksdeutsch*, hearing me speak German, came to our rescue, offered to find us rooms and arranged for our puncture to be mended by his own garage next morning. He also insisted on driving me back to our lodgings. Although he had nothing good to say about the Romanians, he was equally unenthusiastic about joining Hitler's Third Reich and did not hesitate to help us.

We left early next morning and overtook Gubbins, Sword and Dabrowski in Bucau. However, instead of following the main road to Bucharest, Davidson and I decided to turn west and make for the Carpathian mountains, partly to avoid the checkpoints on the main road but mostly on a sightseeing trip for we agreed we might never pass

that way again. It was well worth the detour. After crossing a number
of small streams on elegant eighteenth-century stone bridges, the Imperial
turnpike snaked up the mountainside in a series of hairpin bends, each
corner being carefully metalled with cobblestones. The hillside itself
was thickly wooded and we might have been driving through Bavaria.
In fact, Brasov, a picturesque town nestling in a valley, its market square
surrounded with fine half-timbered houses, was the centre of the German
Swabian minority and seemed in every respect to resemble a German
town in the days before Hitler. It seemed wonderfully peaceful and we
had an excellent lunch of Wiener Schnitzel and Apfelstrudel washed
down with a litre of German beer. The rest of the journey to Bucharest
was on a main road. We drove through Sinaia with its summer palace,
though the Transylvanian Alps seemed rather banal after the Carpathians. We also passed the oil-fields at Ploesti, the main target of
MI(R)'s Romanian Mission should Hitler decide to march south. We
reached Bucharest about 5 p.m. and, having dumped my incriminating
military luggage in the grounds of the legation, I repaired to the Athenee
Palace Hotel for my first bath since leaving the Zamoyskis at Adampol.

That evening Colin Gubbins, Alan Brown and I sallied forth on a
round of nightclubs to celebrate our escape. Starting at the Cina, where
we had some supper, we moved on to the Colorado which was supposed
to have the best 'attractions'. Here to my surprise I was warmly greeted
by one of the bar girls: 'Hallo, Peter, Singst du noch?' It was my friend
Mickey Mouse from Prague who reminded me of my nightly rendering
of 'I Can't Give You Anything But Love, Baby' at the Est Bar. Gubbins
seemed amused, even rather impressed, by my familiarity with the
central European *demi-monde* but he reminded me that we did not want
to advertise our presence to the Germans and this was no time for
reminiscences so, after a drink or two, Gubbins and I moved on while
Alan went home to bed. The last entry in my Polish diary reads as
follows: 'Went to Nippon where Gubbins and I got a bit bottled and
had two very amusing girls and two bottles of fizz for one pound
sterling though this entailed fighting a rearguard action through the
swing doors – and so to bed, scarcely able to remember when I had last
had a full night's sleep.'

CHAPTER 10

France, 1940

My diary of the Polish campaign disappointed my mother who complained that it might have been written by a curate accompanying a party of Victorian spinsters. Having had me educated in the shade of Rupert Brooke, she had expected something more heroic. The War Office was equally dismissive of the dispatch which Gubbins had drafted for General Carton de Wiart describing Rundstedt's double encirclement of the Polish Army and his use of armoured divisions with close air support pressing on regardless to the limit of their endurance. Neither the British nor the French general staff recognized the Polish campaign as a model blitzkrieg and both agreed that such tactics could not possibly succeed on the Western Front.*

Our return voyage to England passed without incident though several ships were sunk in the convoy which followed us. It was made all the more agreeable for me because the troopship was carrying the wives and families of our 1st battalion which had hastily been transferred from India to Egypt. One memory of the voyage is of having to take a two-hour submarine watch in the 'crow's nest' which involved climbing the foremast in the Bay of Biscay in an equinoctial gale.

As part of the BEF the 2nd Battalion Royal Fusiliers had already left for France without me and when I duly reported to the War Office late in October, I fully expected that I would lose my acting captaincy and be posted to some dismal infantry training unit. To my relief I learned that Gubbins was to head a somewhat reduced No. 4 Military Mission which was to be accredited to the Polish and Czech headquarters in Paris and that I was to be attached to MI(R) as his rear link in London. My delight was all the greater when I discovered that I was to share a

---

* So dismissive was the War Office that although both Gubbins and I had been 'mentioned' in General Carton's dispatch it was only after the encirclement of the BEF in 1940 that they saw fit to gazette these awards.

room with Peter Fleming, the author and explorer, and now a supplementary reservist in the Grenadier Guards. My debt to Peter Fleming during the next six months is very considerable, for he gently and tactfully rubbed off many of my rough corners; introduced me to all sorts of people I would not otherwise have met and generally looked after me. We played squash and swam together daily at the Royal Automobile Club where, pathetically, I tried to impress him by doing swallow dives off the high board. Looking back, I suspect that he rather enjoyed my schoolboy hero-worship. I still remember one of his minutes as a model of conciseness: 'Mr A seems to have a good opinion (a) of himself, (b) of his project and (c) of me. Since (a) and (c) appear to be without foundation, I have little confidence in (b).'

Once a month I flew over to Paris and spent two or three days with Colin Gubbins, discussing plans and meeting Polish and Czech personalities. He also introduced me to the representatives of the SIS and the French IIe Bureau. It was at a party with the latter that I was not altogether surprised to meet the elegant young Frenchman, the friend of the Duchesa della Villarosa, with whom I had shared a cabin when returning from Egypt in 1938. This time he claimed to be employed dispatching Red Cross parcels to prisoners of war which, for a healthy young man of military age, seemed an unlikely occupation; but I was learning that, in this company, the fewer questions I asked, the fewer lies I was likely to be told. I had set myself up in bachelor rooms in Clarges Street, off Piccadilly, and I should, perhaps, have felt more guilty than I did about the very comfortable way in which I was spending the war. However, I concluded that I was actually closer to the enemy, dealing with the underground resistance in Poland and Czechoslovakia, than I would have been teaching recruits elementary drill in Lincolnshire or digging trenches on the Franco-Belgian frontier; and as a GSO3 in MI(R), I was certainly better paid.

During the first eight months of the war, when Italy, Hungary, Yugoslavia and Romania remained neutral, Section D of the Secret Service operated a clandestine organization in the Balkans which was our only channel for delivering arms and *matériel* to the underground resistance groups in Poland and Czechoslovakia. When in London, therefore, as much of my time was spent at the headquarters of Section D in Caxton Street as in MI(R). I was given a desk in their Balkan section and allotted the secret symbol DH/M. I was also given a special identity card which seemed of questionable value since I was instructed by the security officer to keep it in a sealed envelope and never to show it to anybody. I never did. However, my relations with George Taylor, the head of the Balkan section, for whom I had great admiration, were extremely cordial and he accepted me unreservedly as a member of his team. At the beginning of 1940, a number of problems arose concerning our secret courier lines and George Taylor suggested, and Gubbins agreed, that I should visit Belgrade, Budapest and Bucharest, our principal dispatch points, and try to sort things out. To provide the necessary cover, I was given a courier's passport and about a dozen bags of diplomatic mail for the three legations concerned. Early in February I set out, travelling once again in luxury in the Simplon–Orient Express. In my personal luggage I was carrying a dozen .45 revolvers for the Poles and some time-fuses for the Czechs. For the former I had had special wooden boxes made in Shepherd Market which had been coated with creosote so that they could be buried. In consequence, the adjoining sleeping compartment, where my personal luggage as well as the non-confidential diplomatic mail was stowed, smelled like a rabbit hutch. Happily, however, wartime austerity had not yet affected the kitchen on the Simplon–Orient Express and, forbidden to leave my confidential diplomatic bags unguarded, I was served a delicious meal in my compartment beginning with a generous helping of Romanian caviar.

Although the archivist at the Paris Embassy observed that I had one more bag than was entered on my Foreign Office waybill, the journey went smoothly as far as the Italian–Yugoslav frontier. I had handed my passport and travel documents to the conductor of the sleeping car and my journey had, so far, been undisturbed by customs or frontier controls. However, at Postojna I was busy reading the German war bulletins in the *Frankfurter Allgemeine*, which I had bought in Switzerland, when I was confronted with an Italian frontier official who questioned the validity of my suspiciously new civilian passport. The sleeping car attendant interpreting, I told him as firmly as I dared that I was travelling on official duty and that he had no right to question me. He seemed far from satisfied and asked me the number of my new passport. I explained that no Englishman knows the number of his passport. To which he replied in an unpleasant way, 'Naturally not, because your passport is false.' With this riposte he withdrew, leaving an aroma of violet brilliantine which mixed incongruously with the smell of creosote emanating from my personal luggage. Glancing at the mirror over the wash-stand I saw that I looked as frightened as I felt, so I tried to pull myself together while awaiting the visit of the Yugoslav frontier officials who, I thought, would certainly have been tipped off by their Italian colleagues to arrest me. However, nobody came and, a few minutes later, the train was winding its way up the hill to the long tunnels over which particular stretch of line, later in the war, I and my partisan friends were to cross and re-cross and watch the German troop trains on their way to the Italian front.

At Belgrade I was met by the Legation archivist who was annoyed at having to turn out after dinner to meet an 'unofficial' courier. Having taken my diplomatic bags, he drove off in the official Humber, leaving me standing in the snow. It was past midnight and the only hotel whose name I knew in Belgrade was the 'Sibsky Kial', where I directed a taxi to take me. The night porter seemed surprised when I handed over my British passport but he provided me with a room without comment. Next morning, on my way down to breakfast, I shared the lift with a nice-looking German woman with two small boys. Since we were in a neutral country, there seemed no reason not to observe normal civilities so we said good morning to each other and proceeded to the dining room. The room was full and the waiter showed me to a table already occupied by, what I took for, two Germans. Barely looking up from their newspapers, they said 'Guten Morgen' and we shook hands and shortly afterwards, having wished me a 'Guten Appetit', they got up and left. Cautiously inspecting the dining room from behind my *Frankfurter Allgemeine*, I decided that not only was there no other Englishman in the room but that almost certainly everybody else was German. I recounted this to the Legation archivist when I reclaimed my bags at the station next day and he replied that, in order to avoid unpleasantness, the Yugoslav authorities had ordained that British travellers should stay at the Hotel Majestic, while German and Italians were to be accommodated at the Sibsky Kial. He added, rather spitefully, that since I was travelling officially, he had assumed that I had been briefed by the Foreign Office. The arrival of my train cut short this conversation which threatened to become personal.

On reaching Budapest I put up at the Dunapalota Hotel. Wartime Budapest in mid-winter was very dismal compared with the cheerful sun-kissed city where Alan and I had spent four anxious days in September 1938. After delivering my bags to the Legation I went in search of Section D's Polish contact to hand over my revolvers. He was not at all grateful, pointing out that they were too heavy and bulky and, moreover, fired rimmed ammunition which was unobtainable in Poland. He said he proposed to drop them in the Danube at the first opportunity but, for the time being, he was very short-handed. His principal agent had recently become infatuated with a certain Countess Krystina Gizycka (alias Christine Granville) who was the representative of an independent resistance group in occupied Poland and he had already made several hazardous trips across the Carpathian mountains on skis. When his advances were rebuffed, he had threatened to shoot himself in his genital organs but, having lost his nerve at the last moment, had succeeded only in wounding himself in the foot. However, this failure made him even more ardent and he had proceeded to throw himself off the Elisabeth bridge. Unfortunately, the Danube was partially frozen and, instead of drowning himself, he had merely broken his remaining good leg and was now in hospital totally immobilized. To add insult to injury, my friend had just received a telegram from Head Office pointing out that this incident was a serious breach of security.

I spent three days in Budapest, hospitably looked after by the military attaché and his wife, whose brother was in my regiment. I then collected what was left of my diplomatic bags and set out for Bucharest, travelling across Transylvania. For extra security, I was accompanied by the assistant naval attaché for this was Dracula country and the route was one usually avoided by King's messengers.

At Bucharest I put up as usual at the Athenee Palace. There were fewer Germans staying in the hotel than I expected and on the evening of my arrival the hotel bar was taken over by a noisy group of British expatriates 'hanging up their washing on the Siegfried Line'. I lunched with Geoffrey and Nora Macnab and they invited me to stay at their villa but I thought that, as an itinerant civilian engineer, it was wiser for me not to accept. So I dined alone at Kapsa which, despite the war, lived up to its reputation of being one of the half-dozen leading restaurants in Europe. I was tempted to go on to the Colorado in search of Mickey Mouse, but thought better of it.

On the way back I stopped off in Paris to report to Colin Gubbins. During that bitterly cold first winter of the war, I had regularly stayed with Gubbins in his flat when I was in Paris. This time I found him unusually fed up with the Poles and Czechs and hankering after more active employment than that of a liaison officer. Consequently, I was not surprised when, a few weeks later, he told me that he was being recalled to London to form and train the so-called Independent Companies, the special raiding parties devised by MI(R) which later became known as the commandos. However, I was struck almost speechless when he added that the War Office (with many reservations for I was aged only twenty-five) had agreed to promote me to acting major and put me in temporary charge of the Mission.

I had been brought up by my step-father to have a low opinion of staff officers and I had little doubt that he would have strongly disapproved of my new appointment. However, since there was no chance of returning to my battalion and the alternatives in this period of 'phony war' were not only unattractive but even more remote from active service than my work with the resistance, I was delighted with my new assignment which I found very exciting. There followed three of the most agreeable months of the whole war. I took over Gubbins's flat at 88 rue de Varenne, opposite the Musée Rodin; his housekeeper, who was an admirable cook; and Corporal Dickinson, who doubled as driver and soldier-servant. I also had at my disposal a large black Renault saloon which I was allowed to drive myself. The exchange rate was extremely favourable and, on my major's pay, I could live extravagantly well in Paris while keeping on my rooms in Clarges Street for my visits to London. Among my friends was Edward Ward whom I had met skiing at Garmisch-Partenkirchen in 1937 and who was now a BBC reporter. There was also Geoffrey Cox of the *Daily Express* with whom I was later to share a house in Crete during the battle in 1941 and meet again on the way to Trieste in 1945. At the Embassy, there was Tony Nutting who was unfit for military service and many years later resigned from his post as Minister of State at the Foreign Office, disgusted by British policy over Suez in 1956. There too were Maurice Petherick, a right-wing Conservative Member of Parliament and Alick Dru, philosopher and writer, whom I particularly admired and who was serving as an assistant military attaché. Alick, who was later to take charge of the Polish section at the War Office, became a close associate and friend. My work was very much as before, doing what I could to provide arms and equipment for the secret army in Poland and keeping in touch with the Czech headquarters which claimed to control a burgeoning underground organization in Bohemia and Moravia. As a result of my recent trip to Eastern Europe, the War Office had agreed to appoint representatives in Budapest, Belgrade and Bucharest dealing exclusively with Polish and Czech matters who would report directly to me in Paris. So did Douglas Dodds-Parker who had taken my place as GSO3 in MI(R).

April slipped by very agreeably; the work was interesting and not particularly arduous; life in Paris went on very much as in peacetime, and bars, restaurants and theatres were all crowded. Various friends from London or from the BEF came to stay, including two of my Cambridge friends whom I met at the races at Auteuil. A slight blot was the arrival of a parliamentary delegation led by Victor Cazalet (later to be killed with General Sikorski returning from Russia in 1943). During Colin Gubbins's time, No. 4 Military Mission had been

exclusively concerned with the work of the resistance and we had had
no contact with the two Polish divisions who had been re-formed and
were now serving under French command in the Maginot Line. The
parliamentarians, ignorant of the true purpose of the Mission, found it
odd, to say the least, that I had not previously visited these two divisions
nor the training camp at Coet Quidan. However, they were so pleased
to have been photographed in France that they made no trouble on
their return to England and I excused my ignorance on the grounds
that I had only very recently taken over from Colin Gubbins. The high
point of their visit was an official luncheon at the Polish Embassy where
I met President Raczkiewicz and General Sikorski for the first time. At
luncheon I sat next to Dr Retinger, General Sikorski's *éminence grise*, with
whom I was to have many dealings in future. On this occasion, he was
as curious about me as I was about him, for with his bleary eyes,
crumpled suit and general scruffiness, he seemed as out of place as I
was in these elegant surroundings. My chief memory of the luncheon
is the Haut-Brion that we drank, the vintage being solemnly announced
by the butler as he filled my glass.

By the beginning of May, Polish intelligence was passing over to us
a steady flow of reports predicting an imminent invasion of the Low
Countries. I duly passed these on to the MI6 representative in Paris
and I should not have been as surprised as I was by the opening of the
German offensive on 10 May. That the French were war-weary – had,
indeed, never recovered from their losses in the Great War – was all too
evident. In the first few days after the German breakthrough, Paris
reminded me very much of Warsaw in September 1939. Superficially
there was business as usual: cafés and restaurants were full; there was
the same lack of reliable news from the front and an ever-increasing
flow of refugees in their dusty and mud-caked motor cars with mattresses
strapped on their roofs, crammed with children and personal belongings.
However, unlike the Poles, the people in the streets already seemed
defeated. They were not a fair sample, for the young and active had
been recalled to the colours and only the elderly and the *embusqués*
remained; but it must be said that there was a disconcerting number of
the latter which, I had to admit, included me. However, I was kept
particularly busy during the second half of May by one of those tiresome
rows, typical of the intelligence community, between Harry Blake-Tyler,
our new man in Budapest, and the representative of Section D. Harry
had secured the support of HM Minister Mr Owen O'Malley and
violent telegrams were being exchanged, many of them requiring to be
personally deciphered by me in the middle of the night, and I made

frequent trips to the Embassy through the darkened and deserted streets.

Fearing that it might be only a matter of days before Italy came into the war cutting our direct overland communication with the Balkans, I sent urgent instructions to Douglas Dodds-Parker to go to the Middle East and set up a supply base in Egypt, and I arranged for Perkins, one of the original members of the Warsaw Mission, to take his place in MI(R). Secondly, remembering my Warsaw experience and the difficulty of obtaining transport if a general evacuation became necessary, I decided to keep in Paris only Truszkowski, another former member of the Warsaw Mission. The remainder of the Mission I packed off to Angers where the Polish general staff were already assembling their rear headquarters. I next summoned Perkins to Paris, intending to return with him for a night to discuss the new situation with Colonel Holland. We booked a flight on 3 June. There had been an air-raid warning before we set off for the air-field at Villacoublay but these were now so frequent that I took no notice of it. I first realized that something was seriously wrong when I saw a row of houses beside the road collapsing like nine-pins as we passed them. The sound of the bombs had been muffled by the anti-aircraft fire and the noise of the car's engine and, before I really took in what was happening, the first wave of aircraft had passed overhead and we were temporarily out of danger. The air-field was obviously the main target so, instead of turning in, I told Dickinson to drive on in the direction of Versailles. However, we had gone barely a quarter of a mile before the main attack started and the bombing became really intense. People starting shouting at us so we abandoned the car and took refuge in a ditch. It was not a moment too soon for a bomb fell on the far side of the road killing a French soldier and wounding several others, and Perkins and I found ourselves lifted about two feet into the air by the blast. Fortunately the car was not blown over on top of us. It was the first of the heavy raids consisting of some 200 bombers concentrating on the air-fields around Paris and both Perks and I were fairly shaken and covered in mud by the time it was all over. The situation at the air terminal was chaotic and the French authorities seemed to have been quite unprepared for an air-raid of this size. To quote my diary: 'It was only at the literal pistol point that we could get them to stop looking on as the wounded were got away and to get on with filling up our plane. It was not a pleasant afternoon.' While we were waiting, a young French soldier came past us in floods of tears. He kept repeating, 'On a tué mon copain.' Finally this got on the nerves of a fellow passenger, Commander Walter Fletcher, MP (later Lord Winster), who replied rather sharply in his schoolboy

French, 'Oui, la guerre est comme ça.' We eventually took off for London in a very ancient De Havilland aircraft, dodging the various bomb-craters on the runway.

I dined that evening with Joan Bright at the Mirabelle to hear the latest news and the following day, after a short meeting with Colonel Holland, I flew back to Paris. I explained to Holland that the military attaché, Brigadier Malise Graham, had held a meeting on 1 June and announced that he could no longer be responsible for warning the more outlying and less regular (this, looking at me) missions of any projected evacuation. When I had protested he had replied that, presumably, I would be warned by the Poles. This amused Holland who said he was sure I would be tipped off by somebody but gave me full discretion to evacuate the Mission whenever I saw fit, if necessary, bringing it back to England. Before leaving London I had a telephone call from Tommy Chamberlayne to say that the battalion had been safely evacuated from Dunkirk and that none of my particular friends was a casualty.

In the event, neither the Embassy nor the Polish general staff let me know that they were leaving Paris on 10 June. Maybe they tried but I was fully taken up with looking after Sir Jocelyne Percy. The latter had arrived the previous day on a special mission from MI(R) to arrange the evacuation of King Zog of Albania. Since there was no other transport of any kind available, I had to spend most of that day driving him to Versailles where His Majesty had a large villa. The King was affable but refused to leave France except in a British destroyer ac-companied by his numerous friends and relations. Having pleaded with him in vain, Sir Percy gave up in disgust and, on 11 June, I got him a seat on the last liaison plane from Bucque, both Villacoublay and Bourget having by now been put out of action. It was midday on the 11th before Truszkowski and I finally left Paris with Corporal Dickinson at the wheel of the Renault. I told Gubbins's housekeeper to sell the typewriters and anything else we had left behind but, in floods of tears, she promised to keep them all intact for our return.*

Remembering the exodus from Poland, I had worked out a careful itinerary avoiding all main roads and towns and, once we were clear of the Paris suburbs, we made excellent time. The occasional road-blocks were manned by reservists who seemed completely apathetic and made no attempt to check us. It was a glorious June day and, as a final

---

* Although the Germans reached Paris on the following day, 12 June, our flat was not immediately requisitioned as it belonged to an American lady who had returned to the United States. I hope the concierge had time to dispose of the typewriters.

gesture, my housekeeper had packed us a superb picnic lunch which we ate in an apple orchard not far from Rambouillet. Truszko agreed with me that it was a great improvement on our exit from Warsaw in September 1939.

The headquarters which Lloyd-Johnes had selected was a small country house about ten miles north of Angers. It was an idyllic situation but as a headquarters quite useless. The British Embassy, on which we depended for our communications, was three-quarters of an hour's drive in one direction, while the Polish general staff was half an hour distant in the other. Indeed, as I sat by the river that evening sipping a glass of Muscadet, I asked myself what on earth we were supposed to be doing; certainly we could not possibly perform our primary function of supporting Czech and Polish resistance. The Germans had by now entered Paris and it seemed that, since communications were so unreliable, the most sensible thing to do would be to return to London personally to seek fresh instructions. Early next morning, I drove to the British Embassy but found nobody in the military attaché's office with whom I could discuss the situation. In the salon of the château, Tony Nutting and Henry Hankey, the Third Secretary, were deciphering telegrams, the former sitting on top of a grand piano. The whole situation was chaotic. The air attaché was sympathetic and gave me a pass for the liaison flight to London but this proved useless as all regular flights had been suspended indefinitely. As a last resort I drove north to St Malo on the rumour that General Brooke's II Division, which had been sent to defend Brittany, was to be evacuated the following day. Hot and scruffy from their forced march, the troops were lining the rail of the cross-channel steamer when I drew up in my sleek black Renault and emerged in well-pressed service dress, with my boots and Sam Browne belt meticulously polished by Corporal Dickinson. I half expected to be greeted with derisory wolf-whistles but instead I found myself suspected of being an enemy agent, probably a 'parachutist', and had not the GSO3 (Intelligence) been an acquaintance from my time at the War Office in 1938, I might well have had to make the crossing under close arrest.

On arrival in London, my first task was to persuade the War Office that some 30,000 Poles might shortly require evacuation from France and accommodation and re-equipment in the British Isles. The general staff were reeling from the return of the BEF from Dunkirk and in no mood to contemplate this new commitment. Feeling rather desperate and passing the Cabinet offices at Gwydr House on my way back from lunch, on the spur of the moment I asked to see Henry Hopkinson of the Foreign Office, whom I knew to be aware of the activities of No. 4 Military Mission. Hopkinson (who later became Lord Colyton) assured me that the situation was under control. General Sikorski had flown over from France that morning and was discussing the situation with the Prime Minister and the Secretary of State for War at that very moment. Realizing that it was now virtually impossible to return to France, I began to worry about the fate of the members of the Mission whom I had deserted. Before leaving, I had instructed Lloyd-Johnes in a rudimentary transposition cipher which he could use in an emergency to send messages to London via the Poles. Sure enough, when I got back to the War Office, there was a message to say that he and the rest of the Mission were safely at Saintes. There was also another and more urgent message saying that I was to accompany General Sikorski back to France the following morning. I immediately telephoned Henry Hopkinson, who confirmed that the Prime Minister had promised General Sikorski one of the Imperial Airways' flying-boats in which to collect the key members of the Polish general staff from Bordeaux and bring them to England.

As instructed I reported to the Dorchester Hotel at 8 a.m. the following day. An Embassy car was waiting with General Sikorski and Count Tyszkiewicz-Lacki, his ADS and we set off at once. We were late arriving at Poole and the captain of the flying-boat, an irascible Australian called D. C. T. Bennett,* was not in the best of tempers for he was fearful of missing the tide. As we were taxiing out for take-off, the general beckoned to me and said, 'Dites au Capitaine que j'ai toute confiance en lui.' In retrospect, this uncharacteristic remark may have had a prophetic signi-ficance, foreshadowing the general's death when taking-off from Gibraltar almost exactly three years later, on 4 June 1943.

Many youthful memories flashed across my mind as we gained height leaving Studland Bay, with the Old Harry Rocks under our starboard wing. We then flew down-channel and away to port, as far as I could see, there was a huge streak of black smoke from the burning oil installations at Le Havre. To avoid interception, we flew well out into the Atlantic before turning south and I had just dozed off when I was woken up by the aircraft banking steeply. Beneath us was a stricken tanker, broken-backed as though it had received a direct hit amidships and rolling gently in a vast slick of brown oil. We made two or three passes over the abandoned ship, but there was no sign of life. However,

---

* Bennett was later to make his name as a path-finder and finished up as an air vice-marshal in the RAF.

about 500 yards away, there was a solitary open ship's lifeboat, with its gunwale shattered. The general watched the proceedings intently and murmured, 'Pauvres gens.' If nothing else, the incident may have brought home to him the extreme vulnerability of his now beleaguered British ally.

When I next awoke, we were circling the lighthouse at Arcachon, the long beach as inviting as ever but now deserted. I expected that we would turn eastwards and fly up the Gironde but, instead, we continued southwards for another twenty minutes and finally touched down in the l'Etang de Biscarosse, a large inland sea, set in the pine trees about 50 miles south-west of Bordeaux. Here there was a French sea-plane base now apparently deserted. Nevertheless we continued to taxi round at high speed allegedly to avoid the attentions of a German dive-bomber.* Finally, we approached the slipway with extreme caution for, although it seemed unlikely that the base was already in German hands, we were uncertain of our reception by the French now that they had surrendered; and the captain kept his engines running. In due course, a scruffy figure approached in a small rowing boat. He said that he was in charge of the deserted sea-plane station and he took Tyszkiewicz ashore to make arrangements. Meanwhile, the general remained on board and Captain Bennett asked me to explain that his orders were that, if attacked, he was to take off immediately, if necessary abandoning the general. This upset Sikorski, who replied rather crisply, 'But I order him to stay.' I conveyed this to Captain Bennett who replied equally crisply in demotic Australian that he took his orders from the Air Ministry and not from some bloody foreign general. I translated this reply as diplomatically as I could, adding that in any case I would be there to explain what had happened and make fresh arrangements. To this the general replied tartly that all that mattered was that the aircraft should be there at his disposal. 'I order it,' he repeated. When Tyszkiewicz reappeared I rowed the general ashore and then returned to the aircraft to make emergency plans.

Late that afternoon there was an air-raid alert but the enemy bombers were far away on the horizon and Captain Bennett decided that we were more likely to escape detection if we remained where we were than if we took off. However, he started up the engines just in case. Otherwise, we had a peaceful evening relaxing on the flight-deck until it was time to turn in after an excellent Imperial Airways dinner. About

---

* This attack is specifically mentioned in Captain Bennett's official log but I have no recollection of it. Certainly no bombs were dropped.

3 a.m. I was woken by the unmistakable sound of tracked vehicles on a metalled road. I roused the captain and, once again, we got ready to take off at short notice. However, the sound of tanks receded and, relaxing, we had some breakfast. At first light, I saw some figures on the slipway and, with my field-glasses, was able to establish that they were in Polish and not in German uniforms. I rowed ashore in the dinghy and ferried them aboard in twos and threes beginning with General Sikorski and General Sosnkowski. With all fifteen aboard, we took off on our return flight. It was an historic passenger list, a copy of which I presented to the general remarking facetiously that it might prove as memorable as the roll of knights who accompanied William the Conqueror in 1066. However, I fear the allusion was lost on him and he was certainly not impressed.

On arrival at Poole, an embassy car was waiting to take the two generals to London but no arrangements had been made for the rest of us. The Imperial Airways staff produced three elderly taxis into which we piled. Now that France had fallen, the Home Guard (or Local Defence Volunteers as they were then called) had been warned to expect German parachutists at any time. There were at least a dozen road-blocks between Poole and London and it took me all my ingenuity to explain away three taxi-loads of unidentifiable individuals, dressed in unrecognizable foreign uniforms and talking in an incomprehensible language. Fortunately, at this stage the LDVs were mostly armed with scythes and pitch-forks so we were not in any serious danger. In London the question arose as to who should pay for the three taxis. On a field message form I wrote out a chit making the War Office responsible for settling the bill, a matter of some thirty pounds. For many months afterwards this chit followed me round from post to post until, eventually, I believe, the sum was debited to the Polish war debt.

Two days later, I formally handed over No. 4 Military Mission to a Brigadier Bridges. He kept me waiting for half an hour and made it clear that he had no time to listen to anything I had to say about the Polish Army or the various personalities with whom he would have to deal. Although admittedly I was at least fifteen years younger than him, I thought his manners left much to be desired. Walking across St James's Park with my nose thoroughly out of joint, I was overtaken by Colin Gubbins who had just returned from Norway where he had ended up commanding not only the Independent Companies but the 24th (Guards) Infantry Brigade. Hearing that I was now out of a job, he asked me whether I would be his GSO2 in a new venture to which he had just been assigned by MI(R). It was to form the nucleus of a British resistance movement in the event, which now seemed likely, that the Germans invaded the British Isles. This sounded not only a job after my own heart but it meant that I kept my major's pay which by now I would have been sorry to lose, if only because I had just received the last instalment of the Army Council scholarship which had been granted to me for five years as a young officer on first appointment!

CHAPTER II

Auxiliary Units

I N early June 1940, army units re-forming in the south of England after their evacuation from Dunkirk reported the presence of mysterious civilians behaving suspiciously in their divisional areas. These were members of Section D who had been given the task of recruiting an underground organization to carry out subversion and resistance behind the German lines in the event of an invasion. The appearance of these strangers in their city clothes, sinister black limousines and general air of mystery caused alarm among the local inhabitants and infuriated subordinate military commanders since they refused to explain their presence or discuss their business except to say that it was 'most secret'. Meanwhile, prompted by Peter Fleming, Lieutenant General 'Bulgey' Thorne, commanding XII Corps, had formed a small experimental unit known as XII Corps Observation Unit to act as guerrillas in the enemy's beach-head. These desperadoes, consisting mainly of local farmers and commanded by Peter Fleming, had a hide-out in the extensive woods overlooking the Stour Valley between Ashford and Canterbury.

GHQ Home Forces, exasperated by the activities of Section D, finally decided that if they were not to become a nuisance all these 'irregulars' must be co-ordinated and placed under military command. Colin Gubbins was given the task of recruiting, organizing and training these so-called Auxiliary Units under the direction of GHQ Home Forces. Although this was to be a civilian and volunteer organization, provision was made for a small professional headquarters staff which Gubbins personally selected. My job was organization and planning and I was also responsible for liaison with my friends in Section D and MI(R) and other secret agencies. The other GSO2, Bill Beyts of the Rajputana Rifles, who had been with Gubbins in Norway, was responsible for recruitment and training. Mike Henderson of the 16/5th Lancers ran the administration and Captain Rodolfo, who had been Gubbins's intelligence officer in Norway with the Independent Companies, was the intelligence officer. Twenty-five years later I was to meet the latter in Saigon when he was serving with the Australian forces in Vietnam.

Our immediate task was to appoint the first half-dozen unit commanders. After East Kent, which was the responsibility of Peter Fleming, the next priority was the sector between the mouth of the Thames and the Wash. Gubbins selected Andrew Croft for this post. He was an old MI(R) hand, a former Arctic explorer who had been on Gubbins's headquarters staff in Norway. Moreover, his father was vicar of Kelvedon so he had many local connections and, before the end of July, he had succeeded in organizing a chain of patrols in Essex and Suffolk. Sussex was scarcely less important than East Anglia and here the choice fell on John Gwynne, a friend of Peter Fleming and a substantial local landowner with many county connections. And so the deployment progressed, extending simultaneously up the east coast and along the south coast wherever invasion seemed likely. Recruitment was made easier when permission was given for Auxiliary Units to draw on the Home Guard, who objected strongly to their best men being poached. With Hitler mustering his invasion forces on the other side of the Channel, there was no time to be lost and, by the end of August, a rather ramshackle organization covering the most vulnerable invasion beaches had been established along the North Sea coasts of England and Scotland as far north as Brechin where the then Lord Dalhousie commanded a particularly enthusiastic patrol composed largely of his gillies and game-keepers. The south coast was similarly covered as far as Lands End, and also South Wales as far as Pembroke Dock.

Patrols varied considerably in efficiency as did the unit commanders, known as intelligence officers. Time was so short that they had to be given a free hand to recruit and plan as they thought fit. Some of them, former members of MI(R) or of the Independent Companies, had some knowledge of explosives and guerrilla tactics, but others had to be trained on the job and two or three times a week, as soon as my office work was finished, I got into a fast car and drove down to a rendezvous somewhere on the coast. While it was still light, I used to give a short demonstration using plastic explosive (still in very short supply) and the special sabotage devices obtained from MI(R) and Section D.* When darkness fell there would be a night exercise in which I would offer expert advice on setting up an ambush or demolishing a bridge. Some-

---

* In the early days, for convenience I used to keep a pound or two of plastic explosive which I used for demonstration purposes on the balcony of my flat in Clarges Street; however, it was a practice I discontinued when the German air-raids began in earnest.

times there were night attacks on friendly units and although they had been forewarned of our intentions, everyone in those days tended to be trigger-happy and I felt most comfortable when the target was a Home Guard unit which had not yet been issued with live ammunition. During the drive back to London I usually managed to snatch a couple of hours sleep. Then, after a bath and breakfast and, if time permitted, a brisk run round St James's Park, I was at my desk in Whitehall Place by 9 a.m.

These excursions into the English countryside were an exquisite pleasure to be savoured before the last bastions fell. Invasion now seemed almost certain and, whether it succeeded or failed, I felt that my personal chances of survival seemed small. So the immanence of English sights and sounds, the sweet smell of green bracken, the splash of a rising trout, the springiness of downland turf and the mustiness of beechwoods, sensations half-forgotten since childhood, suddenly became infinitely precious. However, in that hectic summer there was not much time for such elevated thoughts.

Security was a continuous problem which I seemed to take more seriously than my colleagues. The most that one could hope for was that the actual locations of dumps and hide-outs would remain secret. There was no time to carry out security checks on personnel nor was this really necessary, for each patrol was a brotherhood, more likely than MI5 to detect treachery among its members. Anyhow, it soon became clear that the rules for organizing a secure intelligence network were impossible to apply where guerrilla operations were concerned. Gubbins quite rightly considered security to be of secondary importance since there was little chance of Auxiliary Units surviving in the longer term. All the intelligence officers and many of their patrol leaders knew the names and identities of individual members of the headquarters staff, and Gubbins made a point of getting to know as many of the rank and file as he could; it was not his style to exercise remote control. Nevertheless, it was considered bad form as well as being a breach of security to inquire about people's antecedents or peacetime occupations. Peers of the realm owning broad acres 'kipped down' happily with poachers and convicted burglars, the latter criminals recruited for their dexterity in handling explosives or in picking locks. No two patrols were alike except that all consisted of men who, for one reason or another, were excused military service. In age and experience, they ranged from veterans of the Great War, who took a grim and realistic view of the tasks that lay ahead, to boys waiting to be called up and meanwhile eager for some desperate adventure. However, like countrymen everywhere, they were masters of improvisation and marvellously ingenious in organizing and stocking their hide-outs and dumps.

As the summer wore on and arms and explosives became more readily available, finding secure locations for these dumps became a serious problem. In every case it was necessary to provide the property owner with some plausible story. Most asked no questions and were told no lies but some of the more conscientious citizens reported these approaches to the police or military authorities and both Gubbins and I had to spend quite a lot of our time in allaying suspicions and smoothing ruffled feathers. Senior military commanders were, for the most part, helpful and co-operative; but there were exceptions. Among the latter was Major General Bernard Montgomery. One night the perimeter of his headquarters, which he had declared impregnable, was successfully penetrated by some of John Gwynne's patrols who, to add insult to injury, caused a slight explosion on his front lawn to coincide with his morning staff meeting. It was a silly prank which might have had serious consequences and the general was not amused. Another incident concerned Beddington Behrens to whom Colin Gubbins had, against his better judgement, given a sort of roving commission. He had sought an interview with the GOC Eastern Command and, striding theatrically into the general's office, had tossed a Molotov cocktail through the open french window, incinerating in a flash the general's favourite peach tree. Like General Montgomery, the general was not amused. The most awkward interview which I had was with Sir Will Spens, the Master of my Cambridge College, who had been appointed Regional Commissioner for East Anglia. He listened attentively while I described what Auxiliary Units hoped to achieve. After a moment's thought, he replied that he was not convinced that clandestine resistance of this sort could serve any useful purpose. It was, moreover, bound to provoke severe reprisals against innocent civilians whom it was his first duty to protect. He felt obliged, therefore, to warn me in no uncertain terms that if any member of Auxiliary Units was found acting illegally in his region, either before or after a German occupation, he would be arrested and severely punished. This remark was in stark contrast to Mr Churchill's exhortations to fight on to the bitter end, but its logic was unanswerable and I walked sadly away for I had great respect for my Master's intellectual integrity. It was my first encounter with the *Pétainiste* argument against which SOE was to strive, so often in vain, while trying to fan the sparks of French resistance.

Fortunately, most people's attitude was more visceral and less intel-lectual than that of this distinguished scholar. One or two of the dozens of civilians contacted clearly harboured latent fascist sympathies and we considered means of dealing with them if the invasion came, for we were ruthless young men. However, most of the refusals we encountered were due to unwillingness to put at risk the safety of their families or, more often, their property and possessions. Among the latter were some who should have known better but the vast majority, from the richest to the poorest, reacted splendidly leaving no doubt that had Hitler invaded Britain, these people would have resisted to the bitter end. How the British people as a whole would have reacted to prolonged enemy occupation is a matter for speculation. However, any suggestion that Auxiliary Units could have provided a framework for long-term underground resistance is, in my opinion, absurd.

By the middle of August security was finally thrown to the winds. The units had become too numerous and too widely dispersed for training to be undertaken by members of the headquarters staff. A training school was therefore established at Highworth House, near Swindon, an Inigo Jones mansion belonging to Miss Molly Pleydell-Bouverie. Weekend courses were organized throughout the summer and were attended by patrol leaders from all over the country who exchanged views and got to know each other. With its increased numbers the character of the organization changed and it became virtually a guerrilla branch of the Home Guard. With Colin Gubbins's approval I made plans to recruit an inner core of 'trusties' whose identity would, I hoped, remain secret and who would provide the nucleus of a British resistance movement. By then Gubbins would certainly have been compromised and I saw myself in a key role. I therefore set about providing myself with cover as an electrical apprentice in a Rugby factory. However, this somewhat boyish fantasy was cut short in mid-November when Gubbins was transferred from Auxiliary Units to take up the post of Director of Operations in the newly formed Special Operations Executive (SOE). He asked me whether I would like to go with him as his personal staff officer with special responsibilities for Poles and Czechs. By now there seemed no likelihood of a German invasion taking place in the foreseeable future and I had become bored and disenchanted with Auxiliary Units; so I accepted his proposition with alacrity.

CHAPTER 12

The Special Operations Executive (SOE), 1940–41

B Y the end of September 1940, the immediate threat of a Nazi invasion had been removed, but the prospect of defeating the Germans seemed more remote than ever. With France out of the war, the numerical advantage enjoyed by the Axis forces made any British attempt to invade the Continent impossible for the foreseeable future. The only hope was that aerial bombardment and naval blockade would destroy the German economy and create a revolutionary situation in which the German nation, as well as the people of occupied Europe, would revolt and overthrow the Nazi regime. In this wildly optimistic scenario, propaganda and subversion, hitherto disparaged by the military establishment, assumed strategic importance and were considered by the War Cabinet on 27 May 1940. Neither Electra House, Sir Campbell Stuart's propaganda organization, nor Colonel Grand's Section D was considered up to the job and both were disbanded. So was MI(R) on the somewhat specious ground that it was anomalous that a branch of the Military Intelligence Directorate should have operational responsibilities. The Independent Companies which had been formed by MI(R) and commanded by Colin Gubbins in Norway were transferred to MO4 and re-christened 'Commandos'.

After much inter-departmental wrangling, a new organization was formed in 1940. It was known as the Special Operations Executive (SOE) and was made responsible for both propaganda (SO1) and subversion (SO2), and placed under the direction of Dr Hugh Dalton, the Labour Minister of Economic Warfare in the new coalition government. Dr Dalton envisaged that SOE should be a civilian organization, a 'fourth arm', independent of the Armed Services. However, he soon felt the need for a professional soldier as his director of paramilitary operations and Gubbins whom he had previously met and liked seemed the right man for the job. Perhaps for Gubbins's own good, General Sir

Alan Brooke, the C-in-C Home Forces, strenuously opposed this appointment and the War Office was persuaded only with difficulty to release him. In fact there is little doubt that, in accepting this 'special employment not remunerated from army funds', Gubbins ruined what might have been a brilliant army career. However, he felt it his duty to take the job and I was flattered when he asked me to go with him. I had little to lose as I had no particular desire to return to peacetime soldiering if I survived the war, but I too realized that in accepting this appointment I was burning my boats.

The Ministry of Economic Warfare was in Berkeley Square where Dr Dalton had a small staff dealing exclusively with SOE. It was headed by Mr Gladwyn Jebb of the Foreign Office who was known as the Chief Executive Officer (CEO). SO1 (propaganda) was rusticated at Woburn Abbey and SO2 (subversion and sabotage) was accommodated at 64 Baker Street, in peacetime the head office of Marks & Spencer. The head of SO2, always referred to as CD, was Sir Frank Nelson, at one time a Conservative Member of Parliament, and more recently head of the SIS station at Basle. He was an austere and magisterial figure who in November 1940 stalked the corridors of 64 Baker Street often unrecognized, dressed in the uniform of a 'wingless' flight lieutenant in the RAF Volunteer Reserve.

SO2 was originally mainly staffed by former members of Section D and MI(R) and Nelson appointed George Taylor and Tommy Davies as his two principal assistants. Taylor had been head of Section D's Balkan desk and Nelson made him his Chief of Staff, responsible for SO2's operations world-wide. Tommy Davies, formerly of MI(R) and a member of the original Polish Mission, was put in charge of training, supplies and general administration. Gubbins's appointment as the new Director of Training and Operations necessitated a redistribution of duties which was, in the event, never formalized but, since the three men were personal friends who had previously worked together, there were no serious problems when some of their functions overlapped.

Colin Gubbins, his personal assistant, Margaret Jackson, and I reported for duty on 18 November 1940. My first impression was that SO2 owed more to Section D than to MI(R) and was essentially a civilian organization and, though I pretended not to, I rather enjoyed the Secret Service ambience in which its business was conducted. There was no room for Gubbins's new section in the headquarters' building at 64 Baker Street and we were relegated to a block of apartments opposite Baker Street station, known as Berkeley Court, where we occupied two gloomy family flats. Jack Wilson and Perkins, both from

MI(R), were already installed when we arrived. Jack Wilson was a first cousin of my mother's, one of those who had stayed with us at Camberley. He had been the deputy head of police in Calcutta and, on retirement, had become chief instructor at the Boy Scout training centre at Gilwell Park. In the spring of 1940 he had been recruited by MI(R) to train the Independent Companies in field-craft and he had been transferred to SO2 as head of the training section. Perkins was the surviving member of the Polish Mission. While Gubbins and I had been engaged with Auxillary Units he had kept in touch with the Polish general staff, now established in London at Hotel Rubens in the Buckingham Palace Road. Early in the New Year we were joined by Major R. H. Barry, Somerset Light Infantry. Dick Barry had been one of my anti-tank and machine-gun instructors when I had been a student in the 1930s. He had served with the BEF and been evacuated at Dunkirk. A first-class interpreter in French and German, he was also a graduate of the Staff College and Gubbins made him head of his operations section. With Margaret Jackson and Vera Long, Perkins's secretary who had come with him from MI(R), we formed the nucleus of the future M Section.*

Our arrival in Baker Street was viewed with considerable suspicion by some of the civilian founder members of the organization who feared that it heralded a military takeover. Others were sincerely convinced that army officers were temperamentally unsuited for performing the sort of tasks for which SO2 had been created which, it must be admitted, in those days were usually disparaged by the regular military establishment. So we had to be on our best behaviour. There was also a large element of jealousy for although by the turn of the year SO2 had been running for six months, no country section had yet succeeded in establishing an agent with a radio-set in Western Europe. It therefore seemed unfair that, thanks almost entirely to the previous existence of a well-organized Polish underground army, Colin Gubbins had been able to parachute three agents into occupied Poland on 15 February 1941, within three months of his arrival. In fact, neither Colin Gubbins nor I had had much to do with this first operation to Poland which was the fruit of six months' close collaboration between Perkins, the VI Bureau of the Polish general staff, and the Royal Air Force. Its success was above all a triumph for Flight Lieutenant John Austin and his British air-crew even though the three agents were dropped 50 miles

---

* In accordance with Secret Service practice, Gubbins had adopted the symbol 'M', while as his assistant, I was known for the rest of the war as 'MX'.

short of their target in a part of Poland already annexed to Germany. In those days the formidable difficulties involved in these long-range flights were not fully appreciated by us in Baker Street.

While Perkins was dealing so successfully with the Poles, I was doing my best to wake up the Czechs. Unlike the Polish Government-in-Exile, the Czech National Committee had not yet been recognized by the British Government. However, early in the New Year Dr Beneš invited Dalton and Gubbins to lunch. General Ingr, the Czech Commander-in-Chief, Colonel Moravec, the Chief of Intelligence, and I were also present when it was agreed that some two dozen volunteers from the Czech brigade then forming at Leamington Spa should be given special training by SO2 and then be held in readiness for operations in the Protectorate. However, before any operations could be contemplated, it was essential to establish a new radio link between London and the Protectorate which, for reasons of security, was entirely independent of the Czech intelligence network now operating under the aegis of the SIS. Moravec wasted no time in producing a radio operator named Otmar Riedl and I took him up to Ringway to make a couple of parachute jumps. I also secured Gubbins's approval to let me accompany the first flight to Czechoslovakia and during the February moon period, when the first flight to Poland was taking place, I too was on 'stand-by' with my flying kit stacked in a corner of my office. We were not as lucky as the Poles with our weather, though on the last evening of the moon period we got as far as the air-field only to be 'gazumped' at the very last moment by the SIS who produced an agent who, they claimed, was to be given higher priority than Riedl. When Nelson protested to 'C' about this high-handed behaviour and said that owing to its par- ticular importance I was to have accompanied this operation, he received a curt reply that I should count myself lucky since the aircraft had been lost and there were no survivors. Riedl was finally dropped on 16 April, not as planned in the Protectorate south of Plzen but in Austria. He succeeded in concealing the fact that he was a parachutist and was merely expelled by the Austrian authorities as being an illegal immigrant. He duly reached Plzen; his radio equipment, which he had buried, was retrieved by the Czech resistance. However, by this time I was already in the Middle East.

Despite the high hopes raised by the success of these early operations, I had already learned from personal experience how difficult these were and that, contrary to the popular view, it was quite unrealistic to imagine that secret armies in central Europe could be equipped by long-distance flights from the United Kingdom. I wrote a paper setting out these conclusions and recommending that every effort be made to find alternative channels for transporting arms and equipment. The fall of France had cut us off from the courier lines based on Belgrade, Budapest and Bucharest which we had been developing with some success in the spring of 1940. However, George Taylor was now in Belgrade revitalizing Section D's Balkan organization and linking it with SO2's headquarters in Cairo. So far as M Section was concerned, I pointed out that the operational season was now drawing to a close and it would be six months before it was dark enough to resume long-range flights to central Europe. I therefore suggested, and Gubbins agreed, that I should fly out to the Middle East to see what could be done about reconstituting our former courier line with Poland and Czechoslovakia.

A flying-boat could no longer use the Mediterranean route and since there were indefinite delays flying to the Middle East via Takoradi and Khartoum, our travel section advised me to go by sea to Cape Town and then to fly up from Durban to Cairo by Imperial Airways flying-boat. Although the U-boat campaign in the Atlantic was at its height, so was the London blitz. The risk of being torpedoed seemed no greater than the likelihood of being bombed in one's favourite nightclub – a fate which befell several of my friends in the Café de Paris while I was on the high seas. I looked forward to several weeks travelling in luxury on a Union Castle liner. However, the ship I boarded at Gourock in the Firth of Clyde that cold foggy evening in March 1941 was almost as squalid as the emigrant ship I had joined at Tilbury in 1932. It was an elderly British India liner of about 10,000 tons, built towards the end of the last century for the East African run. The other occupant of my cramped two-berthed cabin had already taken up most of the limited space, the port-hole was heavily blacked out and the walls were plastered with notices about lifebelts and emergency boat stations. Feeling thoroughly depressed, I made my way to the bar where I found a cheerful group of SOE recruits also on their way to Egypt. These included Dick Usborne, at that time a regular contributor to *Punch*, John Connel, alias Jack Robertson, the future biographer of Wavell, Christopher Cadogan who had just come down from Oxford, and his brother-in-law, Sir Anthony Palmer, a contemporary of mine who had been a regular officer in the Northumberland Fusiliers. I could not have chosen more congenial travelling companions. For the first five days we were part of a North Atlantic convoy of some thirty or forty ships with attendant destroyers rounding up the laggards like sheepdogs. However, having sited Greenland's icy mountains, we turned south and set out on our own, sailing at 9 knots down the middle of the Atlantic in defiance of the U-boat packs. Although it was not a comfortable journey, there were compensations. The ship's cellar contained some vintage claret of a quality no longer obtainable in London, while the library held treasures like Compton Mackenzie's *Water on the Brain*, once prohibited in the United Kingdom on account of its disparaging revelations about the Secret Service in the Great War and now long out of print and a great rarity.

Our first port of call was the Cape Verde Islands where we watered and fuelled. It was not at all a healthy spot for there was a resident German consul to report our movements and I certainly expected that when we left we should sail straight into the jaws of a wolf-pack of enemy submarines. However, we had half a day ashore and, for want of anything better to do, made plans to blow up the German Consulate which we duly forwarded to London. Since Britain was dependent on the Portuguese government for the use of the Azores as a staging-post for aircraft crossing the Atlantic from the United States, there was no likelihood that our plan would be accepted, but it relieved the boredom. Our next port of call was Freetown, Sierra Leone, at which passengers were prohibited from disembarking. However, claiming that we had an urgent telegram to send to London, Anthony Palmer and I went ashore in the pilot cutter. It was not a rewarding experience, for Freetown seemed a little more horrible than the Cape Verde Islands. Moreover, on our return we had to climb aboard the ship on a rope ladder in a heavy Atlantic swell to the amusement of our fellow passengers. It was the first time that we had appeared in uniform and the parachute wings which I now wore on my shoulder aroused the curiosity of a group of deep-sea divers bound for the naval base at Simonstown. In fact, I was a bogus parachutist and my experiences so far had been far from happy. Shortly after joining SOE, I went up to the Parachute School at Ringway, Manchester, the first member of the SO2 headquarters staff to learn to jump. In those days, the training was rudimentary. We spent the first morning jumping through a hole in a mock-up of the fuselage of a Whitley aircraft. In the afternoon, under supervision, we packed our parachutes for our first jump, a practice which, in my case erroneously, was supposed to give the novice confidence. The following morning – weather permitting – we jumped. In those days there were no crash-helmets or spine-pads or other protective clothing and, provided you completed your jumps without injuring yourself, you were awarded your parachute wings. The first few seconds after my parachute opened while I was floating silently downwards towards Tatton Park were sublime but unfortunately I was caught by a gust of wind and landed heavily on the frozen ground, wrenching the knee which I had damaged the previous year while skiing in Slovakia. So to the sniggers of my less venturesome colleagues in Baker Street I had to spend the next three weeks with my leg in plaster. However, by the beginning of March I had recovered sufficiently to complete my jumps. With Alfgar Hesketh-Prichard I went up to Ringway for the weekend just before leaving for the Middle East. By now a regular parachute battalion had been formed and we stayed in their mess. On the Saturday, all jumps were cancelled on account of the strong winds. However, since my time was short I persuaded Wing Commander Benham, in charge of the training flights, to allow us to do our remaining jumps on Sunday morning before breakfast, dropping on to the airfield at Ringway instead of going to Tatton Park. All went well, but returning afterwards for a late breakfast we were met by a furious adjutant who accused us of disobeying standing orders, of which we were unaware, and, worse still, of 'bringing parachuting into disrepute'. Almost speechless with rage he threatened us with all sorts of disciplinary action but we caught the morning train back to London and heard nothing more about it. Nevertheless the incident reminded me of the sort of puerility one was apt to encounter from time to time in regimental life.

During the final leg of our passage to Cape Town we twice sailed through wreckage which clearly belonged to a ship recently torpedoed. Since leaving Gourock we had been at sea for thirty-one days, steaming at a maximum of 9 knots, and we considered ourselves fortunate indeed to have arrived safely. We might have been more anxious had we known that the German cryptographers (the B-Dienst) had managed to reconstruct the British convoy code and the movements of British merchant shipping were known to them. Even so, it is worth noting that with gin at sixpence a glass, my mess bill was over £30.

I have only postcard memories of Cape Town but I remember eating some excellent oysters in a garish restaurant with a ceiling dotted with winking electric stars. The following day we boarded the Johannesburg Express. Dismounting briefly at a wayside station on the high veldt, I wondered whether my father, serving with the Mounted Infantry during the Boer War, had felt the same exhilaration. At Bethlehem we changed trains and turned east for the run down to Durban through the most beautiful country I had ever seen. I fell in love entirely with the South African landscape which, sadly, I have never had the chance to revisit. At Durban we were put up at the Durban Club and smothered in hospitality while waiting for the departure of our flying-boat to Cairo.

The evening before we left I was asked to a splendid party where I got so drunk on a lethal milk punch that at dawn next morning when 'weighing out' with my luggage, Dick Usborne kindly held me upright on the scales. Once on board, however, after a couple of horse's necks and an hour's sleep I recovered completely. If I remember rightly, we spent that night at Zanzibar but were advised not to venture into the bazaar and, since we had to be up before dawn, I went to bed without exploring the town, which I regret. The next night we spent at Kisumu, on Lake Victoria. Here I passed an unprofitable evening with a morose British remittance man, paying for his drinks and listening to his fantasies of an England which had gone for ever, if indeed it had ever existed, and which certainly bore no resemblance to the war-torn country of air-raids and rationing which I had so recently left behind me.

The next leg of the journey was the best of all for we flew low over the game reserves, watching the elephants and giraffes feeding quietly and quite undisturbed by the aircraft unless its shadow passed over them. Then we swooped down on the Murchison Falls, scattering the hundreds of crocodiles basking on the hot rocks. From then on we followed the Nile and I remember, at one of our stops, seeing a stark-naked Dinka tribesman standing on one leg and leaning on his spear while he gazed gravely at the flying-boat which had just landed. Douglas Dodds-Parker met me at Khartoum and we spent the evening together. After the disbanding of the Polish Mission he had been working with the Abyssinian guerrillas but his job was now finished and I promised to arrange for him to be posted back to London. On the final leg of the journey, I was already on familiar ground and had a memorable view of the temple at Karnak as we took off from Luxor. Later that same day we found ourselves circling the Pyramids before splashing down on the Nile in front of the Semiramis Hotel where the engines were shut off for the last time. That evening, sitting on the terrace of Shephard's Hotel, sipping a gin and crushed lime, I felt once again that I had really come home.

CHAPTER 13

Crete, 1941

WHILE we had been at sea the situation in the Balkans had changed dramatically for the worse. The German invasion of Yugoslavia had put an end to my plan of using SOE's Balkan organization based on Belgrade. Lines were still open between Budapest, Bucharest and Istanbul. However, these were suitable only for individual couriers and Turkish co-operation could no longer be counted upon. Poland was now virtually cut off from the Middle East and it looked very much as though I had come on a wild goose chase. There was certainly no point in proceeding to Ankara to take up my appointment as assistant military attaché, and I was told to stay in Cairo for the time being in case I was needed in Greece where Peter Fleming had a small group known as 'YAK' Mission harassing the German advance in the Monastir gap. By the time I had tidied up the outstanding matters in Cairo and paid a short visit to Jerusalem, the Greek front had collapsed and the YAK Mission, or what was left of it, had been evacuated to Egypt. However, Ian Pirie, an old colleague from Section D and until recently SOE's representative in Athens, was at present in Crete where he had collected a number of small fishing vessels with which he proposed to keep contact with the Greek mainland and, in particular, with a certain Black Michael who claimed to have an organization able to handle sizeable quantities of arms and explosives as well as agents and couriers. It seemed unlikely in the extreme that these arrangements could be of any value to the Poles but they provided me with an excuse to go to Crete where, according to intelligence sources, a German parachute attack was imminent. Airborne operations fascinated me and this one might provide important lessons for future operations in occupied Poland. A few days before my departure, I lunched with Peter Fleming and Nancy Caccia, the wife of the First Secretary at the British Legation, which was now established at Canea, and they recounted the story of their evacuation from Greece in the British Legation yacht, *Kalanthe*. The ship had been severely bombed and Nancy's brother, Oliver Barstow, a contemporary of mine at Rugby and a member of Peter's YAK Mission, had been killed before her eyes. Since her husband had lost all his kit in the *Kalanthe*, Nancy asked me if I would take him a pair of grey flannel trousers; which is how I first met Harold Caccia who was to have such an important influence on my subsequent career in the Diplomatic Service.

The ship that was to take us to Crete was to sail from Alexandria and I seized the opportunity to spend the night with my parents. News from the Western Desert was bad with the British forces, sadly depleted through the disastrous expedition to Greece, proving unable to withstand the newly arrived Afrika Korps under General Rommel. Although over sixty years of age, my step-father had succeeded in getting himself re-commissioned as a captain in the Royal Engineers and my mother and my two sisters were, therefore, eligible to be evacuated to South Africa as an army family. My step-father and I, anxious to be rid of the responsibility for her safety, both urged my mother to take advantage of this offer now that Alexandria was threatened not only by enemy air-raids from Greece, but also from the advance of the Afrika Korps. Much against her better judgement, she accepted this advice which she was to regret for the rest of her life and for which she never forgave me.

My ship was due to sail on 15 May and my parents drove me down to the harbour and saw me off. I was travelling very light with only a rucksack, though I was also carrying a heavy suitcase containing a radio transmitter for Ian Pirie. I went straight on board and, at the top of the gangway, I remember turning and waving to my parents on the quay-side and thinking that they looked sadly diminished. I was not to see my mother again for five years, by which time I would be married and she would have been widowed for the second time.

Our ship, in peacetime a Dutch passenger liner of some 10,000 tons, was packed with reinforcements for the Crete garrison, including a squadron of the 3rd Hussars. I had a single first-class cabin in which I stowed my luggage and then went on deck while we steamed out of Alexandria harbour, past the familiar landmarks of my adolescence. A stiff sea-breeze was blowing which put me in mind of the happy after-noons I had spent dinghy racing around these familiar buoys. It felt far more than twenty months since we had taken off from here on our way to Poland and it seemed curious to be setting out for the war once again from such familiar surroundings. I stayed on deck thinking senti-mental thoughts until the low line of the harbour breakwater had faded into the distance. I went early to bed and read *The Well of Loneliness* which, for some reason, my mother had pressed on me at the last

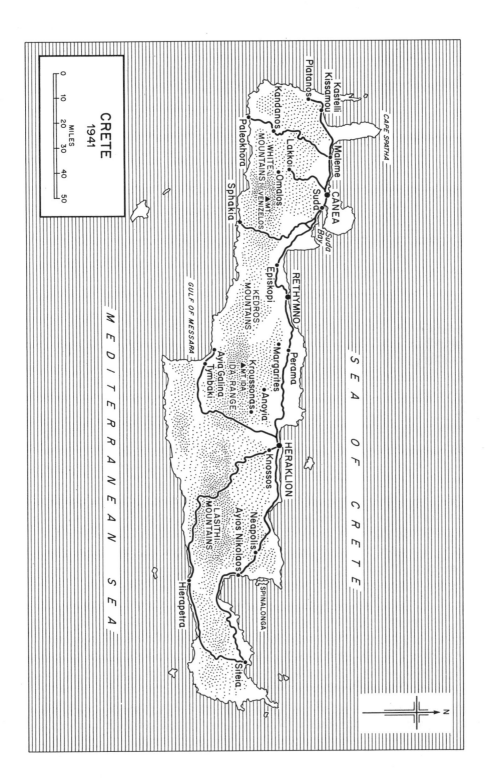

CRETE
1941

MILES

0
10
20
30
40
50

CAPE SPATHA

Kastelli
Kissamou
Platanos
Kandanos
Paleokhora
Sphakia
Lakkoi
Omalos
WHITE
MOUNTAINS
MT.
VENIZELOS
Maleme
Suda
CANEA
Suda
Bay

N

SEA OF CRETE

RETHYMNO
Episkopi
KEDROS
MOUNTAINS
Margarites
Perama
Anoyia
Kroussonas
MT. IDA
IDA RANGE
Ayia Galina
Tymbaki
HERAKLION
Knossos
Neapolis
Ayios Nikolaos
LASITHI
MOUNTAINS
SPINALONGA
Hierapetra
Siteia

GULF OF MESSARA

MEDITERRANEAN SEA

N

moment, surprised that I had never heard of it or of Radclyffe Hall, its unhappy author.

Our passage was largely uneventful except for an attack by a single aircraft which dived out of the setting sun, dropped several bombs into the sea and made off at zero altitude fired at by every gun in the convoy that could be brought to bear. It was, I noted in my diary, rather like a single partridge escaping from a farmer's shoot. Two days later, we arrived at Suda Bay, a large inlet on the north side of the island and the main British base. We had approached in darkness to avoid the enemy bombers, but as we berthed the air-raid siren went. This caught me in my bath but I hurriedly dressed and went on deck. The troops were forming up in their air-raid stations but there seemed no reason for me to stay on board, especially since the ship was clearly the main target. So, as soon as the gangway was rigged, I shouldered my rucksack, seized the suitcase with the radio transmitter and made my way across the deserted dock. Shortly afterwards an army truck came by and I hitched a lift as far as Canea. The intelligence report which I had seen in Cairo had predicted that the parachute invasion would take place in the very near future but there were few signs of military activity in the olive groves through which we drove. In Canea too, people seemed to be going about their business much as usual. The only signs of war were some slit trenches in the parks and public places and here and there signs indicating air-raid shelters. With some difficulty, I located the house taken over by SOE. It was a large villa standing in a small garden on the side of a hill in a suburb known as Halepa, about a kilometre west of the old town of Canea. The lilac trees in the front garden were in full bloom and concealed a shallow air-raid trench. The house overlooked the bay of Canea and enemy Stukas, levelling out after dive-bombing the Akrotiri peninsula and Suda Bay, flew past at eye-level a mere 250 yards away. Having our evening drinks on the terrace, it was good sport to take pot-shots at them with a rifle. I doubt if we ever hit one, though we sometimes made them 'turn'.

The British Legation, housed in a less elegant villa than SOE, was within five minutes walk and, having settled myself in, I went in search of Harold Caccia. I may be excused for having failed to recognize the fair-haired, rather thick-set young man standing in the garden for, apart from the Eton Rambler hat-band on his panama hat, he was un-conventionally dressed for a British diplomat. His grey trousers had a purple stripe and his alpaca jacket was of the sort worn in England by elderly clerical cyclists; on his feet he had patent leather evening shoes with rubber soles. However, he introduced himself and I gave him his trousers and the messages from his wife and Peter Fleming. In return he asked me to lunch the following Sunday.

I was the latest arrival at Fernleaf House which was an unusual establishment even by SOE standards. In charge was Ian Pirie, a tubby little man with a baby face of ageless guile and fair curly hair. He sometimes wore an Old Harrovian tie and, before joining Section D in 1940, where I had first met him, had already had a number of colourful business careers. With him was his latest wife, Niki, until recently the leading attraction at one of the Athens nightclubs, whom he had married on the eve of the evacuation and brought with him to Crete in an SOE caique. She was a dusky beauty who spent most of the time in Ian's bedroom, emerging only occasionally to scold the Greek servants. Nevertheless, it was thanks to Niki's housekeeping that we had such excellent food and drink. Other residents included Bill Barbrook, a retired major in the Sherwood Foresters with Great War medal ribbons, whom Ian had recruited in a belated effort to organize Greek irregulars. Barbrook was assisted by an agreeable young subaltern from the Northumberland Hussars, called MacFarlane, who was to be killed a few days later fighting with the Greek gendarmerie. There was also Geoffrey Cox, the New Zealand journalist whom I had last known in Paris in 1940 when he was working for the *Daily Express*. Now an intelligence officer at Creforce HQ, he was also editing the *Crete News*, a daily newssheet for the troops. Besides these permanent residents, there were several honorary members of the mess who included Monty Woodhouse, Nick Hammond, David Pawson and Michael Forrester, all of who were to become important figures during the forthcoming battle and in the subsequent German occupation.

The day after my arrival, Ian took me to see his flotilla. This consisted of two caiques and a 30-foot motor cabin-cruiser which were now berthed at Kastelli Kassamou, a small fishing village at the head of a mountain-locked fjord at the extreme western end of the island. The coast road ran through the New Zealand defensive position south of Maleme but there were few signs of activity and the defenders seemed to me to be widely dispersed and extremely thin on the ground. The Greek crews of the caiques, having reached the comparative safety of Crete, were in no mood to return to the mainland and there seemed no point in keeping them at Kastelli Kassamou where they were daily exposed to enemy dive-bombing. I urged Pirie to have them refuelled and watered without delay and sent round to Sphakia on the south coast where they were to play a useful role in the evacuation. The more I saw the less confident I felt of the island's ability to survive an airborne invasion now that the enemy had achieved complete air superiority, and I confess that I thought Ian's caiques might yet provide us with a means of escape to Egypt.

When Sunday came, I had an excellent lunch with Harold Caccia in a Greek restaurant in Canea after which he proposed that we should walk to Venizelos's birthplace which, he believed, was a village about three miles distant. Our walk took us through the Australian lines south-west of Canea where the troops were enjoying their day of rest lazing in the olive groves, stripped to the waist, smoking and drinking beer from empty cigarette tins. Although Harold was wearing his new flannel trousers, we must have looked a rather bizarre pair and were subjected to some good-natured ribaldry which Harold clearly enjoyed though, conscious of my major's uniform, I felt rather uncomfortable. Many of the Australians had left their arms and equipment in Greece and had neither the tools nor the inclination to dig defensive trenches. For the time being, it was sufficient for them to have escaped from Greece and they seemed to take little account of the invasion which, as Harold and I knew, was expected at any moment. The situation was far from reassuring and, over drinks that evening, I confided my misgivings to Ian Pirie who thought me unduly alarmist. However, he agreed that we ought to have some emergency plans and proposed to have a staff meeting the following day. But by then it was too late.

The Germans were in the habit of bombing the island every morning. On 20 May I woke up at about 6 a.m. and noted that the bombing had begun slightly earlier and seemed slightly heavier than usual. However, since most of it appeared to be directed at Suda Bay, I was not par-ticularly worried. At about 7.30 the bombing stopped and I took my breakfast out on to the terrace. I was reading the latest issue of Geoffrey Cox's *Crete News* when I became aware of a loud throbbing. Suddenly, the air to the north-west was swarming with Junkers 52 transports, flying at about 400 feet and disgorging parachutists until the whole cloudless sky was filled with parachutes floating earthwards. It was such a remarkable sight that for several minutes I did nothing but stand and stare. Some of the parachutists were landing about a thousand yards away near General Freyberg's headquarters. None was within rifle range but I collected the rifle which I kept handy for taking pot-shots at passing Stukas and stuffed a couple of clips of ammunition into the pocket of my shorts. Ian Pirie also emerged from his bedroom followed by Niki, the latter complaining bitterly 'Where are Hurricanos? No good RAF.' She might well ask, for the last Blenheims and Hurricanes had been sent back to Egypt the previous week.

My Parents

The author at Studland with
his uncle, Frank Wilkinson,
1916.

The author, 1936.

My Wilkinson aunts' house at Longcross, 1938.

The author *en route* for Poland, 1939.

Marshall Tito (signed photograph given to the author at Jajce, December 1943).

Major Alfgar Hesketh-Pritchard, MC.
Royal Fusiliers 1943.

Major General C. McV. Gubbins,   KCMG,
DSO, MC in 1944.

Völkermarkt 1996, Carinthia Memorial to Partisans including Alfgar, killed in Saualpen.

The end of the road - the author in Vienna, 1945.

Carinthia, 1944. River Drau (Drava) crossed by Alfgar and partisans in rubber boats, October 1944.

Lake Phoimj

The summit of the Saulapen, Carinthia.

Our wedding in Rome, 1945. Left to Right: Gerard Holdsworth, Delia Holland-Hibbert, Author, Theresa, Charles Villiers, Lavinia Lascelles.

The Author as H. M. Ambassador, Vienna 1970.

"Aufmachen" 1996. Virginia, the author, John and Peter Zorz and Florjan in front of the hay-barn in which we were sleeping in 1944 until disturbed by Peter then aged 14 pretending to be the Abwehr.

It was not Ian Pirie's style to issue decisive orders but the first priority was obviously to send a flash signal to Cairo and arrange for emergency radio schedules. The next task was to destroy incriminating signals and other documents which Ian had brought with him from Athens and, in a few moments, we had a blaze burning amid the lilac trees in the villa's front garden. The nearest parachutists we could see were about 500 yards away and not advancing in our direction so I propped my rifle against a tree and, since it was hot work in the morning sun, took off my shirt and, strapping my Browning pistol in its shoulder holster under my left armpit, busied myself with the burning. By far the most incombustible as well as being the most compromising objects were the twenty-four German uniforms which Ian Pirie had brought with him from Athens *à toutes fins utiles*. It proved almost impossible to get the nasty ersatz material to burn and it took about an hour and a half before the job was complete. I then collected the metal buttons, dug a hole and buried them amid the lilac bushes. All this time the German parachutists were exchanging fire with the Northumberland Hussars covering Freyberg's headquarters. None of it was directed at us but it occurred to me that even Ian Pirie, who could talk his way out of almost any scrape, would have been hard put to it to have explained the presence of those German uniforms had we been overrun.

All day the battle raged at Maleme for possession of the air-field but the New Zealanders were reported to be holding their own and by nightfall the situation, though serious, appeared to be under control. So were we for, except for our emergency ciphers, we had burned all the incriminating material which had been brought from Athens. From our terrace, we could see the German transports and gliders coming in to land and the red dust and smoke of the battle. However, there was no longer any fighting in our residential suburb and Ian was reluctant to abandon his radio station which was still in contact with Cairo. Air-raids on Suda Bay were continuous, mostly Dornier 17s and Junkers 88s, flying at 6,000 feet or more. In the bright sunlight, one could see quite clearly the clusters of bombs as they came out of the bomb bays; few dropped very near us but there was a great deal of noise and dust.

The following morning I decided to visit Creforce HQ to find out what was happening and see if there was anything useful I could do. It was about half an hour's walk up the hill and I made my way circumspectly for although the area had been cleaned up by the Northumberland Hussars there were still individual snipers lurking in the olive groves. Creforce HQ had a magnificent view across the Bay of Canea with the battle taking place at Maleme airfield some twelve

miles distant clearly visible. I had hoped to see Geoffrey Cox to offer
my services as a supernumerary intelligence officer. However, he was
not there and instead I saw a captain who I have always claimed was
David Hunt, though he strenuously denies it. In any case, I told this
captain that I was a trained intelligence officer, a qualified parachutist
and spoke reasonable German and I offered to help interrogating German parachutists or to do any other job that they might have for me.
Whether he believed me or thought I was a German spy my offer was
curtly refused, somewhat to my surprise and indignation. Nor was
anyone prepared to tell me about the progress of the battle and the
general atmosphere reminded me of the Polish campaign where, so
often, headquarters seemed completely out of touch with their forward
troops and no longer cared very much what was happening.

On 23 May, the general situation worsened dramatically and the New
Zealanders having been forced to withdraw from Maleme air-field, the
enemy gliders and transports were now landing continuously and almost
unopposed. Since I could no longer be of much assistance to Ian Pirie,
I asked Bill Barbrook if I could help him with the Cretan gendarmerie
which he hoped to organize as guerrillas. The following morning, at his
request, I drove down to Suda Bay in search of some arms and equipment which he was expecting from Alexandria. By now, most of the
parachutists had been mopped up in the Akrotiri sector and the road
was clear but Suda Bay itself was not at all a healthy spot. Bombed
incessantly, the splendid harbour was littered with half-submerged
wrecks. Amid this scene of desolation Captain J. A. V. Morse RN, the
senior naval officer, seemed the only person entirely unperturbed. He
said that nothing had arrived from Alexandria but that a mine-laying
destroyer was due in late that night and that if it had anything for us,
he would try to let me know. I left my name and, as I turned to go,
he said, 'You aren't by any chance Major Peter Wilkinson of the Royal
Fusiliers?' He went on to say that he had received, that very morning,
a secret telegram from the Admiralty instructing him to ensure that I
was evacuated by the first available ship. I had no idea what this was
about and thought I was possibly to be charged with having gone to
Crete without orders. Only later was I to learn that groundless fears
had been expressed that while head of the Polish Mission in Paris I had
learned more than I should have about the 'Ultra' secret.

My first instinct was simply to ignore the signal. However, I had
second thoughts when Monty Woodhouse arrived later that afternoon
and reported that Creforce HQ was withdrawing to a new location
south of Suda Bay and that it was high time that we moved before

Canea was overrun by the Germans. It was obvious that time was
running out and with few regrets I packed up my kit. After supper one
of Ian Pirie's staff, whose name I have unfortunately forgotten, offered
to drive me down to Suda Bay. It was a generous act on his part for
in the general confusion of the blackout he was as likely to be shot by
our own patrols as by the German parachutists. He left me on the dock
and, about two hours later, HMS *Abdiel* suddenly loomed out of the
blackness and berthed alongside. Within minutes the two battalions of
commandos comprising 'Layforce', commanded by Colonel Robert Laycock, had disembarked and formed up on the quayside. I caught a
momentary glimpse of George Young, an old MI(R) hand who, bound
for the Romanian oil-fields, had travelled out to Alexandria with us in
HMS *Shropshire* in September 1939.*

Some wounded were taken on board, mostly stretcher cases, but a
splendid Maori NCO, his magnificent torso entirely encased in a blood-
soaked plaster cast, insisted on walking up the gangway unaided. Twenty
minutes later *Abdiel* had cast off and, nosing her way through the half-
submerged wrecks, was making for the open sea. With daylight, the
bombing started and we began to zigzag, the ship heeling over at every
turn and everything movable sliding across the deck. One of the other
passengers, a Fleet Air Arm pilot from Maleme, remarked cheerfully that
at this speed even a near miss would send us to the bottom like a stone.
However, after a couple of hours the bombing stopped and he and I
were allowed on deck where we watched the tremendous bow-wave
swirling past us at 40 knots and the huge wall of the stern-wave which
left a phosphorescent wake as far as the eye could see. We reached
Alexandria the same evening and berthed at the Messageries Maritimes
quay from which I had set out full of martial enthusiasm barely ten days
previously. It was an ignominious return for I had achieved precisely
nothing except to shed my last remaining illusions about the war.

In my absence, my mother and my two half-sisters had already left
for South Africa and I found my step-father, who had had a few days'
leave from the desert to see them off, alone. At dinner that evening he
listened while I recounted my adventures. Then, his mind going back
to his own experiences of front-line heroism and staff incompetence a
quarter of a century earlier, he remarked, 'What a bloody awful
shambles. It sounds just like Gallipoli.'

---

* Colonel George Young, DSO RE and his battalion were to be taken prisoner a week
later, having been left behind to cover the withdrawal and evacuation of the remainder
of Layforce from Sphakia on 31 May.

CHAPTER 14

Polish Frustrations, Heydrich's Assassination and the Formation of the Jedburgh Parties

O N my return from Crete I found a telegram instructing me to break off all contacts with any Polish organizations which had previously been in touch with Section D's Balkan network. This included the Budapest group run by Christine Granville (Countess Gizycka) and Andrew Kennedy (Kowerski) which the VI Bureau alleged had been penetrated by the enemy. Both Christine and Andrew were now in Cairo hoping to reconstitute their line via Istanbul and they vigorously rejected the VI Bureau's allegations as being politically motivated; which they probably were. It proved a painful interview which I handled badly; I was just back from Crete, more over-stressed than I cared to admit. Impatient with their special pleading I made lifelong enemies of both of them, which I was later greatly to regret. However, I neglected to have them struck off the SOE pay-roll so both of them were able to subsist in Cairo for the time being. Later Andrew became the chief instructor at the SOE parachute school in Palestine and, despite the fact that he had only one leg, insisted on jumping with every new group of students so as to set them an example. Christine, while serving with the French Resistance, effected the escape of a group of British officers arrested by the Gestapo by an act of outstanding courage for which she was awarded a George Medal. They were a glamorous pair who deserved better of their fellow countrymen.

Less edifying was my involvement in the case of a Polish double-agent in Istanbul which occupied me for the next three weeks and in which I narrowly avoided becoming an accessory in a 'liquidation'; for in such matters the Poles were ruthless. However, by the beginning of July I had had enough of Cairo and, leaving Guy Tamplin as the liaison officer with the Polish VI Bureau in Egypt, I took off for home.

In the summer of 1941, air travel was still a battle of priorities in which, as in much else, SOE had a well-deserved reputation for over-calling its hand. So I was only held up for three days in Khartoum, one night at El Fashr, a romantic oasis in the middle of the Sahara Desert, and a fortnight at Lagos. Then, travelling as a civilian, I succeeded in getting a seat on the *Clipper*, a United States flying-boat which flew a regular service between South America and Lisbon via the west coast of Africa. I spent a pleasant day shopping in Lisbon and had an excellent fish dinner. Then I flew across the Bay of Biscay in a DC3, arriving at Bristol at dawn the following morning in the aftermath of an air-raid. My fellow passengers on the *Clipper* had included Harold Caccia on his way back to the Foreign Office and Colonel Bob Laycock, who had commanded Layforce in Crete and was returning to the War Office to report.

I found that many changes had taken place in Baker Street during the four months that I had been away. M Section, greatly expanded, had moved to an office block called Norgeby House directly opposite the headquarters at 64 Baker Street. George Taylor was still interned in Italy with the staff of HM Legation at Belgrade and, in his absence, many of his responsibilities as Chief of Staff had been assumed by Colin Gubbins with Dick Barry, head of the Operations Section, as his principal assistant. I was still nominally responsible for liaison with the Poles and Czechs but apart from importuning the Air Ministry to increase the allotment of long-range aircraft, I had little part to play in the operational planning, which was in Perkins's hands. However, be-sides the VI Bureau of the General Staff which dealt with the Home Army, there was also a civilian organization under Professor Kot, the Polish Minister of Interior, which was responsible for the clandestine civil administration inside occupied Poland and also for the Polish *émigré* communities world-wide. Among the latter were half a million Polish coalminers in north-east France, an area of particular strategic import-ance in the event of a future invasion of the Continent. Liaison with the Kot organization was in the hands of Ronald Hazell, a former member of the Polish Mission, and his opposite number was Jan Librach, a young Polish diplomat. During the winter of 1941–42 detailed plans were worked out for using this large Polish community in the Pas de Calais for paramilitary operations in support of regular troops. It was at this time, potentially, by far the largest resistance group in occupied France and was of considerable interest to the Joint Planning Staff.

Meanwhile, however, the Chiefs of Staff had lost interest in Secret

Armies since Hitler's invasion of the Soviet Union and the declaration of war on the United States meant that the Western Allies were no longer numerically inferior to the Axis powers, at least in the longer term. During the summer of 1941 studies undertaken by SOE and the Joint Planning Staff had virtually ruled out the support of patriot forces in Eastern Europe on any significant scale as requiring too great a diversion of effort from the bombing of Germany. This conclusion was politically unacceptable to the Poles who were facing national extinction at the hands of both the Germans and the Russians. The success of the initial flight to Poland had encouraged the Home Army to think in terms of the liberation of their country by a major airborne invasion as soon as German resistance started to crack. The Polish secret army was at that time SOE's most important asset and Dalton and Gubbins and, for that matter, Perkins, Hazell and I, were so deeply committed to the Polish cause that we funked facing them with the realities of their situation. Anyhow the staff officers of the VI Bureau dared not adopt anything but the most positive attitude in their dealings with the Home Army. So we played along with them and, on Gubbins's instructions, over the next twelve months I wasted hours in make-believe joint planning with the Polish general staff working out the logistic requirements of a full-scale airborne invasion of German-occupied Poland which both they and I knew could not possibly take place. Crete had brought home to me that, without complete air superiority, any airborne operation of this sort was doomed to disaster. This conclusive argument was not acceptable to the Home Army who had to keep up their hopes regardless. For my part it was a thankless task and I felt deeply frustrated and depressed by the futility of the whole exercise.

Despite a five months start, the Czech underground movement was not nearly as efficiently or as securely organized as the Polish Home Army. Whereas the Poles faced national extermination, during the summer of 1939 many Czechs had come to terms with the German occupation which at that time was by no means onerous. They considered that they had been deserted by the West in 1938 and saw no reason to make any further sacrifices in the common cause. The Germans had installed a puppet government in the Protectorate and only a minority accepted the leadership of the discredited Dr Beneš and the Czech National Committee in London. Moreover, despite protestations to the contrary, the Czech general staff had very little actual control over the Czech underground army. Based on the pre-war Sokol organization it was largely autonomous and, though directed by former Czech officers, not all of these accepted orders from Beneš and his committee even when it had, at last, been recognized as the Czech government-in-exile. It was in these circumstances that Beneš had agreed to allow SOE to train the twenty-four volunteers from the Czech Brigade for special operations in the Protectorate; and he doubtless had in mind particularly those which for one reason or another the Czech resistance movement was unwilling to undertake on his orders. Just such an operation was the assassination of Reinhardt Heydrich, the newly appointed Reichsprotektor of Bohemia and Moravia, an operation rejected by the Czech resistance as carrying too great a risk of reprisals against the civilian population. In September 1941 two volunteers for this almost suicidal mission were chosen by Colonel Moravec from the twenty-four Czechs undergoing SOE training in Scotland.

Before leaving for the Middle East I had secured Gubbins's approval for the appointment of Alfgar Hesketh-Prichard as the future head of the newly formed Czech Section. Alfgar was a brilliant young man who, after leaving Cambridge, had gone to work in Prague as a hydraulic engineer. He had had a bad fall steeple-chasing during his last year at the university which not only robbed him of a first-class degree but also caused him to be rejected, on medical grounds, by both the Royal Air Force, although he was a qualified pilot, and by the army though the Scots Guards employed him as a civilian to train their recruits in sniping and field-craft. He was still graded C3 but I had got him appointed for a probationary period as a field-craft instructor at one of our new training schools in Scotland, and when I returned from Egypt I put him in charge of the Czech Section which at that time consisted of one elderly officer. Alfgar took over the personal training of the two agents for the Heydrich assassination and, with characteristic energy, tackled the technical problems of the operation which had been code-named 'Anthropoid'. Chief among these was the difficulty of providing a bomb which could be concealed in a briefcase, used at short range without killing the operator but which was nevertheless sufficiently powerful to penetrate the armour-plating of the Reichsprotektor's official motor car. With the help of Nobby Clark, one of SOE's explosive experts, Alfgar succeeded in adapting a percussion grenade of a type used in the Western Desert as an anti-tank weapon. The prototypes were ready by early October and at Aston House, near Stevenage, which had formerly been Section D's experimental station, we spent several arcadian afternoons in the autumn sunshine carrying out 'field trials' on an ancient Austin saloon. This vehicle had been rigged up with armour-plated panels and was towed behind a tractor. Alfgar, whose father had played cricket for the Gentlemen versus the Players at Lords just before the Great War, had no difficulty in hitting the moving target at speeds of up to 25 mph; I was less successful and the two Czechs, not having been reared in a cricketing tradition, did even worse than me and were profoundly distrustful of this percussion grenade. As it turned out, without consulting us, they decided as a first choice to depend on a sten-gun, a weapon which they had learned to use in Scotland. Sten-guns were mass produced and notoriously unreliable and the one they had taken with them jammed at the critical moment with nearly disastrous results. Fortunately the bomb in the hands of the second agent functioned perfectly, fracturing the side of the car and wounding Heydrich with a splinter of bodywork which caused the septicemia from which he died.

During the November moon period the weather was too bad to fly to Czechoslovakia and the parachute drop did not take place until the morning of 28 December. A fall of snow had obliterated the landmarks and made map reading impossible and the unfortunate agents, instead of being dropped in a disused airfield near Plzen, were carried on for some 70 miles and finally landed in the open country south of Prague where no arrangements had been made for their reception. The adventures of these two men, culminating in the assassination of the Reichsprotektor on 27 May 1942 is one of the epic stories of the Second World War. However, it has been told elsewhere* and forms no part of my personal narrative.

In a general reorganization of the Baker Street headquarters in November 1941, I had been promoted to Lieutenant Colonel and, in addition to the Polish and Czech sections, I was given the German and Austrian Section to supervise. I found this embarrassing for I knew very little about Germany and nothing whatever about Austria which I had only once visited as a tourist. On the other hand, the head of the German and Austrian Section, Ronald Thornley, was one of the most experienced and certainly one of the ablest section heads in SOE. A scholar of Winchester and Clare College, Cambridge, until the outbreak of war he had been the managing director of a branch of Ideal Boilers in the Ruhr and certainly did not need me to teach him his business. However, we became close friends and, two years later, he was my 'Controller' at the Baker Street headquarters when, as head of 'Clowder' Mission, I was engaged in running agents into Austria. So far as I was concerned, it

---

* Callum MacDonald, *The Killing of Obergrubbenfuhrer Reinhardt Heydrich* (Macmillan, 1989).

was an extremely profitable partnership and I strongly supported Thornley in his rejection of the popular view that economic collapse would produce a revolutionary situation in Germany leading to the downfall of the Nazi regime. He maintained from the outset that the German armed forces, the *Wehrmacht*, was the only element in contemporary Germany strong enough to overthrow the Nazi regime and that so long as Hitler's luck held there was little chance of mutiny by the German generals against their Führer however much they disliked and despised him. I therefore had no hesitation in endorsing Thornley's recommendation that the approaches of Adam von Trott and Dr Willem Visser t'Hooft in the spring of 1942 should be rejected.

By the summer of 1942 I was feeling stale, frustrated and fed up with central Europe. Dick Barry had returned to the regular army and I realized that if I intended to continue my career as a professional soldier it was time that I did likewise. However, it would have meant reverting in rank, attending the Staff College and subsequently being swallowed up in anonymity. In SOE, on the other hand, thanks to Gubbins's patronage, I was sure of a good job and had by now acquired considerable expertise in the specialized forms of irregular warfare with which we were now experimenting. My post-war career was not within the foreseeable future and I was confident that something would turn up.

Dick Barry's successor was Group Captain C. McK. Grierson, who had no previous experience of special operations, and Gubbins proposed that I should assist him by taking over the forward operational planning. Freed from departmental responsibilities it was a job after my own heart. To assist me I recruited Charles Villiers, Theresa's brother, who was in the Supplementary Reserve of the Grenadier Guards and who had been seriously wounded in a training exercise and was unfit for active service. He had a good analytical mind and a healthy scepticism about SOE which sometimes got on the nerves of the more dedicated members of the organization. We were both a good deal quicker witted than Grierson who, unlike Dick Barry, had not had the advantage of an expensive education and spoke no foreign languages. He found himself fully occupied dealing with the Chiefs of Staff, planners and the service ministries and gave me a free hand. In the autumn of 1942 our plans were based on the assumption that an invasion of the Continent would take place during the summer of 1943 and would trigger a wave of spontaneous insurgency in occupied Europe. Moreover, we were receiving reports of increasing numbers of young men taking to the

French *Maquis* in order to avoid forced labour in Germany. In the six months likely to be available there was no time to organize and train the latter, nor indeed were many of these Maquisards suitable for incorporation in the various secret networks which SOE was building up in occupied France. The problem seemed to me to be two-fold. First, how to harness this considerable resistance potential so as to support the regular invasion forces; and secondly, and no less important, how to prevent these volunteers getting in the way both of the regular operations and of SOE's clandestine actions. My proposal was that small groups, each consisting of an organizer with the rank of captain or major, a demolitions expert and a radio operator, should be dropped in uniform in the enemy's rear at the time of the invasion with the task both of mobilizing and providing support for any resistance groups which they encountered and co-ordinating their activities as far as possible under the direct orders of the local corps commander. At corps headquarters there would be a small special force detachment as part of the operations staff. The assumption was that these parties would be employed on purely tactical assignments – securing or demolishing bridges, cutting rail and telegraph communications and so on – and that after a few days they would be overrun and picked up by the advancing regular troops. Colin Gubbins liked the idea, which was given the code-name Jedburgh, and during the autumn of 1942 I and Mike Rowlandson, a new addition to his headquarters staff, put some flesh on the original scheme by working out, in considerable detail, the probable requirements of aircraft, arms, demolition stores and radio equipment. In February or March 1943 there was an opportunity to give the plan a dry run. Canadian I Corps, under General McNaughton, held a full-scale exercise in the Thames valley. Charles Villiers and I were attached to corps headquarters where we reported directly to the BGS. Meanwhile, Mike Rowlandson, operating from an SOE base in Essex with some half-dozen of the so-called 'Jedburgh' parties, transported by motor bus, carried out various tactical assignments, most of which I made up myself as the exercise developed. The experiment proved more successful than we expected. First the BGS, Brigadier (later Lieutenant General) Guy Simmonds was very intelligent, immediately grasped what we were trying to do and gave us every help and encouragement. Secondly the chief umpire was my old friend Gerald Templer, now a major general, who had been a colleague of Colin Gubbins in the War Office and closely associated with MI(R) in the summer of 1939. Thirdly, unbeknown to us, orders had been issued that the exercise was to be 'dry'. In all innocence we arrived with a hamper from Wellington

Barracks well stocked with 'medical comforts' and as the only (and secret) source of hard liquor our popularity with the operations staff was assured. Gerald Templer gave me a free hand to improvise tactical situations involving local resistance groups and reported favourably on the results both to the War Office and, even more important, to Cossac HQ which was planning the invasion and was persuaded to accept the Jedburgh concept. General McNaughton, a radio enthusiast, was fascinated with our ionospheric transmissions which for verisimilitude I had arranged to have relayed via an SOE station in the Shetland Islands.

By the spring of 1943, I was getting bored with Baker Street and my conscience told me that as a healthy young man I ought to be playing a more active role. The turn of the tide on the Eastern Front raised questions about the Soviet attitude to Poland's frontiers, the role of the Home Army in defending them and above all the propriety of SOE supporting the Home Army in circumstances which might involve confrontation with the advancing Soviet forces. At one of our periodic dinners at the Ecu de France, Retinger had told me that Sikorski was becoming very anxious about the future of Polish–Soviet relations and proposed shortly to visit the Soviet Union to discuss these matters personally with Stalin. Retinger thought that a British presence on his staff would be useful and suggested that I should join the party in an unofficial capacity. Colin Gubbins agreed and, much to my surprise, the Foreign Office, consulted at departmental level, raised no objection. So I lost no time in handing over my current work to Jack Beevor and getting ready to leave. I was, therefore, mortified when I learned about three weeks before our date of departure that Mr Churchill wanted Major Victor Cazalet to accompany General Sikorski as his personal representative and that the general had given him my seat on the aircraft. I had met Victor Cazalet in Paris in 1940 and knew him to be an ardent supporter of the Poles so I bore him no ill will but I felt very let down. In the event it proved one of my many lucky escapes for, on its return flight, the aircraft crashed taking off at Gibraltar, killing all the passengers including General Sikorski and Victor Cazalet. On learning the news I recalled how, almost exactly three years previously, when we had set off from Poole in June 1940 General Sikorski had sent me forward with the somewhat embarrassing message assuring the pilot of his complete confidence and I wondered whether he had given a similar assurance to the Czech pilot of the ill-fated Liberator at Gibraltar. I mourned General Sikorski who had always shown me great kindness and whose untimely death at this juncture was a catastrophe for the Polish nation.

I was now out of a job, but not for long. Colin Gubbins had paid a short visit to North Africa in January where he had an important discussion with General Eisenhower and Colonel Donovan, the head of the United States OSS, about the future shape of special operations in the Mediterranean. He had returned convinced of the urgent need to establish an operational base in Tunisia (and in due course in Southern Italy) which would significantly shorten the flights to Yugoslavia and Eastern Europe. Meanwhile he wanted to transfer SOE's Mediterranean headquarters from Cairo to Algiers. He now proposed to dispatch Bickham Sweet-Escott and me to discuss this proposal in Algiers and Cairo in general terms. I was given the further task of setting up an operational base and packing station in Tunisia for which he had already secured the approval of the Air Ministry, since Tunis had already been chosen as the base for the additional long-range aircraft which the Chiefs of Staff had recently allocated for Balkan operations.

On 6 July Bickham Sweet-Escott and I boarded a civilian DC3 at Lyneham. The only other passenger was Roger Makins of the Foreign Office, the deputy to Mr Harold Macmillan, the Minister Resident at AFHQ. For reasons of security, the windows of the aircraft cabin had been covered up so that it was impossible to look out. Not so the window of the lavatory from which, by chance, I had a magnificent bird's-eye view of Bath as a precious 'last glimpse' of England. Over the years, I had become less sentimental about these 'last glimpses' but this time my thoughts were heavy with the death of General Sikorski at Gibraltar two days previously.

We landed at an undisclosed airfield in north Devon. It was probably Hartland for we were taken in a tender to dine in a neighbouring town which Bickham immediately recognized as Bideford. As soon as it was dark we took off on our flight across the Bay of Biscay and after a short stop at Lisbon flew on to Fez. Here we spent two days in the greatest luxury in the best hotel before continuing our journey to Algiers in the comparative discomfort of a US transport DC3 with hard metal seats – a timely reminder that 'there was a war on'.

CHAPTER 15

The 'Muddle East', 1943

I N peacetime, SOE's headquarters in North Africa, code-named 'Massingham', had been a luxurious beach camp set on the seashore some 10 miles west of Algiers. Besides a number of well-appointed bungalows it contained a substantial villa where Douglas Dodds-Parker lived and entertained a succession of well-screened VIPs, of whom the most eminent was King George VI when His Majesty was on a visit to his troops in North Africa. Set on the beach, and projecting into the sea on piles, was a restaurant and bar which now served as the officers' mess. Despite its sybaritic surroundings, Massingham was a highly efficient headquarters. The working day began with a compulsory run and PT before breakfast which was led by Douglas himself, and the sea-bathing, bare knees and general atmosphere of *mens sana in corpore sano* was somewhat reminiscent of a well-run prep school; but I found it a welcome antidote to the grim streets and weary cynicism of wartime London, and felt young and optimistic again.

Characteristically, Douglas had anticipated the purpose of our mission. He had already obtained General Alexander's permission for SOE to collect the arms and other *matériel* which had been surrendered by the Italians in Tunisia; and he had secured General Eisenhower's and Air Marshal Tedder's endorsement of the plan to transport this *matériel* direct to the Balkans from a dispatch station in Tunisia. Moreover, he had requisitioned a farmhouse some 10 miles south of Tunis for this purpose and installed Donald Hamilton-Hill, a veteran of Auxillary Units, to set up the packing station and supervise the collection of the arms. With Dick Barry, now GSO1 in the planning branch of AFHQ, to prepare the ground, it took only one meeting with Brigadier Sugden, the British BGS, to obtain approval in principle for Baker Street's proposal to move SOE's Mediterranean headquarters from Cairo to Algiers and place it under the operational direction of AFHQ. After

three days at Massingham, Bickham took off for Cairo and I left for
Tunis to see how Donald Hamilton-Hill was getting on with organizing
the new packing station at Protville.

The site which had been chosen for the establishment was a farmhouse set in a vineyard, a square whitewashed building with green
shutters and a terracotta roof. On two sides of a shady vine-covered
courtyard were large stone barns while the third was open to a wide
view of the red-earthed vine-covered hills stretching into the blue
distance. This idyllic scene was spoiled by a plague of vicious blow-flies
which settled on everything. In the closing stages of the campaign, the
farmhouse had been used by the Germans as a first-aid post and the
discarded dressings and medical detritus had to be collected and burned
before attacking the flies with DDT (not yet a prohibited weapon). A
party of locals was engaged in the unsavoury task. The two large barns
where the surrendered weapons were to be stored and packed contained
some vats of liquid which, on investigation, had proved to be the *fortifiant*
used to strengthen the local red wine. Donald described how some of
his other ranks had tried to drink this liquid with dire consequences.
However, excellent local wine was abundant and army rations could be
exchanged for chickens and eggs and, on occasions, a leg of lamb.
Donald encouraged these illegal transactions, arguing that he was
running an operational station and that agents departing for the field
needed to be well-fed. I did not dissent and wrote a report for Gubbins
on the success of our mission so far. I then followed Bickham to Cairo.

I was glad to be back in Cairo among the familiar sounds and smells
but much had changed since my last visit in the spring of 1941. Instead
of a small villa on the banks of the Nile which SOE had inherited in
1940 from Section D, the Cairo office was now housed in Rustum
Buildings, a large block on the Kasr el Aini Street and known to every
Cairo taxi-driver as 'Secret Building'.

From its inception, SOE had aroused the envy of the regular military
establishment. In Cairo this jealousy was almost paranoid and had led
to a series of annual purges and attempts at a military takeover. The
present head of SOE was a civilian, Lord Glenconner, and his military
assistant and Chief of Staff, imposed on SOE by GHQ (ME) in the
most recent purge, was a certain Brigadier Keble. Keble, a regular
infantry officer, was a martinet, reputed to have been at one time
commandant of a military prison in Malaya. More recently he had been
removed from his appointment in the intelligence branch of GHQ for
a fatal miscalculation of the strength of General Rommel's armour at
the time of the latter's spring offensive in 1942. Keble terrorized the

staff of Rustum Buildings, including Lord Glenconner, by his ruthless military bureaucracy. If the motive force, as some people alleged, was primarily his own advancement, he had nevertheless infused the organization with new energy and enormously extended SOE's operations in the Balkans where it now boasted having more than fifty missions attached to guerrilla groups of every political complexion. In consequence, Rustum Buildings was a hive of activity in marked contrast to GHQ (ME) which, now that North Africa had been cleared of the enemy and the battle had moved on, seemed pervaded by a sort of post-coital sadness. Keble was not noted for his social graces but Bickham and I were somewhat taken aback when he received us, having discarded his shirt, in his shorts and undervest. He was a dumpy little man, his hair cut short *en brosse* and, so it seemed to me, his eyes bulging with animosity. Not only were Bickham and I representatives of the Baker Street headquarters which he had never visited but regarded as his personal enemy, but he rightly sensed that we posed a threat to his ambition of taking charge of all Balkan guerrilla operations and becoming a major general. Nevertheless, his opposition to moving SOE's main dispatch centre for Balkan operations from Libya to Tunisia was reasonably well founded, for the present organization at Derna was well established and extremely efficient. Besides, at this time SOE was principally involved in Greece and operations to Yugoslavia were confined to General Mihailovic's Cetniks in eastern Bosnia, no decision having yet been taken to support Tito's communist Partisans on any significant scale. There was, therefore, no appreciable advantage in terms of range to be gained from basing operations at Protville. There were, however, two other considerations which we put to him. The first was the availability in Tunisia of an almost unlimited quantity of captured Italian arms. The second was the Air Ministry's recent decision to base the additional long-range aircraft at Tunis. The latter was a *fait accompli* to which, Keble reluctantly conceded, he would have sooner or later to conform. However, he dismissed the proposal to transfer the direction of Balkan operations from Cairo to AFHQ out of hand as being not only politically unacceptable, so long as the King of Greece and his government were in Cairo as well as King Peter of Yugoslavia, but also as being militarily impractical so long as the main radio transmitter was at Heliopolis, the SOE training school on Mount Carmel and the parachute school at Ramat David. These were well-founded objections which were echoed by Guy Tamplin, whom Keble had promoted to full colonel and put in charge of Balkan affairs.

Meanwhile, a major crisis was blowing up over Greece, SOE having included a number of anti-monarchists in a delegation of resistance leaders which they had brought secretly to Egypt. The demands of the anti-royalists had outraged the Greek Government-in-Exile and caused King George of the Hellenes to threaten abdication. While Bickham stayed on in Cairo to sort out this latest development, I set out for home. The invasion of Sicily had just taken place and there was a long waiting list at Algiers for passages to the United Kingdom. However, with John Anstey, Douglas Dodds-Parker's deputy, I hitched a ride in an RAF Lancaster bomber which was flying home to refit. Owing to a mechanical defect we were held up for a couple of days at Fez where, instead of the comfort of a luxury hotel, we slept as GI aircrews in a US transit camp and, for the first time, I experienced the horror of waffles and maple syrup for breakfast.

On our flight across the Bay of Biscay we made ourselves as comfortable as we could on the hard floor of the fuselage but there was no heating and we were cramped and frozen stiff by the time we arrived, early next morning, at an airfield somewhere near Peterborough. Revived by an 'operational' breakfast of bacon, eggs and sausages in the officers' mess, we caught a train for London.

In the United Kingdom and in the United States, guerrilla resistance in Yugoslavia in 1943 was attributed almost exclusively to General Mihailovic. This romantic guerrilla leader whom the royalist government had appointed as its Minister of War *in absentia* and the courageous exploits of his Cetniks were given full propaganda treatment by the Ministry of Information. I was therefore both surprised and slightly shocked that SOE Cairo rated Tito and his communist Partisans far higher than Mihailovic and his Cetniks and that the latter was increasingly suspected of collaboration with the enemy. I was not alone in my suspicions of a left-wing bias in SOE Cairo appreciations, but I could not deny that the territory Tito claimed to control not only in Bosnia but also in Croatia and Slovenia was now strategically more important than the Athens–Belgrade railway which had hitherto been the main target of Mihailovic's guerrilla operations. Moreover, I learned that these reports were confirmed by Bill Deakin who had been parachuted to Tito's headquarters in May and that SOE Cairo also had liaison officers at the Croat and Slovene headquarters of Tito's National Liberation Army.

Croatia and Slovenia were of particular interest to me since they had common frontiers with Austria and while in Cairo I spent some time briefing myself in the Yugoslav Section. Here I learned that in 1941

Hitler had incorporated a large slice of Slovenia in the Third Reich. This area, roughly speaking, extended northwards from Ljubljana to the Austrian frontier in an inverted triangle, and the Slovene Communist Party was reported to have an efficient underground organization operating throughout the province. At first sight this looked like the back door into central Europe for which I had been searching for the last two years. This conclusion was supported by Captain Klugman of the Yugoslav Section, whom I found exceptionally well informed about communist organizations in central Europe, and who claimed that the Slovene Partisans had links with the Austrian Freedom Front (OFF) which was reputed to be active in Styria and Carinthia. Had I then known that Klugman was a member of the Communist Party and that my conversations with him were almost certainly being reported to his Soviet controller, I might have been more reticent about disclosing my plans and would certainly have discounted much of the information he supplied. As it was, in my excitement, I took it all at its face value and laid my plans accordingly.

Immediately on my return to London I wrote a planning paper recommending that we should investigate the possibility of working into Austria from Yugoslavia and that Hesketh-Prichard and I should be given the task of organizing this penetration. Colin Gubbins backed my recommendation and, somewhat to my surprise, it was immediately approved by the SOE council and tacitly accepted in principle by SOE Cairo. Alfgar, who had made several unsuccessful attempts during the previous summer to escape from Baker Street, was delighted at the prospect. He was an expert, if unconventional, radio operator but to be on the safe side I added Sergeant-major George (Ginger) Hughes, Royal Signals, to our party.

We spent August briefing and equipping ourselves – I had no time for any leave – and finally left England on 6 September, flying overnight to Gibraltar and then direct to Algiers. There was an air of conspiracy about Massingham which had not existed four weeks previously when I had passed through on my way back from Cairo. Douglas Dodds-Parker waylaid us and regretted that the villa where I had expected to stay was temporarily out of bounds. Later, when we were alone, he told me, in strictest confidence, that it was being used for the Italian armistice negotiations which were being conducted by means of an SOE radio link with Rome. News of the Italian surrender broke the following day and we first heard it when we touched down at El Adem to refuel. My jubilation was tempered with regret for the time and effort wasted in setting up the packing and dispatch station at Protville which was now obsolete; and also by Alfgar's fury at not having been let into the secret.

Since the operation, now codenamed Clowder, was being controlled directly from Baker Street, for I had no confidence in Cairo's radio and cipher facilities, we could expect little help from Rustum Buildings though, until his untimely death from a heart attack some six weeks after our arrival, my old friend Guy Tamplin did his best for us. Brigadier Keble's nose had been put thoroughly out of joint by the appointment of Fitzroy Maclean as Mr Churchill's personal representative with Marshal Tito and on learning that we proposed to operate from Tito territory under Maclean's aegis, Keble gave Clowder the lowest priority in everything and did not conceal his animosity. Fortunately Fitzroy, who had recently returned from his first visit to Tito, was lunching with Peter Stirling and Charles Johnstone, two of his former colleagues in the Diplomatic Service, to celebrate his promotion to brigadier and Peter Stirling, who was a distant cousin of Alfgar's, kindly asked us to join the party. I was somewhat apprehensive about this meeting for Fitzroy had been treated disgracefully by SOE in London and had been the victim of some scandalous and quite unfounded allegations which Keble had used in an attempt to discredit him and prevent his appointment. However, my fears were entirely groundless and, far from showing resentment, Fitzroy listened carefully to our plans and promised to do everything he could to help. Understandably he was not prepared to draw on his own limited fund of good-will with Tito in order to further our plans but he suggested that I should fly to Bosnia and put the proposition to Tito myself. Alfgar and I could not have hoped for more. After an excellent lunch we went racing at Gezirah, several of the guests having borrowed money for the purpose from Mo, Peter and Charles's Egyptian servant and one of the more notable members of the Cairo scene.*

From time to time garbled reports reached us of a titanic struggle which was taking place in Whitehall about SOE's future as an independent organization and SOE Cairo's relationship with GHQ (ME) in particular. This confrontation culminated on 30 September in a meeting of ministers presided over by Mr Churchill which resulted in Keble's dismissal and the resignation of Hambro, who had succeeded Nelson as Chief Executive, and Glenconner. Colin Gubbins was appointed CD in Charles Hambro's place and it was agreed that Keble

---

* This actual luncheon party is described in Charles Johnstone's biography of Mo who remained in his service after the war. Mo's signature was indelibly inscribed in the cellar of the house which I inherited from Charles when, in 1955, I succeeded him as Head of Chancery at the British Embassy in Bonn.

should remain temporarily in charge of SOE Cairo until a replacement could be found for Lord Glenconner.

Gubbins lost no time in flying out to the Mediterranean. His arrival in Cairo on 15 October changed my status for he immediately installed me in Keble's outer office with instructions to monitor everything that went in and out of it. Keble accepted this arrangement with a surprisingly good grace and, so far as the day-to-day work was concerned, we got on well enough for I found him extremely efficient with a remarkable mastery of detail; and with Gubbins to back me I could easily hold my own. However, my new responsibilities meant that our departure for the field was further delayed until Glenconner's successor arrived and took over from Keble. This left Alfgar at a loose end and I was fearful lest he should get into mischief and fall foul of Keble who had a vindictive streak. Sure enough, one afternoon Keble returned from lunch in particularly good form and told me that Alfgar had committed a serious breach of security, having failed to lock up his confidential papers. When admonished, Alfgar had replied that it was barely worth putting the papers away since any fool could open his steel cupboard in ten minutes with a paperclip. 'So,' said Keble triumphantly, 'I have locked his press and given him a paperclip and told him that unless he has it open in ten minutes' time, he will be in serious trouble.' Keble's triumph was short-lived for he had barely finished recounting this story when Alfgar telephoned to say that he had succeeded in opening the press. I was reasonably sure that Alfgar's original reply had been intended as a statement of fact and not as an act of insubordination which he would have thought beneath him in dealing with someone like Keble. Nevertheless, I was fearful of the latter's vengeance and told Alfgar to make himself scarce. So he arranged with the RAF to take a course of flying twin-engined aircraft which kept him out of Keble's sight. He also decided to adopt the pseudonym of Squadron Leader Cahusac as his *nom de guerre*.

Not wishing to live in the SOE mess at Heliopolis, popularly known as 'Hangover Hall', Alfgar and I had spent our first month staying at the Continental Hotel. Now that our departure seemed likely to be delayed, we started to look for somewhere else to live. Arnold Breene, a young captain in the Royal Engineers who was a leading light in Rustum Buildings, came to our rescue and invited us to join his mess at 'Chateau Tara'. This was a large villa in Zamalek with a marble hall and a ballroom which had been leased by a group of friends, mostly British liaison officers serving in Crete and Albania, as somewhere to live when they were in Cairo on leave. The occupants at various times

included such *kondottieri* as Paddy Leigh Fermor; Billy Moss of the
Coldstream Guards, who was to be Paddy's accomplice in the kid-
napping of General Kreipe from Crete in April 1944; Billy Maclean of
the Scots Greys; David Smiley of the Blues; and Rowland Winn (later
Lord St Oswald) of the 8th Hussars. Even by Cairo standards the
lifestyle at Chateau Tara was extravagant, arousing both envy and
malice. Its dinner parties were renowned, not least because they were
presided over by the elegant Countess Sophie Tarnowska who had a pet
mongoose which she released in the dining room when the conversation
became tedious or the guests outstayed their welcome. An epic story
was told of King Farouk standing on a dining-room chair and defending
his ankles with a napkin and a table fork from the attacks of this
ferocious small animal. Although we had several memorable dinner
parties, there were no royal guests while Alfgar and I were at Tara, for
royalty was Paddy Leigh Fermor's speciality and he had recently returned to Crete. Being somewhat older than the others, and already a
lieutenant colonel, I fitted less easily than Alfgar into this Hell-Fire
society. Besides, as Keble's assistant, I was identified as a staff officer,
a category particularly derided by these boy adventurers whose motto
was 'A bas les culs de cuir'. So while I was grateful to them for accepting
me as a member of their tribe, I was as eager as Alfgar to be off.

Fortunately, relief was in sight. A brigadier called Stawell was selected
as Glenconner's successor and was due at the end of November. I
guessed that Colin Gubbins would have liked me to have stayed on
after Keble's departure until Stawell was settled in. However, the first
winter snows had already fallen in Bosnia and Operation Clowder was
several weeks overdue. So I sent Alfgar to Italy with instructions to see
Fitzroy Maclean and organize our visit to Tito without further delay.
Stawell, now a major general, took over from Keble on 30 November.
Two days later, with only a slight twinge of conscience, in Gubbins's
absence and to Stawell's dismay, I shook off the dust of Cairo for the
last time. As the aircraft circled the Pyramids and I settled down to
sleep off the excesses of my farewell party at Tara the previous evening,
I little thought that within seventy-two hours I would find myself in a
blizzard, knee deep in snow, pushing a stalled Italian army truck up an
icy mountain road in central Bosnia.

CHAPTER 16

A Safe Landing, December 1943

I WAS somewhat disconcerted to discover that we were to fly in a small Italian three-engined aircraft still sporting Italian roundels. Nor did the pilot inspire confidence, arriving on the tarmac in a pair of filthy shorts, smoking a cigarette and wearing an Italian Air Force cap on the back of his head. The Italian armistice was very recent history and I did not at all relish approaching Malta in an aircraft with Italian markings. However, as soon as we had taken off I fell asleep, only to be woken up half an hour later by an elderly major on the other side of the aisle who gestured towards the pilot's cabin. Its door had swung open revealing, sprawled across the co-pilot's seat, a pair of bare female thighs which the pilot was fondling with his spare hand. 'It's disgusting,' shouted the indignant major above the roar and rattle of the aircraft, 'you ought to report him.' I nodded non-committally, thinking our recognition by the Malta anti-aircraft batteries was of more immediate importance. However, we landed safely and a blowsey blonde emerged from the cockpit, waved to the censorious major and vanished into the crowd.

It was only a short flight from Malta to Bari and Alfgar was there to meet me. I noted that he had the expectant look of a spaniel who had just retrieved a doubtful bird and was hoping for some reassuring sign of approval. 'It's all right,' he said, 'I've fixed everything with Fitzroy and we're booked to fly in with him first thing tomorrow morning.' This was rather more than I had bargained for and, if truth be known, I had been looking forward to a quiet week in Italy making Clowder's administrative arrangements and perhaps spending an afternoon or two on the beach recuperating from my exertions in Cairo. However, I recovered from my initial shock after a good lunch and a bottle of Chianti at the Hotel Imperiale. It was a delight to have escaped from Cairo and to be back again in Europe and, for the time being, I was content to leave our fate in Alfgar's hands.

Massingham had established its advance headquarters at Monopoli, a small seaside town some fifteen miles south of Bari, hitherto notable only for having been the birthplace of the American gangster Al Capone. In command of this detachment was Commander Gerard Holdsworth, DSO, RNVR, an original member of both Section D and SOE. Gerry was an old friend of mine and a veteran of many operations, who had just been awarded his second DSO for conspicuous gallantry in North Africa. He cheerfully undertook to act as Clowder's rear link for the time being, and told me not to worry about details but to leave 'all standing' and he would sort it out after we had left. So we had a convivial farewell dinner, my second in two days, interrupted by a loud explosion which shook the table and spilt the wine in our glasses. This was caused, as we later discovered, by a German aircraft bombing a ship loaded with ammunition and explosives in Bari harbour, and it provided an authentic background for Gerry's stories of ferrying agents to and from Brittany during the early months of the Occupation. The party broke up about midnight but since a car had been ordered at 3 a.m. to pick us up and take us to the airfield at Leece, there seemed no point in going to bed. So having packed my rucksack with my few belongings I spent the rest of the night writing letters to my family, my lawyer and my bank to say that I should be *incommunicado* for the next few months.

Dawn was breaking over the Adriatic by the time we reached the outskirts of Leece and stopped to ask the way to the airfield. After a cup of coffee at the officers' mess, we drove out to the dispersal point where our DC3 was standing and joined a small group, none of whom we knew; nor did anyone take any notice of us. In due course a jeep drew up containing Fitzroy Maclean and a youthful and be-medalled colonel commanding the US 82nd Fighter Group which was providing six Lightnings to escort us, for our destination at Glamoc was beyond the range of RAF fighters.

At 9.40 a.m. we took off, flying northward over a sunlit, white-capped sea, the Lightnings circling and swooping above us. As we approached the mainland, the Dalmatian Islands, Hvar, Vis, and many others looked particularly inviting. However, as we flew inland, the sun vanished and we ran into wispy cloud giving only an occasional fleeting view of the coastal plain and the barren uplands; caught in down-draughts, the DC3 began to lurch and yaw. By now I had had time to take stock of my fellow passengers. These included Hilary King, a cheerful curly-headed young man who was to act as Fitzroy's signals officer and who later became a close friend of mine when we served together in HM Embassy at Washington in the early 1950s. There was also a United States major called Selwig from the Office of Strategic Services who told us that his voluminous kit, besides including almost every item of camping equipment known to Abercrombie and Fitch, also contained a selection of automatic pistols which he proposed to present to Partisan notables, including Marshal Tito.

Distancing myself as far as possible from the garrulous Major Selwig, I buried my nose in a book on classical architecture, a subject of which I was entirely ignorant, which I had bought at Cairo airport, and hoped it gave an impression of nonchalance. Then, all at once, we started a steep descent through the scattered clouds and a few minutes later we were bumping over the rough landing strip which the Partisans had prepared. The aircraft swung round into the wind with its engines still running and, seizing our kit, we tumbled out. I had just time to exchange a few words with Bill Deakin, who had spent the last six months as a liaison officer with Marshal Tito and was now returning to Cairo. Then he boarded the aircraft; the door banged shut; Fitzroy waved to us from the co-pilot's seat and within a matter of minutes the DC3 had taken off, joined the Lightnings which were circling overhead, and headed back towards Italy.

It was a grey day with a freezing north wind which fretted the snow on our barren plateau known as the Glamocni Polje. The small group of newcomers stood there rather like new boys on the first day of term, uncertain what to do next until a tall figure in a white sheepskin coat detached himself from the reception committee and introduced himself as John Henniker-Major. I asked him if he knew Squadron Leader Cahusac. 'Yes,' he said with a weary smile, 'we were at school together.' Alfgar, dressed in his immaculate Huntsman riding breeches, an old leather flying jacket and his Royal Fusiliers beret looked rather crestfallen that his disguise had been penetrated so early in our adventure. Nevertheless, John Henniker seemed genuinely pleased to see him and took us both to lunch at Livno with the Partisan corps commander.

Livno had only recently been liberated by the Partisans and was unlikely long to remain so, for a German offensive in Dalmatia had already begun. It had been badly knocked about and there were still many traces of the Italian occupation. A blank wall, pock-marked with rifle bullets, bore the half washed-out inscription 'Il Duce ha sempre ragione', and across this had been scrawled in red paint the Partisan slogan, 'Smrt fasismu – Svoboda Naroda' ('Death to fascism – freedom to the people').

The corps commander was a surprise. In his early thirties, with a black moustache and the wary eyes of a veteran guerrilla, Koca Popovic was an attractive man. He spoke excellent French and we had an entertaining and civilized lunch. On the way back John Henniker, who had the highest regard for him, explained that Popovic was the son of a wealthy Serb. He had been educated in Switzerland and, to the dismay of his father, had joined the Communist Party while still a student and had served in Spain during the civil war. In 1941, as a member of the Royal Yugoslav Army, he had fought the Germans, later joining a Partisan resistance group during the early days of the Occupation. His fighting record was legendary and, with his intelligence and ability, he soon reached high rank in Tito's National Liberation Army. He made a deep impression on me for he was as different as I could possibly have imagined from the stereotyped communist guerrilla which I had pictured in Cairo.

John also described a tragedy which had occurred a few days previously on the plateau on which we had just landed. Fitzroy had agreed with Tito to fly out two Partisan representatives for discussions in Cairo. He had made three previous attempts to land at Glamoc which had been aborted each time owing to bad weather. Finally, in desperation, the Partisans had suggested flying the delegation to Italy in an aircraft which they had recently captured from the Germans, piloted by a German air force deserter. With great difficulty it had been brought down to Glamoc under cover of darkness. On the final morning, while the engine was being warmed up before take-off, a small German aircraft had appeared and dropped two bombs. The first had killed Robin Whetherly who had been in charge of the air-strip party; a second bomb had destroyed the aircraft, killing another British officer as well as one member of the Partisan delegation and severely wounding his colleague. Replacements had immediately been found and it was thought that they had already arrived in Italy. Happily, neither Alfgar nor I had realized how hazardous our operation, the first landing in Occupied Yugoslavia, had been; and Henniker's account explained why the reception committee had seemed to us to have been unnecessarily fraught while our DC3 was on the ground.

We rejoined the party in a neighbouring village where they had been given a meal. A recently captured Italian truck had already been loaded with our radio equipment and Major Selwig's assorted *impedimenta*. We piled into the back where we were joined by half a dozen Partisans and, having waved goodbye to John Henniker, we set off in the half-light up the steep mountain road.

It now began to snow quite hard and it was bitterly cold in the open truck. From time to time it came to a halt, skidding on the frozen road.

We all jumped out, shoved and then ran after the truck, climbing aboard as best we could for the driver dared not stop. Sometimes as the truck disappeared around the next bend, I had rather the feeling of a sailor who has fallen overboard and watches his ship vanishing over the horizon. At the top of the pass we halted while the engine cooled and were immediately invaded by an entire brass band who piled their musical instruments on top of us. I found my leg wedged under an enormous brass euphonium and its owner and was unable to move until we reached our destination at Bugojno half an hour later. Bugojno where we were to spend the night was a straggling town on the road between Jajce and Mostar and about 50 miles west of Sarajevo, the provincial capital. Even in the darkness it looked a wretched place. It had seen a lot of fighting in recent weeks and scarcely a house was undamaged. About half a dozen of us slept on straw pallets in a large room heated by a wood stove. I was glad to turn in, for I had not been to bed at all the previous night and it had been a long and eventful day.

The next morning we learned, to our considerable astonishment, that we were to continue our journey to Jajce by train. Apparently the Partisans had recently captured the railway line between Bugojno and Jajce intact. It was a stretch of only twenty miles but the Partisans were understandably proud of it even though, for fear of air attack, it was possible to travel only under cover of darkness. It was a nasty grey day with a cold drizzle and Alfgar, Hughes and I spent it indoors calibrating the radio-sets and making up for lost sleep. I began to take a very good view of Sergeant-major Hughes, our radio operator, who seemed extremely adaptable. I was also much impressed by his technical ability when, at dictation speed, he took down a news bulletin which was being transmitted in high speed automatic Morse. Our Partisan escort assured us that the nearest enemy was 15 miles away and it was safe to take off our boots. Alfgar and I were such greenhorns that it had never occurred to us not to.

As soon as darkness fell we were taken down to the station. The single platform was lit by a paraffin flare and the station building was in ruins, but there, puffing and snorting and periodically belching showers of sparks out of its smoke stack, was a toy engine, a wooden passenger coach and two open trucks, the latter already half-filled with Partisans. We were ceremoniously received by the station-master; then, amid a fanfare of whistle and horn-blowing, we set off. The journey to Jajce took less than an hour but was unforgettable. Indeed, the whole experience seemed so improbable that I would hardly have been surprised if Alice and the White Rabbit had been on the platform at Jajce to meet us.

CHAPTER 17

Tito Approves

J AJCE station was a grizzly place. Before vacating it, the Germans had burned a number of civilian hostages in the station buildings. These blackened ruins were now lit by a flickering kerosene flare under which stood David Satow, as immaculately turned out as if he had just come off adjutant's parade, Gordon Alston, Fitzroy's intelligence officer and Major Mackenzie, the resident medical officer. They led us across a roaring mountain torrent, walking gingerly along the girders and slippery sleepers of the half-demolished railway bridge. In the moonlight we could just discern the outlines of a ruined castle and, in the distance, there was the roar of an unseen waterfall. It was a frosty starlit night and there was a smell of wood-smoke in the air.

The British Mission had been allotted a substantial house which had formerly belonged to the German manager of the local mine. Jajce itself was a Muslim town, dominated by the ruined castle. The marketplace, which I wandered through the following day, resembled a bazaar with its open shops which were well stocked with local produce notwithstanding the war; the charcoal braziers gave off a delicious smell of grilled maize, and a few old men played tic-tac in half-deserted cafés. On one side of the square was a mosque with a tall minaret, so far unscathed by the war, on which an Imam was calling the faithful to prayer. It was an altogether Middle Eastern scene.

Gordon Alston had wasted no time in arranging the meeting with Marshal Tito. On the morning of 6 December, he took us down and introduced us. Tito shook hands and welcomed us in excellent German. He was wearing a grey tunic with a high collar after the fashion of Stalin, neither military nor altogether civilian, and well-cut riding breeches. Although slightly below medium height, he was very strongly built with broad shoulders, thick-set but not yet showing a tendency to corpulence. He had good, rather mobile features and intelligent bright eyes. Above all, he had the easy manners of someone accustomed to authority. These were my first impressions but as our conversation progressed I became aware of a very sharp intelligence together with a breadth of mind which surprised me.

He suggested that we should dispense with the interpreter and talk German. I agreed somewhat reluctantly, knowing my linguistic limitations, and explained as best I could that our object was to seek the help of the National Liberation Army in establishing contact with anti-Nazi resistance groups in central Europe. I stressed that we had no evidence that any such groups existed at the present moment but now that the Italians had surrendered and the tide of war had turned in the Allies' favour, one could expect a growing disenchantment with the Nazi regime even in the Third Reich itself. Our mission was not to take action but merely to investigate the possibilities.

Tito replied that the Italian surrender had radically changed the situation but it was too early to say what effect it would have throughout Occupied Europe. So far as he was concerned, sufficient arms and equipment had fallen into his hands to enable him to establish the National Army of Liberation as an effective military force. However, to bring the latter up to strength, he needed vastly increased support from the Western Allies and, now that the Germans had occupied the coastal plain, this could only be brought in by air. Summoning from an adjoining room his Chief of Staff, a cadaverous individual whom he introduced as Arso Jovanovic, he recited a list of his immediate requirements. The equipment of patriot forces and the availability of long-range aircraft were two subjects with which I was familiar and, within the limits of my German, I gave an account of our future plans for providing logistic support from bases in Southern Italy. For the present, however, I stressed that our capacity fell far short of Tito's expectations and, as a stop-gap, I asked whether the Partisans had any organization for buying arms direct from the Germans. It was, I said, a practice which the Polish Home Army followed in Poland with considerable success and that, while we were limited in the quantities of arms that we could transport to Bosnia, we had the capacity to send in an almost unlimited supply of gold and convertible currency if he had the organization to handle it. Tito replied rather haughtily that the Partisans had no need to buy arms from the Germans since they could capture them in battle if they needed them. However, his face then relaxed and, turning to Jovanovic, he said in Serbo-Croat, 'Did you hear the Englishman suggesting that we should buy arms from the Germans?' A wintery smile crossed the Chief of Staff's lugubrious features and, turning to me with a laugh, Tito said that this was an interesting suggestion and that he would give it his immediate attention. Refreshments were brought in and he suggested that we should continue our conversation over lunch.

During luncheon we discussed at some length the characteristics of the various European countries and their capacity for active resistance. Hoping to ingratiate myself, I stressed the leading part played by communist underground organizations about which Tito proceeded to question me closely. Not being aware that between the wars Tito had attended the Comintern school in Moscow, I was astonished by the breadth of his knowledge as, I dare say, he was by mine. Anyhow, he hesitated only slightly before agreeing when I asked him for a *laissez-passer* which he told Arso Jovanovic to prepare. He hesitated rather longer when I asked him for a signed photograph but he promised that this too would be delivered to me later in the afternoon. Finally, I raised the question of 'black' propaganda, explaining that this was subversive material ostensibly emanating from resistance groups inside the Third Reich, and asked if he had the means of disseminating it among the German troops. He grasped the idea immediately and promised to arrange for me to discuss the possibilities with his Minister of Information, Dr Ribnikar.

We returned to the Mission very satisfied with the outcome of the meeting and I was greatly relieved that we had negotiated this important hurdle so successfully. Next morning came a message fixing up my meeting with Dr Ribnikar and saying that arrangements were in hand to escort us northwards to Croat headquarters at Otocac. We heard nothing more until three days later, on 9 December, when suddenly at lunchtime we were warned to be ready to leave at three o'clock that afternoon. It was generally assumed that we should proceed by captured truck, at any rate as far as the headquarters of the North Bosnian Corps at Ribnik, where there was a British liaison officer who was warned by telephone to expect us. To everyone's surprise, a captured motor-cycle combination with a side-car and a sort of trailer appeared and my mind went back to the motor-cycle rally I had witnessed at Garmisch in 1937. Alfgar and I climbed into the side-car, Hughes mounted the pillion seat, our packs and radio kit were loaded into the trailer and we set off. After about half an hour we had a puncture and Alfgar and I were invited into a cottage for refreshments while the tyre was repaired. We were given thick Turkish coffee which took about twenty-five minutes to prepare and we drank it with due ceremony, for it was clearly very precious. There was a further delay while a fresh brew was made for the driver. Alfgar, who had yet to learn to control his impatience, became restive, for night was falling and so far we had travelled only 10 miles. At least under cover of darkness we were unlikely to be strafed by enemy aircraft. We set off again and half an hour later our driver said that we were now entering Cetnik country and advised us to keep our pistols handy. He himself had an Italian rifle slung across his back which he loaded and cocked. We reached a high plateau after a long climb and, having stopped to allow it to cool, the overheated engine refused to start again. Some 500 yards back along the road there was a ruined bothy, doubtless destroyed during some Cetnik raid, so we sought what shelter we could find there from the cruel wind and waited while our driver wrestled with the engine by the light of my torch.

It was an inauspicious start to our journey north and Alfgar's patience was just beginning to run out when we heard the hum of an approaching truck. Confident that it was friendly, our driver flagged it down and explained our predicament to the Partisan in charge. The truck was absolutely crammed, including some wounded Partisans who were lying on the floor. There was no room for us inside the truck but we secured a toe-hold on the outside to which we clung as best we could until we reached Ribnik the following day at 2 a.m.

It would be tedious to describe in detail our five-day journey from Jajce to the Croatian headquarters at Otocac but it was the first and not the least adventurous of our many marches, and I can do no better than to quote extracts from my first report to Colin Gubbins which I sent out by hand of an escaped British prisoner of war.*

Fungus, 16 December 1943: Party well and prospects reasonable. Limitations are weather (as there is snow already lying, and sleeping out is impractical), the continued co-operation of the P'zans, and our reception by Jones [Major William Jones, the BLO at Slovene HQ] who is considered by the P'zans to be mad (but holy). Jones is getting rather outside his brackets as according to all accounts he has become a rabid Slovenian Nationalist. Think life with him will be unbearable and we shall have to push forward either to Darewski [Darewski was a BLO in the Trieste area who had, in fact, already been withdrawn as *persona non grata*] or strike out on our own. Future mobile parties must have much less kit – one large knap (not ruck) sack is max: weight personal clothes. We have already had to jettison almost everything including one w/t and charging motor (left with Ballinclay) and are now almost as poor as P'zans. Also one arouses resentment and comment by appearing too 'rich' (i.e. with spare clothes) and over difficult stretches one has to carry everything on

---

* I have before me this scrap of paper, covered in minute handwriting, which Gubbins returned to me as a memento thirty years later.

one's back. Our second w/t set batteries hand generator went west when our pack-horses developed excessive hydrophil [*sic*] tendencies and plunged into local stream. MYO and self both stripped, MYO gallantly swam stream and rescued horses and I paddled about and tried to salve what I could. Local inhabitants amazed to see two stark-naked Englishmen coping with mountain stream in spate, two half-drowned pack-horses, snow on the ground. But we gained much face and the rumour of the exploit went rushing up the valley ahead of us and we had tremendous reception everywhere. Spent two nights in P'zan front-line – uneventful. This journey though perfectly feasible should not be undertaken lightly (anyhow under 'offensive' conditions). In four days we marched thirteen, nine, seventeen and eleven hours consecutively and all across mountains, which precipitous here ... Weather was good. Doubt if we could have brought w/t kit anyway as among other things, we had to cross fast-flowing river in no-man's-land by dug-out canoe ...

Air arrangements with Cairo appalling. No drops for two months most places and chaps waiting every night in intense cold. P'zans feel game not worth candle in view minute quantity stores received. Hughes seems very satisfactory and ADZ equipment excellent. Cairo has done very poorly about keeping chaps in the picture, and the lack of inf: (for instance provincially complete ignorance of existence of Jungle [code-name for a new SOE base in southern Italy]) is appalling. My trip well worthwhile if only to put chaps in the picture. Also whole Cairo set-up obsolescent and, from this end most urgent and pressing need is transfer of everything to Italy. OSS seem to be overlapping and becoming rather a nuisance ... They seem trying to run independent lines rather selfishly and not v. skilfully. P'zans have been charming to me and particularly happy with our recognition of their government. King Peter is not at all popular and Emigré government and Mihailovic continually publicly and universally condemned. Our friends from [Soviet Union] are pretty influential. Suggest you should not overrate Yugoslavs. They have grave limitations and much resemble the Poles in character and capacity. There is a lot that is very interesting, much of which seems to have escaped previous observers. Especially Russians. As soon as I get things organized I must try and get back to Italy. However, meanwhile, I will try and condense my thoughts into a telegram but must be careful not to cross Fitzroy Maclean. He has done well and would have done better if he had taken on one or two of our officers. As it is, there is no, repeat no, sabotage work being done though the possibilities are enormous. My best wishes to all – especially Margaret and Patricia [Jackson] and the old MX boys. Ask Margaret to let my aunts and my mother know I'm in the pink also for MYO – his mother. CSM Hughes is doing well and party is daily growing less green.

The incident with the horses remains vividly in my memory. We had discarded most of our spare kit at Ribnik. Even so, we had to have two pack-horses to carry the SOE radio transmitter and 'portable' generator with which we were still lumbered. Our way out of Drvar ran beside what looked like a very promising trout stream. About halfway up the valley, Alfgar and I had gone on ahead when looking back we saw the leading pack-horse, which was carrying our precious radio equipment, straying off the road and heading for the river. I shouted to Hughes, 'Catch those bloody horses' but he was not familiar with animals and merely frightened them so that they plunged into the stream and the leading horse was soon out of its depth. Alfgar and I stripped off as quickly as we could and Alfgar struck out for the leading pony which was now in mid-stream pinned against a rock by the current. He caught hold of the animal's bridle and dragged it ashore. Meanwhile, I had caught the second horse and rescued some of our belongings which were floating downstream. Several onlookers appeared but, though impressed by the sight of two naked Englishmen immersed in a fast-flowing and icy mountain stream, showed no disposition to help. Taking stock after we had dressed again, we realized that our 'portable' generator was now at the bottom of the river and, after a cursory inspection of the radio-set, Hughes pronounced it damaged beyond repair, so we left it at the nearest farmhouse with instructions that it was to be taken down to Drvar. Meanwhile, our escort was giving a highly coloured account of our adventures and while we warmed up, sitting with our backs to the stove, the farmer's wife gave us each a cup of hot soup. Fortunately, we were none the worse for there was a foot of snow on the ground and a bitter north wind blowing down the valley and, altogether, it was far from 'jolly boating weather'.

Otocac had not been so badly damaged as Drvar; shops were open and there seemed to be an abundance of fresh food, though little else. Partisan headquarters had been told to expect us and offer help but they declared that the Croatian Partisans had no direct courier lines running to Austria or Hungary and that if these were our object, we should do better to consult Slovene headquarters. This information was a disappointment, for in our original plan we had envisaged operating from Croatia and if we went further north our lines of communication with Italy might become unduly extended. Nevertheless, on the open ground, known as the Lika, which we had just traversed, there seemed every possibility of establishing airstrips on which DC3s and other transport aircraft might land provided that the Partisans could keep the area safe from the enemy. This possibility we discussed at some length with Owen Reid, the BLO, and the corps commander.

Alfgar and I decided that our only option was to push on. We were encouraged in this decision by the presence in Otocac of Major Gibbon,

RTR, who had brought down a group of some eighty prisoners of war who had escaped at the time of the Italian armistice from camps in Northern Italy. With enormous courage and determination, they had made their way to Croatia through successive German offences and were now waiting in Otocac for the Partisans to arrange for a boat to take them secretly to Italy. The Kommandant of the Croatian Corps insisted on giving all eighty of them a sumptuous farewell dinner and, as the senior British officer present, I had to make a speech of thanks. I found it a very moving occasion and typical of the generosity with which, in those days, the Partisans acted towards the British.

Gibbon and his escaped POWs left by truck on 19 December for Senj and, although the Adriatic coast was by now heavily occupied by the Germans, a fishing boat was found for them and they returned safely to Italy. They left behind the Partisan guide who had brought them safely down from Slovenia. Florjan, to give him his Partisan name, was a twenty-two-year-old university student who had fairly recently joined the Partisans. His father was a judge and his mother an Irish woman and he claimed to have two cousins flying with the Royal Air Force. He was not only an agreeable young man, but he spoke almost perfect English and undertook to conduct us to Slovene headquarters. Florjan was to remain with me as my personal liaison officer during the three and a half months that I spent in Slovenia and he was the source of most of the information contained in the final report which I wrote on my return to the United Kingdom.*

---

* After the war Florjan, whose real name was Franc Miklavcic, became a judge. In 1976 he was arrested and sentenced to six years' imprisonment as an enemy of the state. However, he was released after two years, rehabilitated and in good health by the time that I visited Ljubljana and gave him lunch in December 1985.

CHAPTER 18

The Journey North,
Christmas 1943

O WEN Reid's headquarters was well found, hospitable and appeared relatively secure. It would have been a comfortable base from which to direct our operations according to our original plan. However, since it had no links with central Europe, there was no excuse for remaining there. Our journey north presented problems. We had no specific authority from Tito to proceed beyond Croat headquarters; nor had we obtained permission from the Slovene authorities to enter Slovenia. To have sought to regularize our position might have caused weeks of delay besides excessive use of the Partisans' extremely insecure ciphers which would almost certainly have revealed our plans to the Germans. We therefore decided to entrust our fortunes to the youthful Florjan, our new interpreter, who seemed confident of being able to deliver us safely. We entertained the Croat corps commander to dinner and he promised to give us every assistance as far as the Slovene border.

He was as good as his word and we set forth on stage two of our journey northward on 20 December, six of us and our baggage crammed into a small Fiat saloon. For the first three or four hours all went well and we covered a distance which would have taken us at least two days to have traversed on foot. However, as we climbed the foothills of the Velika Kapela the snow grew deeper and our stops to dig the car out more frequent. Finally, we skidded into a deep snowdrift and our driver conceded that he could go no further. There was nothing for it but to shoulder our overweight packs and continue on foot. We were now in the middle of the forest and it was quite dark. The snow was only two feet deep but it had a breakable crust and every fourth or fifth step we sank up to our knees without warning. The lower branches of the pine trees were heavily laden with new snow which drenched us with an icy douche every time we brushed into them in the dark. It was altogether a nightmare march and poor Sergeant-major Hughes came off worst and needed constant encouragement. It was past midnight before we finally got above the tree-line and emerged from the forest on to a windswept plateau. We had now climbed about 4,000 feet and were drenched in sweat and melted snow, our shoulders aching from our oversize packs. However, before long we came across an isolated farm-house where we were allowed to spend the night. We were now a few miles south of Mrkopalj, a small mountain resort on the Velika Kapela and the farmhouse had a number of bunk beds on which, in peacetime, they used to put up skiers for the night. We brewed up some hot tea (Hughes's contribution) and slept late into the following morning secure in the knowledge that the road to Delnice was blocked with snow and that we were unlikely to be surprised by the Germans.

We set off again that afternoon, re-entering the forest and this time the track led downhill all the way and the snow was well trodden. Emerging after a couple of hours on to a secondary road we found, to our agreeable surprise, a small Fiat car waiting to take us to Delnice.

Delnice was a sizeable town on the main road between Zagreb and Fiume which was regularly patrolled by the Germans by day while by night it was 'liberated territory'. All the same, it was not a safe place and our hosts were evidently relieved when, early the following morning, we crossed the river Kupa by a bridge on which, surprisingly enough, there was no police checkpoint and entered Slovenia.

In Bosnia and Croatia, where there were extensive liberated areas with their perimeters defended by major Partisan formations, we had become used to travelling freely by night and even by day taking only the minimum precautions – and those mainly directed against Serbian Cetniks or Croatian Ustase.* In the liberated areas, despite chronic wartime shortages, life went on more or less normally except when the Germans were carrying out one of their periodic offensives.

In the heavily cultivated areas of Slovenia, with its vine-covered slopes and wooded hills, the circumstances were different. Here too there were nominally 'safe areas' but everyday life was considerably more insecure than in the liberated areas of Bosnia and Croatia. Outside these safe areas, the countryside was controlled by the Germans by day and by the Partisans by night. We could no longer count on getting lifts in motor cars or captured Italian trucks, for in Slovenia the main roads were regularly patrolled by the Germans and the side roads and tracks had been mined and cratered and bridges demolished by the Partisans.

---

* Referred to by one of the British WTOs as 'those bloody Worcestershires'.

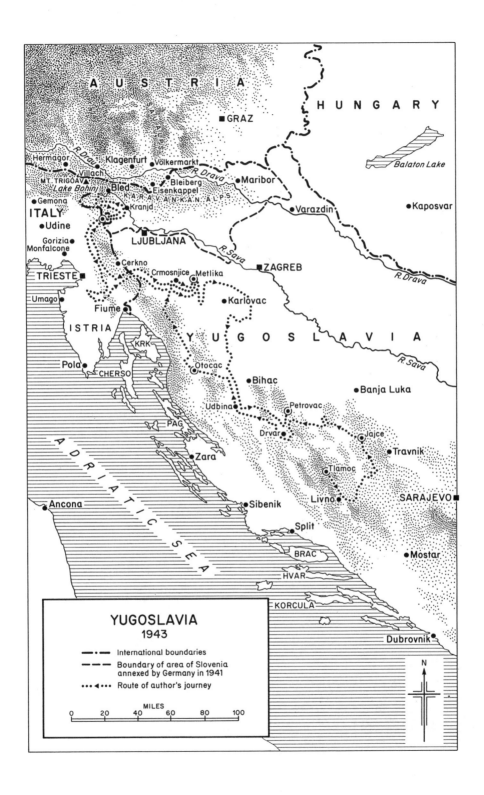

AUSTRIA

HUNGARY

■GRAZ

Balaton Lake

Hermagor
R. Drau
Klagenfurt
Völkermarkt
R. Drava
Maribor
Kaposvar
Villach
MT.TRIGOAV
Lake Bohinj
Bled
Bleiberg
Eisenkappel
Varazdin
Gemona
KARAVANKAN ALPS
Kranjd
ITALY
Udine
Gorizia
Monfalcone
LJUBLJANA
R. Sava
ZAGREB
Cerkno
Crmosnjice
Metlika
TRIESTE
Karlovac
R. Drava
Umago
Fiume
Y U G O S L A V I A
ISTRIA
KRK
R. Sava
Pola
CHERSO
Otocac
Bihac
Banja Luka
PAG
Udbina
Petrovac
Jajce
Zara
Drvar
Travnik
A D R I A T I C   S E A
Tlamoc
Ancona
Sibenik
Livno
SARAJEVO■
Split
BRAC
Mostar
HVAR
KORCULA
Dubrovnik

YUGOSLAVIA
1943

—·—· International boundaries

— — Boundary of area of Slovenia
annexed by Germany in 1941

•••◄••• Route of author's journey

MILES

0   20   40   60   80   100

N

Unlike Bosnia, pack-horses were a rarity in Slovenia and we realized that in the future we were doomed to carry all our possessions on our backs. Moreover, our packs had to be light enough so that we could take to our heels if we bumped into a German patrol. This minimalist lifestyle was more congenial to Alfgar than to me who cherished such small luxuries as a dry shirt, a change of underclothes and clean socks.

Meanwhile, faced with our superfluous kit, the resourceful Florjan had somehow managed to secure the loan of a farmer's gig and we set off at a spanking trot along the road to Kocevje, a German strong-point some 25 miles distant from Delnice. Although this secondary road was not regularly patrolled by the Germans, it was a foolhardy thing to do and we were fortunate not to run into trouble. Our driver thought so too and after a few miles he put us down and we continued on foot as far as a village called Morava, some eight miles south of Kocevje. We spent the night with a cobbler, sleeping in his workroom surrounded by worn-out boots and pieces of harness awaiting repair. We were warned on no account to show ourselves, for a German division was quartered in the neighbourhood en route for the Italian front and we might encounter German soldiers in the street.

As soon as it was light and the curfew was lifted, we set forth again led by our host, the cobbler, a diminutive man in a black suit and hat, carrying a black umbrella almost as large as himself. He looked, if anything, even more incongruous than we did making our way across the frozen fields. After a couple of hours we reached the safe area and henceforward the track we were following was well cratered and there was no possibility of being overtaken by a German patrol. Having delivered us to a prosperous-looking farm where, he assured us, we would find someone who would guide us to Slovene headquarters, our host left us. He was a brave man and we waved to him as he set off homeward along the frozen track, an incongruous figure in his long black overcoat like someone out of a fairytale by the Brothers Grimm. I remember that it took two hours to prepare a hot meal for us on which our hosts insisted, and it was late afternoon before we set off again on the remaining three hours of our march. Our destination turned out to be a large farm on the edge of the Bela Krajina, a fertile and heavily cultivated saucer, rich in vineyards. Though in the centre of a so-called safe area we were to learn that it was frequently raided by German foraging parties. It was already 23 December and the women of the household were busy with their Christmas preparations. Before we left the following day, the farmer's daughters insisted on giving us each a slice of the family Christmas cake. Layered with ground almonds and honey, for there was no sugar, I remember it as the most delicious cake that I had ever eaten. More important, the farmer provided us with a pack-horse to carry our kit and one of his farm workers to act as our guide.

Our arrival at Slovene headquarters at Sredna Vas that afternoon was inauspicious. To begin with we looked incredibly scruffy. Our rucksacks were tied on with string to a girthless Italian pack saddle and the peasant leading the horse was already three parts drunk for we had stopped to celebrate Christmas Eve at several farms on the way. Having foolishly decided to discard our uniform jackets, Alfgar and I were dressed in grubby sweaters and our only distinguishing feature was the elegance of our Savile Row riding breeches which was barely enough to convince Major Jones, let alone the smartly dressed Partisan staff officers, of our bona fides. Jones made no effort to conceal his justifiable annoyance at having received no warning of our arrival, for only a few days previously he had had to deal with the case of Major Darewski, the British Liaison Officer in the Trieste area, whom the Partisans had declared *persona non grata*, alleging that he had been in touch with the fascist White Guards. Jones was also socially embarrassed about whether or not we should be included in the headquarters' Christmas dinner. He decided against it and, having introduced us to President Vidmar, he packed us off to find our own accommodation in a neighbouring village.

By this time night had fallen and the drunken peasant had lost the horse with our belongings. Nevertheless, the resourceful Florjan found us somewhere to sleep and we settled down to the most miserable Christmas dinner that I have ever eaten: a stew of cold saltless tripe and a hunk of black bread (salt, though plentiful in Croatia, could not be procured in Slovenia).

Two days later, on 26 December, Jones took us to call on the Kommandant, Stane Rozman, and the Kommissar, Boris Kraigher. The former, like so many of Tito's commanders, was a youthful veteran of the Spanish Civil War with a formidable fighting record and clearly knew his business. He received us courteously but explained that until he had obtained instructions from Tito's headquarters regularizing our position, we must remain in Crmosnjice in what amounted to polite house arrest. However, Sergeant-major Hughes was allowed to join the other British radio operators at the radio station, and we were to be permitted to send telegrams.

In the officers' school at Crmosnjice, Alfgar and I shared a large bunk bed with four Partisans. We also had our first experience of living on unsupplemented Partisan rations. These consisted of a thin stew, once a day, a hunk of coarse bread, and occasionally some maize fried in pig's fat. Later, on 27 December, a small patrol drove us out of Crmosnjice and with the other inmates of the officers' school we had a night march in a snow storm to Metlika. This incident is important only in that it finally decided me to follow Alfgar's example and discard every article of kit that was not absolutely essential. This left me as poor as any Partisan – even poorer for I had not yet acquired an Italian aluminium mess-tin which was an essential item of Partisan equipment.

The enemy prevented us from returning to Crmosnjice but on New Year's Eve Alfgar and I were invited to attend a gala dinner given by the farmers of the Bela Krajina to members of the Slovene Government and general staff. In all there were thirteen dishes on the menu, washed down with countless bottles of the local white wine. After six days of Partisan rations, Alfgar and I gorged ourselves like hungry schoolboys. I do not remember where we spent the following nights but on 2 January I was summoned to the general staff where I was informed that instructions had been received from Tito that we were to be given every assistance in making our way to Austria and I was invited to move down to the village in which the general staff was billeted. A conference with the Kommissar was arranged for the following day at which, once again in inadequate German, I explained the purposes of our mission. On 4 January, Alfgar joined me at headquarters just in time to attend a Slovene cultural congress at Semic which lasted the whole night from 6 p.m. until 8.30 the following morning. Fiery political speeches, including one by Major Jones which was loudly cheered, were interspersed with recitations of patriotic verse and two one-act plays extolling the virtues of communism. Later in the session there was folk dancing to a concertina, hand-grenades dangling dangerously from the belts of the dancers. It was an excruciating evening not improved by the US liaison officer, a rabidly communist Slovene American called George Wuchenich who shared Major Jones's colonial prejudices concerning British officers and tried to pick a fight with me.* George Wuchenich's loutish behaviour coupled with Jones's paranoid suspicions that I was plotting to supplant him made it impossible to contemplate operating from Slovene headquarters.

On 8 January, the Partisans called an important meeting. It was

---

* When I was serving the British Embassy in Washington in the early 1950s I saw a press report that Wuchenich had fallen victim to one of Senator McCarthy's anti-communist purges. I felt no sympathy.

presided over by President Vidmar who was the most anglophile of the participants, an intellectual who was inordinately proud of his pre-war membership of the PEN Club. The Kommandant and the Kommissar were also present; so was Boris Kidric. Now in his early thirties, Kidric had been a pre-war communist with Tito and a founder member of the Partisan movement in 1941. He was now Secretary of the Slovene Communist Party, a member of the Slovene Liberation Government and the most powerful man in the Slovene Partisan movement. Having listened to my description of the Clowder operation, it was Kidric who replied. He said that the slice of Slovenia which the Germans had incorporated into the Third Reich was strictly policed by the Germans and although there were underground courier lines running northwards from Slovene headquarters, these were, he thought, of such a tenuous nature as to be of little use to us. On the other hand, the headquarters of the Partisan IX Corps which was operating in the Slovene-speaking regions of north-east Italy maintained fairly regular contact with the substantial Slovene minority living in southern Austria, south of the river Drava (Drau). He recalled that after the Great War, a plebiscite had resulted in the Slovene minority being incorporated in Carinthia and denied independence. It was, however, one of the most important war aims of the Liberation Front that this historic Slovene territory, including the towns of Villach and Klagenfurt, should be reunited with post-war Slovenia. In practical terms, moreover, the existence of this substantial and well-organized Slovene community within the pre-war frontiers of Austria was an important asset and might constitute a reliable base for special operations inside Austria. He therefore advised Alfgar and me as a first step to proceed to Headquarters IX Corps and see for ourselves what the possibilities were. The Headquarters, he told us, was located in the foothills of the Julian Alps, a Slovene-speaking region which, together with the port of Trieste, had been ceded to Italy only in the aftermath of the Great War. There was a regular courier line and, though strenuous, it was not particularly hazardous apart from a stretch in the vicinity of Trieste; the journey would take about three weeks in each direction.

I realized that I was getting into very deep water, particularly if acceptance of help for Clowder was taken to imply recognition of Slovene territorial claims in southern Austria. On the other hand, it was far too good an offer to turn down flat so I temporized by saying that I was obviously not empowered to discuss post-war territorial settlements. Nevertheless, if the Slovene Liberation Government would prepare a detailed map of their territorial claims, I would pick it up on my return journey and ensure that it was duly transmitted to the Foreign Office as an expression of the Liberation Government's views. This reply seemed to satisfy the Slovenes and I then raised the question of organizing a systematic exchange of intelligence, particularly concerning German railway traffic passing through the Ljubljana Gap on the way to Italy. The Kommissar said that this was another subject which I might usefully discuss with Headquarters IX Corps but, in the meantime, he would see what improvements could be made in the collection of that sort of intelligence.

Jones had already reported on the Slovene's territorial claims which he had signalled to Cairo in such extravagant terms that they had not been taken seriously. It was not a subject in which I wished to involve myself more than necessary since it crossed wires with the Maclean mission and, having talked it over with Alfgar, I decided only to refer to it in very general terms in my regular situation report to Baker Street. However, I reported that, on the recommendation of the Partisans, Alfgar and I intended to proceed to HQ IX Corps as soon as possible, leaving Sergeant-major Hughes for the time being at Slovene headquarters.

CHAPTER 19

The Journey North:
The Third Stage

W E set out for Italy on 9 January, leaving Semic at 10 a.m. and heading due west. It was a clear frosty morning, the track was frozen hard but only lightly covered with snow and led through wooded hills. Every mile or so the road had been cratered and there was no risk of being surprised by an enemy vehicle. We had left Sergeant-major Hughes behind to collect the replacement radio equipment which we had ordered from Italy but an addition to our party was Captain Davies who had been designated to replace Darewski as the BLO at HQ IX Corps. Neither Alfgar nor I had much in common with Davies, a red-faced young Welshman, whose lack of social graces as well as his total ignorance of any language but English (and possibly Welsh) made him an awkward travelling companion.

Slovene headquarters had selected Major Gregor to accompany us, be responsible for our safety and, more important, report regularly on our doings and contacts. The son of a former mayor of Ljubljana, Gregor had embraced left-wing politics as a student and joined up with the Partisans early on. He was about my own age but looked much older. He had a deeply lined face, a straggling moustache and untidy dark hair; but his lugubrious expression was illuminated every now and then with a warm smile. Both Alfgar and I felt that this was a man whose judgement we could trust and we were soon on easy terms with him; he spoke slightly better German than we did. Gregor brought with him his personal 'patrol' consisting of Comrade Mundo, a burly peasant in his early thirties with a fine selection of hand-grenades attached to his belt, and Comrade Panter, a cheerful teenager who spent much of his inexhaustible energy playing practical jokes on Mundo to whom he was obviously devoted. Our new friend, Florjan, had been attached to me as an interpreter for the duration of my stay in Slovenia and one or two other Partisans who were going our way joined our party at various times for short stages.*

That day we covered a lot of ground, marching almost without a halt, but when darkness fell we were still four hours from our destination which we did not reach until after 9 p.m. It turned out to be the large farmhouse to which the little cobbler had taken us on our way up and once again we were welcomed with a meal of stewed lamb. Any hope we had of a night's sleep, however, was disappointed for we left again at 1.45 in the morning, the excuse being that we had to get past the German strong-point at Kocevje before daybreak. There was continuous firing a few miles to the north and, from time to time, the night sky was illuminated with star shells. However, Gregor assured us that the Germans were merely firing on fixed lines to keep up their spirits and that they rarely ventured forth on night operations except in force. Even so, we did not dally and it was 8 p.m. the following day before we finally arrived at Briga where we spent the night in a cow shed, having been nineteen hours on the road without food. The third day was easier for we were in safe territory and we overtook a farm cart which carried our packs for several miles. We were glad of this relief for both Alfgar and I had begun to feel pretty seedy and were suffering from slight attacks of nausea from time to time due to the altitude and to the unaccustomed food – or, more likely, to the unaccustomed lack of it.

We arrived at Hrib about midday on the third day. Hrib was a substantial stone-built farm standing at the head of a long valley. A telephone ensured that there would be ample warning of any German approach. There was plenty of food including honey, eggs and cream and Gregor encouraged us to make the most of it for we were about to embark on the toughest stage of the journey in the heavily occupied area east of Trieste. There were comfortable beds and we slept and ate most of the next day. Nevertheless, in the early hours before dawn both Alfgar and I awoke to what we took for the sound of a motor vehicle grinding up the pass. We both leapt out of our sleeping bags and put on our boots which, for once, we had felt safe enough to discard. Cautiously we waited outside to listen before giving a general alarm and here we were discovered by the farmer's wife who was coming from a cow shed with two buckets of milk. Seeing us with our pistols drawn she hastened to assure that the noise we had heard came from the electric separator in the dairy which was making the cream. Although

---

* One of them, Ziga Vodusek, I was to meet again in 1953 in Washington DC, when we were both serving in our respective embassies.

she clearly found our anxieties hilarious and I feared that her laughter would waken the household, she forbore to tell the story against us.

Keeping us on the road for thirty-one of the first thirty-six hours seemed to me at the time to have been excessively strenuous but I see now that Gregor needed to test whether we were fit for the rigours of the journey to Italy before he committed us beyond the point of no return. As it was, our two days 'rest and recreation' at Hrib gave us our second wind. On the afternoon of the second day two farm boys suddenly appeared to act as our couriers on the next stage and we set off without delay for the Italian frontier. Our paths lay across the Karst, a barren rocky plateau much fought over during the Great War by the Italians and the Austrians. I have no clear memories of this stage for we marched mostly by night in single file always, it seemed, uphill stumbling over rock-strewn paths and leaning all the while against the merciless wind. Occasionally we came across a village, several of them with white sheets hanging from the windows to signal neutrality. We dozed when we could – it was too cold to sleep – sheltering from the wind behind a rock or in a fold in the frozen ground. Sometimes by day sheltering in the woods we dared to light a fire and stew some potatoes or lentils. But most of the time we were cold, hungry and desperately tired. Nowadays the memory of the thirty-six hours we spent on the Karst returns to me only in nightmares. It was a hard winter.

We crossed the Italian frontier on 15 January. There was not much to mark it, merely a ragged barbed-wire fence and a half-demolished block house. No human soul was to be seen or any sign of shelter and we spent an exceedingly cold night in the forest for the area was in a state of alert. We spent the next day in the forest, too, waiting for our new courier. He arrived shortly after dark and took us across the Fiume–Ljubljana railway where the track ran under a long tunnel between San Pietro di Carso and Ilyrska Bistricka. After a short rest we turned north and crossed the main Trieste–Ljubljana railway.*

We still had to cross several main roads converging on Trieste; these were not as heavily patrolled as the railway and we encountered no enemy. By the time we had reached the emergency courier station south of Senosecchia (Senozoce) at first light on 17 January, we were dangerously exhausted; and not very welcome either for a German offensive

---

* I had been here before for we were only a few miles from Postojna where, in February 1940, when travelling as a courier for Section D, I had been accused by the Italian frontier guard of using a false passport. How different was my present mode of travel from that of former times, when I was cocooned in the luxury of the Simplon–Orient Express.

was in progress. We spent a rather miserable day there in the open hidden in a bramble thicket feeling hungry, cold and tired and were thankful when darkness fell and we were able to resume our march. There were still a number of main roads to cross but the night was very dark and we had little fear of running into German patrols. Nevertheless our courier, a boy of about fourteen, kept us moving very fast. It was a miserable night for me for I had blisters on the soles of both feet, having been unable to change my wet socks for days, and every step was painful. We arrived at Goce, overlooking the Vipava valley, just as dawn was breaking. It was far warmer here with a smell of the sea, and Alfgar and I wasted no time in climbing into our sleeping bags and snatching an hour's real sleep, almost the first we had had since leaving Hrib.

There were four teenage courier boys and their camp consisted of two ragged pup tents half-hidden in the wood. They viewed us without much curiosity and gave us each a hot drink and a hunk of bread. Down here at sea-level the trees were already beginning to leaf and spring flowers were appearing shyly in a corner of the meadow in which Alfgar and I sat in the pale sunshine picking lice out of our shirts, having previously bathed in the icy brook which ran at the bottom of the field. It was a wonderfully still, fine day and we could hear the German traffic on the main road. On the other side of the Vipava stretched the long abutment of Mount Angelska Gora rising sheer 4,500 feet from the river valley. Alfgar, who had done some rock climbing before the war, was looking forward to the prospect of scrambling up this cliff-face with more enthusiasm than I was, though I consoled myself that since we should have to do our climb in the dark, I need not worry unduly about my distaste for heights. This escarpment was the last major obstacle before we reached the foothills of the Julian Alps where the headquarters of the Partisan IX Corps was located. Nevertheless, our immediate situation was somewhat precarious for the Germans were conducting one of their periodic 'search and destroy' operations and the regular courier line had temporarily 'frozen'. One of the local couriers would have taken us across the valley if necessary, though they did not relish the prospect, but the goat paths by which we should have to climb the escarpment were beyond their ken. Meanwhile we had nowhere to go since the courier boys in their emergency camp in the woods could not support a party of our size. In the prosperous Vipava valley, only a dozen or so miles from Trieste, there was a mixed population and only limited support for Tito's communists; many of the local inhabitants collaborated openly with the Italian and German authorities. It was asking a lot of any Slovene farmer to put his life and property at risk by hiding and feeding us during an active German offensive. Alfgar and I spent the morning sitting in the sun and talking about England and, as soon as it was dark, we set out to cross the valley.

The courier rendezvous was a fisherman's bridge over the river Vipava. We waited for an hour or two, hidden in the long grass in a water meadow beside the river, but nobody came to the rendezvous from the other side to take charge of us. It was now past midnight and all was quiet except for an occasional barking dog and, after a short discussion with Gregor, our youthful courier led us down a deserted village street and shut us in a hay-loft above a cow shed for the night. We remained at Slap for the whole of the next day and the two daughters of the house brought us steaming bowls of pasta and bottles of white wine. I lay dozing in the hay listening to the singing of the German troops as they passed by on the main road. Many were songs which I knew; had sung myself in happier times in youth hostels and mountain huts with German boys of my own age, linking arms and pledging 'brotherhood'.

That night we returned to the fisherman's bridge but again there was nobody to meet us and we were obliged to return to the hay-loft and were settling down when we were disturbed by a thunderous banging on the doors of the cow shed and a shout of 'Aufmachen!' I slipped my feet out of my sleeping bag and crouched down in the hay with my pistol cocked. It was pitch dark but I sensed that Mundo had interposed his bulky figure between me and the barn door and I heard him pull the safety pin from one of the grenades which he always carried slung on his belt. Meanwhile Panter had slid down the hay hoist to take the enemy in the rear and had found himself confronting the son of the house, a youth of thirteen, who was peering through a chink in the boards to see the result of his practical joke. I tried to settle down again, but it was no good for the adrenalin was racing through my veins and before daybreak, leaving Mundo and Panter to administer summary punishment to the luckless youth, we set out for Erzej, a hill village about two hours distant where there was a 'battalion' of Partisan Home Guard and we could spend a day in comparative safety. It was a wise move for we heard that a detachment of Germans arrived at midday at both farms and that two of the corporals had spent the afternoon 'chatting up' the farmer's daughters who had looked after us.*

---

* In 1996, accompanied by Florjan and my daughter and son-in-law, I revisited Slap and the 'luckless youth', now in his seventies and a prosperous wine-grower, and his wife and son entertained us to a lavish lunch.

The Erzej Odred consisted mainly of boys and girls of about sixteen. They sang Partisan songs in close harmony (one-third above and one-third below) as they lounged about cleaning their rifles in the afternoon sun. We also had a surprise visit from Sergeant Hammond, a British radio operator who had been dropped in north-east Italy with Major Darewski and who had unfortunately developed acute appendicitis the following autumn. The Partisans had arranged for him to be operated on in a private clinic in Trieste in total secrecy but he was judged too ill to accompany Darewski when the latter left for Slovene headquarters on his way south in December. Since then Hammond had been living in the suburbs of Trieste with the parents of one of his Slovene nurses. I do not know what became of Hammond but rumour has it that he stayed on living under cover for the rest of the war and had subsequently married his Slovene nurse.

While we were at Erzej news came from the valley that the German offensive was over and the troops were returning to barracks. Gregor enlisted one of the local Partisans as a guide and, just before dusk on 21 January, we left Erzej for the valley. This time we crossed the footbridge and, moving cautiously, made for the hills. We met nobody, but the barking of the dogs at each farm we passed must have alerted the whole neighbourhood to our presence. For the next four hours we scrambled up a steep goat path, overgrown and very rough going, and at two places we had to traverse a rock-face, edging our way along a ledge not more than a couple of inches wide. With a heavy pack on my back I found this a frightening experience and Alfgar clearly enjoyed my discomfort. We reached the top of the escarpment just as dawn was breaking and had a magnificent view down the valley towards Trieste and the Adriatic Sea beyond before we turned north again and made for the everlasting snow.

There were many signs of the recent offensive; smouldering barns and hay ricks, deserted villages and the local population too disorganized and cowed to offer food or shelter. So despite our exhaustion there was nothing for it but to push on. About midday our guide made contact with the regular courier line and handed us over. Four hours later we reached Gornja Trebusa and were just settling down to our customary bowl of soup when a courier arrived to say that he had orders to conduct us to the secret hide-out of the Slovene Primorskan Executive Committee where we were to spend the night. Both Alfgar and I had had enough for one day but we dutifully shouldered our packs and followed our guide into the night. After we had been going for about half an hour, the rough track we had been following came to an end and our guide explained that, for the next 500 metres, our path lay along the crest of a narrow ridge with a sheer drop (which fortunately I could not see) on either side. It was pitch dark and he enjoined us to keep hold of the man in front at all costs. In this way we shuffled along the path like blind men until we had negotiated this obstacle, were challenged by a sentry, and shortly afterwards found ourselves in a comfortable farmhouse kitchen lit by electricity. Half a dozen men in a variety of uniforms were gathered round the stove drinking. They rose as we entered and one of them, addressing us in impeccable English, introduced himself as Ales Bebler and invited us to join them.

I might have described this as a memorable evening had I not been too tired to remember much about it. A delicious Italian meal was produced, for the Partisan senior officers always did themselves proud, and Bebler then engaged me in a political conversation offering me a choice of French, German, Spanish or Italian in which to conduct it. I chose French and found myself describing British support of resistance movements not only in the Balkans in which he was particularly interested but also in Italy and France about which he seemed remarkably well informed. Bebler was a wiry-looking man in his middle thirties with an intelligent face and a most attractive manner and I was later to learn that, before serving with the International Brigade, he had spent two years as a student at the Komintern school in Moscow. This certainly explained his interest in hearing about the exploits of the many international communists and their resistance groups with whom SOE had now made contact throughout Occupied Europe. He next launched into a discussion of the theory and practice of underground resistance and I remember him stressing the need for at least six months' 'psychological preparation' before any resistance group was asked to undertake active operations. We were now joined by another veteran of the Spanish Civil War, Franz Leskovsek (Luka). Switching to German for the latter's benefit, Bebler then cross-questioned me about our plans for Austria. All this linguistic dexterity was too much for Alfgar who slipped away to bed, but they kept me up until past midnight refilling my glass with a light and delicious red wine from the Vipava valley. By the end of it I was utterly exhausted but I remember Bebler's final injunction to me when he saw me to bed: 'It is quite safe to take your boots off here'; and I was amused to note that he spoke English as easily as he spoke French and German and could only assume that, as a well-trained communist, he had chosen not to converse in it for fear of giving me a linguistic advantage.

We were left undisturbed until midday to make up for lost sleep.

Then, having taken our leave, we descended a steep slope to the valley of the river Idrija where, to our surprise, we found a horse and gig waiting for us which, according to my journal, 'Drove us up to Cerkno at a spanking trot. It was picturesque but bitterly cold, and for the last three miles, Alfgar and Davies (the new BLO) ran ahead of us like link boys, which much impressed the Partisans, who were all (like me) in a fairly advanced state of exhaustion, and could scarcely have run to have saved their lives.'

CHAPTER 20

A Short Walk in the
Third Reich

AFTER the straggling, war-torn villages of Croatia and Slovenia, Northern Italy seemed very prosperous and peaceful. We spent the night at Cerkno where Alfgar and I were billeted in a comfortable modern flat with, luxury of luxuries, a bathroom with ample hot water. Our host was Slovene and his wife Italian and, formerly, they had owned the leading outfitters and clothing store. Their stock was now sadly depleted and all that was on display was a selection of red silk neckties which, we were told, were worn in secret by the local anti-Fascists. Early next morning a guide arrived to take us up to Headquarters IX Corps which was situated in a mountain village about forty minutes distant. Somewhat reluctantly we said goodbye to the bourgeois comforts of Cerkno, where the shopkeepers were already taking down their shutters and sweeping the snow from the pavements, shouldered our packs and followed our guide up the steep track into the morning mist.

General Ambrosic, the Kommandant of IX Corps, was a young schoolmaster who made us immediately welcome. Over lunch he explained that his primary task was to mobilize and equip the Slovene population in Venezia Giulia. Unlike the Partisan units in Croatia and Bosnia, IX Corps in north-east Italy had not benefited from the Italian surrender and he realized that to arm and equip his new recruits he would be largely dependent on supplies of arms and equipment being brought in by air from Southern Italy. He was fully aware of the strategic importance of the Ljubljana Gap and implied that as a *quid pro quo* he would increase his intelligence-gathering and would even be prepared to undertake a modest programme of railway sabotage when opportunity offered, provided that this did not prejudice his long-term plans. I had no doubt that these long-term plans envisaged seizing Trieste from the Italians as soon as the Germans showed signs of collapse.

I explained to Ambrosic that within the next few months it should prove possible for Brigadier Maclean's Mission ('Macmis')to organize the air transport of arms and *matériel* to the liberated areas of Bosnia and Croatia on a massive scale. However, delivering arms in the heavily occupied area of Northern Italy required altogether more sophisticated techniques than those employed by Macmis in Bosnia and Croatia. Fortunately, Clowder officers had considerable previous experience in organizing secret air-drops in enemy occupied territory. Alfgar backed me up with a largely incomprehensible but none the less impressive description of some of the latest electronic gadgetry shortly to be available to SOE in the Mediterranean theatre. It was a shameless piece of salesmanship and rather bad luck on poor Davies who was the official BLO and the accredited representative of Macmis. However, since he spoke neither German nor Italian, he had no means of taking part in this discussion.

Immediately after lunch Alfgar, Davies and the Partisan Chief of Staff left to inspect possible dropping areas in the neighbourhood previously reconnoitred by Darewski, and to visit the radio station where there were two of Darewski's original Slovene operators who had opted to join the Partisans when he was recalled to Italy. Alfgar soon left Davies behind and during the next twenty-four hours covered some sixty miles on his feet, on horseback and on a bicycle. The Kommandant was no less impressed when, immediately on his return, Alfgar personally enciphered, and transmitted to London on his miniature Polish radio, a detailed load list and other operational details for the next moon period. Fortunately, for the time being Davies was content to leave these arrangements in Alfgar's hands.

We now had the basis for a working arrangement and I felt reasonably confident that, so long as we could provide regular parachute drops of arms and supplies from Italy for re-equipping IX Corps, we could count on Ambrosic's support for our activities in Austria. It seemed, as indeed it was to prove, too good to be true.

Moreover, Alfgar and I felt pleasantly secure at HQ IX Corps and set about making ourselves comfortable. This misplaced sense of security was given a rude jolt early next morning when we received an urgent message that a police battalion had arrived in Cerkno and that we must be ready to move at once. We finished dressing as quickly as possible and Alfgar set about packing up his radio kit. When I protested to the Nacelnik (chief of staff) at having been given such short warning the latter, mistaking my indignation for anxiety, assured me that we were in no immediate danger, except possibly from mortar fire, for police battalions rarely ventured above the snow-line. Nevertheless, for the sake of the villagers it would be prudent to move up the hill. I noted with approval that HQ IX Corps on the march was smaller than a British battalion headquarters. The Kommandant, the Nacelnik and the Kommissar had already gone to their command posts to keep watch on the enemy in the valley, and the rump of the headquarters staff consisted merely of the Intendant who was the quartermaster in charge of provisioning, the Agitprop section which included two muscular girls with large typewriters strapped to their rucksacks and a small patrol to provide local security. The smallness of the headquarters group brought home to me that any Clowder element which we wished to have attached to the headquarters would have to be limited to one or two officers at most and they would have to be all-rounders.

We spent a miserable morning high up on a windy col until soon after midday when the police battalion withdrew from Cerkno. Nevertheless, they remained in the valley until 1 February, keeping us in a state of *Hochstbereitschaft*. Alfgar was downcast that we had lost face with the Partisans by being caught so unprepared, but the incident provided a timely reminder that, even in apparently secure surroundings, it was wise to pack away the radio transmitter, dismantle the aerial and burn the used one-time cipher sheets as soon as the transmission had finished – and to sleep with our boots on.

HQ IX Corps had detailed information about the Slovene community in Venezia Giulia, but news from Austria was very scanty. The regular courier line had been disrupted during a minor German offensive in the autumn of 1943 and had not been rebuilt. Tito activists were busy among the Slovene population south of the river Drau (Drava) and a skeleton Slovene organization existed in many of the villages of the Rosental and even in the market towns of Villach and Klagenfurt. Although this Slovene underground was unlikely to offer any overt resistance, it promised to provide the staging facilities we were seeking and, possibly, later a secure advanced base inside Austria. Although time was pressing, I felt I ought to see for myself what conditions were like before returning to Italy. Both Gregor and Ambrosic were against this, doubting whether the courier lines would be open until the winter snows had melted and pointing out that I was unlikely to get very far or achieve anything useful without careful and lengthy preparation. I sought instructions from London and Ronald Thornley replied that he must leave the decision to me but that I should not delay my return to Italy unduly. He added that to shorten my journey south, No. 1 Special Force would try to arrange for a submarine to pick me up from the coast of Istria during the last week in February. This timetable left me with a fortnight in which to see how far I could get along the road to Austria and, leaving Alfgar and Florjan at IX Corps headquarters, Gregor and I, accompanied by the faithful comrades Mundo and Panter, set out on the afternoon of 6 February.

We spent the first night just short of the Reich frontier which we crossed the following day about noon, having had a stiff climb up the Black Mountain in deep snow. I confess to having felt a modest satisfaction that I was probably the first British and possibly the first Allied officer to have taken an active patrol into the Third Reich during the Second World War. Even though, I told myself, it was only in annexed territory, a black and yellow signpost on the main road pointing to Munchen proclaimed my proximity to the *Vaterland*.

Our path lay over the most eastern spur of the Julian Alps and, although we occasionally dipped down into the forest, most of the time we were above the tree-line at an altitude of about 4,500 feet. The weather was fine, the going good and we saw no living soul until we came to Podlonk, an isolated hamlet nestling in a small valley 6 kilometres west of Zelesniki. We spent the night there but my sleep was interrupted by an old man lying on top of the stove whose agonizing spasms of coughing and noisy expectoration so nourished my fears of tuberculosis that I was glad when, shortly before dawn, the time came to leave. We had a stiff climb up to the Ratilovec saddle and for the rest of a long day followed woodcutters' tracks through the forest. That afternoon, from the security of the woods south of Banska Bystrica, we watched the German soldiers drilling on the square 1,000 feet below, hearing plainly the words of command in the still mountain air. So far we had made excellent progress and arrived well ahead of time at the rendezvous where we hoped to pick up a guide to take us across the valley and into the high Alps.

At this point our luck changed. We learned that the Germans had begun one of their periodic recruiting drives for foreign workers and were visiting outlying farms and villages on the Pokljuka, a snowy wilderness at the foot of Mount Triglav which we had to cross. Moreover, there were now standing patrols in several of the villages along our route which were usually considered 'safe' during the hours of darkness. Then, too, the weather changed and it began to snow. This was a disaster for, if the snow persisted, whatever courier lines there were would be bound to 'freeze' for they dared not leave tracks in the fresh snow leading to their hide-outs and rendezvous points.

We could not stay where we were but decided to trust to luck and push on as far as we could before the snow settled. In the twilight we started to make our way cautiously towards the valley and had just reached the outskirts of Fuzina, a small village at the eastern end of Lake Bohinj, when we were met by a small mephisophelean figure with a pointed black hat and a long black cloak hastening up the path to intercept us. He warned us that a German patrol was just leaving the village. Indeed, the village street down which we passed twenty minutes later was still heavy with the rank smell of German cigarettes and the body-odour composed of garlic sausage and sweaty ersatz clothing which I shall always associate with the presence of German troops. Having taken us safely through the deserted village and across the railway line, our guide vanished, leaving us facing a derelict wooden footbridge spanning a sizeable river which was flowing out of the east end of Lake Bohinj. The bridge was as rotten as it looked and at the far end a plank broke and tipped me into the stream. It was quite shallow but icy cold and I was soaked from the waist down by the time I had struggled to the bank. However, this was no place to hang about and we set off at once up the hill on the other side of the valley. We reached the courier rendezvous on the edge of the Pokljuka shortly before midnight. It was a bleak spot at the best of times and while we waited we turned our backs against the driving snow. I noted dispassionately that the moisture on my soaking Burberry was turning to ice.

After we had waited half an hour our courier said he had to return to his base before it became light. Gregor asked me whether we should go on without a guide in the hope of finding a mountain hut or a hay-croft where we could spend the night, or whether we should go back with the courier. Without hesitation I replied, 'Endgultig zuruck!' Gregor looked at me with great relief and one of his rare smiles crossed his melancholy face. Grasping my hand he said, 'Ich bin kein Feigling aber dass ist ein guter Entschuss!' ('I am no coward but that is a good decision'). We stumbled down the mountain following our own tracks, crossed the river by the rotten wooden bridge and warily approached the village. The snow had stopped and I felt horribly conspicuous in the bright moonlight. It was bitterly cold and when I drew my pistol my skin stuck to the metal. A few dogs barked but otherwise there was no sign of life and we had soon regained the cover of the forest.

Of the next hour I remember little except that I was very near exhaustion and I was lagging fifty yards behind the rest of the party when I slipped on some ice and rolled head over heels down the hillside for 100 feet or more. Nobody came back to look for me and all I wanted was to go to sleep in the snow where I lay. However, after a minute or two some urge of self-preservation compelled me to claw my way breathlessly up the slope until I reached the path and then to follow in the party's footsteps. The courier station where we were being taken consisted of a small cave in which two boys were sleeping and a bare ledge on which a fire was smouldering. I spent the remaining hour or so before first light standing astride the fire hoping to dry my breeches and putties. The boys had little food to spare but they gave us each a small hunk of bread, some salted pig fat and a hot drink. It was the first meal we had had during the twenty-three hours we had spent on the road.

We could not stay at the courier station and our first task was to lay a number of false trails in the snow to mislead any inquisitive gendarme who might have thought to follow our tracks from the village. Then, taking refuge once more in the forest, we retraced our steps eastwards along the way we had come. About midday it started to snow again and, as dusk was falling, we came upon a small clearing in the forest and a deserted hut. We were now dangerously exhausted and, casting caution to the winds, we built a huge fire, lay down beside it and went to sleep, reasonably confident that no German would venture into the forest on such a filthy night.

February 10 dawned clear and, much refreshed, we continued through the forest until we reached Potok, a small village near Zelesniki, where we spent the night. Our host was a carpenter not, surprisingly enough, a Slovene but of *Volksdeutsch* origin who had as little time for the Partisans as he had for the Nazis. The kindness which he and his wife showed us in risking their lives to shelter us could only be attributed to the hospitality which mountain people since the beginning of time have offered to travellers in distress.

We left Potok while it was still dark. A blizzard was blowing with driving snow as we started the long climb up to the col. We had no ice axes or crampons and it was hard to get a foothold in the ice. As we climbed it became even harder to stand up against the wind. I felt the frozen flakes of snow cutting my face like razor blades. Eventually we reached the saddle. Here the wind was shrieking but after we had descended on the other side, conditions eased and we made a brief halt. My right cheek was frost-bitten and Comrade Mundo rubbed it tenderly with fresh snow to restore the circulation. It was now downhill all the way and once we had crossed the Reich frontier into Northern Italy, our spirits soared and, glissading like schoolboys down the snowy slopes, we pushed on at breakneck speed, reaching HQ IX Corps near Cerkno shortly after dark. We were welcomed by the Kommandant who cheerfully admitted that he had never expected to see us alive again.

CHAPTER 21

The Submarine
Fiasco

I N my absence Alfgar had been busy arranging for me to be picked
up by submarine from the coast of Istria. It was an operation after
his own heart and I returned just in time to prevent him setting out for
the coast to reconnoitre a suitable beach. However, everything depended
on the safe arrival from Italy of a second radio transmitter and a new
set of crystals and, until the present snowstorms abated, air operations
were impossible. On the night of 14 February, three days after my
return to Cerkno, the first Clowder parachute drop took place near
Cepovan and the stores were brought up to Cerkno the following day.
It was a triumphant moment and Alfgar insisted on opening one of the
metal containers, a treasure chest of arms and explosives, in the presence
of the Kommandant and the Kommissar who beamed with satisfaction.
The new radio transmitter was undamaged by the drop but, by the time
Alfgar had tested it, our departure had been so delayed that in my
judgement it was impossible to organize the submarine operation by the
end of the month. To the disgust of Alfgar who, in my absence had
been sending characteristically peremptory telegrams to Italy stressing
the urgency of the operation, I telegraphed to Gerry Holdsworth post-
poning the submarine for a month.

Meanwhile a new complication had arisen. Late on 15 February, a
fair-haired young man was brought into the headquarters who claimed
to be an American pilot of a flying fortress which had been shot down
near Udine. I interrogated him as best I could and was reasonably
satisfied that Flying Officer Joseph Perkins was genuine. Nevertheless,
the *Abwehr* had recently made several attempts to use double-agents
posing as escaped prisoners of war and shot-down pilots to penetrate
the Partisan courier lines. Since the safety of a submarine was also at
stake, I felt obliged to telegraph to Italy for corroboration of his story
before agreeing to take him with us, and it was not until the late

afternoon of 17 February that we set off from Cerkno. The Kommandant and Kommissar had placed their own horses at our disposal for the first short stage of our journey and we left in style.

This time we travelled twice as fast as we had on the journey north, reaching Goce in the Vipava valley after a nineteen-hour march; poor Alfgar having suffered agonies of stomach cramps for much of the way. At Goce Alfgar managed to make radio contact with Italy and I was asked to confirm that I wanted to stand down the submarine pick-up for another month. We had made such good progress so far that, against my better judgment and for the first and only time, I allowed Alfgar to persuade me to change my mind. This meant abandoning Perkins, the American pilot, who had damaged his knee when his aircraft was shot down. He could not have kept up with the series of forced marches to which we were now committed, and I arranged for Florjan to take him back by easy stages to Slovene headquarters. However, once again, we were stuck in the Vipava valley having failed to contact the courier line. Probably unjustly, I blamed Gregor who, I sensed, was not keen on our Istrian excursion. However, the following night the courier turned up and during the next forty-eight hours we made up for lost time doing a double march, crossing the Trieste–Ljubljana railway and arriving at the headquarters of the Istrian Odred (Home Guard) just north of Vodice at dawn on 22 February. Here I began to have renewed mis-givings about the submarine operation. We were now about twenty miles south-east of Trieste. Little was known at IX Corps HQ about conditions in Istria and I learned for the first time that the Istrian coastline was mainly populated by Italians and, even in the interior, the population was mixed and the Partisan organization still rudimentary. Moreover the anti-aircraft defences along the coast had been doubled to protect Trieste from daylight raids by the US Air Force and there were rumours of an impending German offensive.

There was no electricity available in the next village but Alfgar found a motor truck in a farmyard and was able to extract enough juice from its batteries to make radio contact with London. To Alfgar's disappoint-ment and to my relief, the first message that we deciphered informed us that the submarine operation had been cancelled but that if I could reach Croatia by the March moon period, an attempt would be made to pick me up by Lysander. The next radio schedule contained an extraordinary series of apparently irrelevant personal questions such as the name of my aunt's dog which we laboriously deciphered and which, to Alfgar's disgust, I insisted on answering in full detail. This was just as well for it was only after my return to England that I learned that, grossly over-tired, Alfgar had omitted the security checks in two successive telegrams and that for twenty-four hours it was feared in Baker Street that we had fallen into enemy hands and that our transmitter was being 'played back'.

Now that the submarine operation had been cancelled we had a little time in hand and decided that, having come so far, we should attempt a reconnaisance of the beaches in order to gauge whether future submarine operations seemed likely to be feasible. In any case I wanted to form some idea of the Partisan organization in Istria which was of obvious strategic importance and had not yet been reported on by a British officer. From Vodice we skirted Trieste and made our way across hilly country in the direction of Umago at the north-western tip of the Istrian peninsula. The Trieste–Pola railway, like the main roads, was only lightly patrolled and we crossed both without incident. Early on the morning of 23 February we arrived at Petrovija, a small village about five miles from the sea. This was a mainly Slav community and the village boys had organized themselves into a Partisan Odred.

That afternoon we were disturbed by the arrival of the Odred commander, a burly youth of about seventeen who had escaped from a convoy taking him to forced labour in Germany. He reported that he and his section had that morning ambushed a party of Germans on the Trieste–Pola road and had taken prisoner four Mongols and a German. He had brought the latter with him to show us. This was the worst possible news for it meant that the Germans were almost certain to send out a retaliatory expedition during the next twenty-four hours and that all able-bodied villagers would be obliged to take to the hills. Even the old and sick who were left behind might be taken hostage and we could certainly not remain where we were. Meanwhile the young Maquisards insisted on my seeing their prisoner. He was a farmboy from Schleswig-Holstein aged about nineteen, who stood there blindfolded. He was too confused by his recent capture to provide any useful information and I urged his captors to take him up to the main road and set him free. However, they were proud of their prisoner who was the first German that they had captured and one of the escort assured me that he would shortly be posted to the 'Thirteenth Battalion'. This seemed to reassure the prisoner but I knew that the grisly euphemism meant that the Partisans would shoot him as soon as we had left. That evening I tried to get some rest but was too tired to sleep and, sickened by the murderous innocence of these young boys, I lay awake in my sleeping bag until it was time to leave.

I had intended to entrust the actual reconnaissance of the beaches to

Alfgar who was much better qualified than I was. An enthusiastic yachtsman, he had received some training in beach landings from the Small Boat Section under Gus March Phillipps in 1941. However, in the present circumstances, without a local guide to take him through the minefields and with no time to observe the enemy patrol routine, I thought the venture not worth the risk; particularly since I had already made up my mind that submarine landings in Istria were not a viable option for the time being. So I gave the order to retrace our steps.

After crossing the main road we had to climb an escarpment which rose steeply from the coastal plain. Thereafter the going was level but extremely rough and, stumbling over a rock in the darkness I fell, severely gashing and bruising my left kneecap. It was the same knee that I had damaged skiing in Slovakia in 1939 and again parachuting in 1940. Remembering that on both occasions I had had to wear a plaster cast for several weeks, I took a gloomy view of my immediate prospects. Fortunately, however, we were not far from a Partisan outpost about a dozen miles south of Trieste, into which I limped at first light.

The camp was concealed in a crater on the top of the hill and looked reassuringly permanent. There were about thirty Partisans in the Odred, mostly evaders from forced labour aged in their late teens or early twenties. Their commander gave up his pup tent to Alfgar and me and I spent the next thirty-six hours there dozing and resting my knee which was very swollen and sore. One of the Partisans was a barber and Alfgar seized the opportunity to have his hair cut. Spring was in the air and although after dark we could see the lights of Trieste, we felt warm and secure and very relaxed. On writing this half a century later, I remember those two days, almost the last that Alfgar and I were to spend together, as a time of great contentment.

We were too near to Trieste to travel safely by daylight but as soon as night fell on 26 February we set out for the HQ of the Istrian Odred at Vodice. I had bound up my knee tightly with a crepe bandage and, except when going downhill, it was not nearly as painful as I had feared. Although I did not relish the prospect of having to run for it if we were unfortunate enough to bump into an enemy patrol, I was reasonably confident of being able to manage the return trip to Slovene HQ. The damage might so easily have been worse and the relief of poor Gregor, who was responsible for my safety, was almost palpable.

CHAPTER 22

The Long March
South

W E spent the day at Vodice making up for lost sleep, and late that afternoon I said goodbye to Alfgar who was to leave for Cerkno the following day to set up the Clowder advanced base. Then, accompanied by Gregor and the faithful comrades Mundo and Panter, I headed for Yugoslavia. It would be tedious to recount in detail our return journey to Slovene HQ for, though most of the actual courier stations were different, we followed very much the same route that we had used on our way north. This time we were travelling very much faster and our march across the high plateau of the Karst lasted twenty-three hours. We were once again above the snow-line and we spent the night of 28 February at Kosarsce in a wattle hut in the forest. Here, to my relief, we found Florjan and Flying Officer Perkins who had made their way south from the Vipava valley and had successfully negotiated the two main railway lines. Once we had crossed the Italian–Yugoslav frontier, the going was easier and we travelled by daylight, reaching Hrib on 29 February.

Before leaving for Istria, Alfgar had sent instructions to Sergeant-major Hughes to join him at Cerkno and, after the submarine operation had been cancelled, Hughes had been told to await my arrival at Hrib. Unfortunately his radio battery was flat and he had no means of recharging it so I remained out of touch with London and Italy and unable to report my progress. Hughes had adapted very well to Partisan life and I was sure that he would be of great help to Alfgar, relieving him of much of the routine radio contacts. He was to remain with Alfgar for another six months, most of it spent inside the Third Reich in difficult conditions and earning a well-deserved Military Medal.

After Hrib we were on the home stretch. It snowed heavily all the way but we were in liberated territory and had no fears about leaving tracks. As we passed each familiar landmark, our spirits lightened and our pace quickened and, three days later, on the afternoon of 4 March, we finally reached Slovene HQ at Crmosnjice.

We were warmly welcomed by the general staff, none of whom had recently travelled as far and wide as we had, and our impressions were eagerly sought. I was subjected to another presentation of Slovene territorial claims in north-east Italy and southern Austria and was duly presented with the map which I had asked for in January and had promised to transmit to the Foreign Office. Jones, his suspicions now allayed that it was my intention to supersede him, was reasonably co-operative in handling my signals traffic. However, for some reason I cannot remember, Perkins, Florjan and I moved down to Semic where, for five days, we were snowbound waiting for a courier to take us south. The Partisans were good enough to give a farewell dinner in my honour which was attended not only by the Kommandant and the Kommissar but also by the leading political personalities including President Vidmar, Edvard Kardelj and Boris Kidric, both of whom were members of Tito's Central Committee and of national importance. Gregor gave a lengthy and, so far as I could gather, unvarnished account of our adventures and many toasts were drunk. I have only a blurred recollection of the evening but I remember driving back to Semic in an heroic mood. The clouds had lifted and, in the bright moonlight, the valley was brilliant with its covering of new snow. The wind had dropped and it was completely still; the only sound being the clip-clop of the horses' hooves and the rasp when the runners of the sleigh met an icy patch on the road.

I parted from Gregor with great regret, having said goodbye the previous day to his faithful patrol, Comrades Mundo and Panter, with whom Alfgar and I had shared so many adventures. I had come to realize how skilfully Gregor had handled us, pacing us as carefully as any racehorse trainer without our being aware of it, to ensure that we did not overtax our endurance. He and his patrol had assumed absolute responsibility for our safety while, at the same time, he had trained us to cope with the exigencies of Partisan life. Throughout he had remained courteous and completely unruffled, coping with every crisis as it occurred with an ease born of long experience. Once we got to know him, we found that his lugubrious expression hid a nice sardonic sense of humour. So far as Alfgar and I were concerned, he exercised the same infinitely tactful authority with which a long-serving platoon sergeant guides the steps of a newly joined subaltern. From the outset I had insisted on keeping our relations formal although, in practice, there were few intimacies that we did not have occasion to share at one time or another. I believe that after the war Gregor, whose real name was Ravnikov, came to London as a member of the Yugoslav Mission. Unfortunately, I was abroad at the time and we never met again. I later heard that, deeply depressed by Tito's break with the Soviet Union, Gregor had shot himself.

Our new guide was called Jose, a swarthy man of medium height in his middle thirties. I do not know whether he was of Slovene or Croat origin but he was a regular courier carrying dispatches between Slovene and Croat headquarters. Florjan, Perkins and I left Semic on 9 March and, for the first stage in our journey which lay in liberated territory as far as Crnomelj, Jose had procured a sleigh and a fast-trotting horse. However, though we travelled in style and it had stopped snowing, it was bitterly cold and I was literally frozen stiff when we stopped at a farm a few hours later for some hot soup. Poor Perkins, who had nothing but threadbare clothes which had been given him by the Italian peasant who had rescued him when he baled out, fared far worse than I did but he never complained about this or anything else and his cheerful acceptance of whatever hardships befell us made him an agreeable travelling companion. Nevertheless he had the limited interests of a mid-western high-school boy and I sorely missed Alfgar's more sophisticated company.

Since the heavy snowfall was reported to have confined the enemy to barracks, Jose had decided to take the direct route over the Kordun by which we should have reached Croat HQ in less than three days. However, on reaching Vinica, we heard sporadic shooting at the far end of the town and learned that a German offensive was in progress and that the road south was blocked. Jose immediately turned back and we retraced our steps, this time heading for Metlika where we were obliged to spend the night. Although the direct route over the Kordun was blocked, Jose was convinced that it was only a local offensive which we should be able to outflank. Accordingly, next morning we set off on foot, heading north-east in the direction of Zagreb. We were now in Croatia where we found no signs of unusual enemy activity. However, we were only a dozen miles from Zagreb and, turning eastward, we had to cross the main road and the railway between Zagreb and Karlovac which was a corridor we knew to be heavily patrolled by the German Cossack Corps. Fortunately, at this juncture we fell in with a Croat divisional commander who intended to make the crossing that night and agreed to let us join his 'patrol' which consisted of a dozen heavily armed Partisans. We consequently felt reasonably secure although it was a moonlit night. Having crossed the road and the railway without incident, we went our separate ways but the local guide whom Jose had recruited soon lost his way in the marshes south-west of Zagreb. These consisted of a labyrinth of small streams and feeders which drained into the river Kupa. At one point it was necessary to strip and wade and I was thankful when, about midday, we were rescued quite by chance by a boat. Once on dry land we marched on to Lasinja about 15 miles east of Karlovac on the river Kupa, wet through and having been twenty-two hours on our feet without a meal. However, relief was in sight, for having spent a day lying up in the village we learnt that a motor truck was coming through that same evening which would take us south. It proved to be an ancient wood-burning Fiat and, after about three hours, just as we were congratulating ourselves on our good fortune, it broke down, obliging us to spend another night in the open. As soon as it was light, we set off for Virgin Most on foot but, later that morning, the resourceful Jose managed to commandeer a farm cart which carried us and our belongings for the remaining ten miles. We were now well within liberated territory and the following day, 16 March, we had no difficulty in getting a lift on a motor truck as far as Croat HQ.

The headquarters had moved from Otocac and was now located at Plitvice about 25 miles on the other side of a range of hills known as the Mala Kapela. Plitvice was, in peacetime, a lake-side resort. There was a small hotel and several villas in one of which the British Mission was comfortably installed.

Owen Reid, the British Liaison Officer, welcomed our party as warmly as he had welcomed Alfgar and me at Otocac the previous December on the first leg of our journey north. There was no shortage of fresh food locally and the Mission's rations were by now regularly supplemented by supply drops from Italy. My first glass of whisky for four months, a hot bath, a comfortable bed and, not least, a breakfast of eggs and bacon fulfilled the dreams which so frequently obsessed my mind during our long night marches when I had sometimes found myself thinking continuously of food for hours on end. However, there was no time to savour such luxury. Owing to the detour which we had been obliged to make our journey had taken eight days, which was twice as long as we had taken on our way north. This delay was crucial to the plans to pick me up by Lysander, for we were now already halfway through the March moon period. An RAF corporal, a specialist in Lysander pick-ups, had arrived by parachute to supervise the operation and had chosen a landing strip near Udbina which Alfgar and I had already reconnoitred and recommended on our journey north. For the last week he had been impatiently awaiting my arrival. Although I would gladly have spent a few days at Plitvice, discussing my plans with Owen Reid and recovering from the journey, there was no time to be lost and, having made radio contact with Italy, it was arranged to attempt the Lysander operation the following night.

Before leaving I arranged with Owen Reid to look after Florjan who was suffering from severe conjunctivitis in both eyes which needed urgent medical attention. I was sorry to leave him in such a poor state for we had been constant companions for two and a half months and I felt personally responsible for him. However, I knew that Owen Reid would look after him in the British Mission, would feed him up and ensure that he was not sent back to Slovenia until he was fit. As a parting present, I gave him my .38 Browning automatic pistol which I had bought in 1938 to take with me to Prague; it had my name and the address of my club on the flap of the holster and I feared that this might get him into trouble but he seemed glad to have it. I was not to see Florjan again for fifty years. I was indebted to him for much of the detailed information on which I based the lengthy report I wrote on my return to England. It was, therefore, a particular pleasure for me that he, against all the odds, should have come to London for the first time in May 1995 as one of the two representatives of the Slovene Veterans' Association attending the celebration of VE Day in St Paul's Cathedral and I was able to introduce him both to my daughter, Virginia Worsley, and to Alfgar's niece, Venetia Lascelles.

Early next morning we set off for the landing strip. It was a desolate spot about eight miles north of Udbina but ideal for its purpose for the wind had blown away most of the snow and the ground underneath was hard as iron. Our operator had difficulty in making radio contact with Italy but the weather was fine and there seemed no reason at our end why the operation should not take place. So about 10.30 in the evening we set out full of confidence for the landing strip. For the first two hours or so I waited wide awake and listening intently for the hum of the approaching Lysander while rehearsing in my mind the boarding drill in which I had been carefully instructed. After that I got into my sleeping bag and tried to sleep but the frozen ground was too hard and it was too cold to do anything more than doze. With the first streaks of dawn we gave up and returned to the ruined schoolhouse we had made our base.

It proved impossible to restore our radio contact and for the next two freezing nights we stood by on the airstrip. On the fourth day we received a garbled signal that no further attempt at a Lysander operation would be made but that I could be picked up from Bosnia during the April moon period. So there was nothing for it but to say goodbye to Owen Reid and continue our weary way south on foot. At 8 the following morning, with a local guide to take us over the mountains, Perkins and I set out for Tito's headquarters which, having been driven out of Jajce, was now located at Drvar.

Having marched all day we were taken across the no man's land separating Bosnia from Croatia the same night. However, this time we did not cross the river Unac by water-logged canoe as Alfgar and I had done on our way north; instead, we used the bridge at Martin Brod. Here we picked up a Bosnian guide who took us as far as Bobljusk where we spent the night, having been over thirty hours on the road. We were both of us too tired to sleep properly; we shared a tiny room with an iron stove which had been stoked up in our honour until it was red hot and the heat was stifling. Out of habit we rose early but our departure was delayed until 9 a.m. as the village Kommandant insisted on telephoning for instructions to his superiors at Drvar who naturally knew nothing about us. In the end we set off on our own. I did not need a guide for the way lay straight up the valley along which Alfgar and I had come the previous December on our journey north. I paused at the place where our pack-horses had plunged into the mountain stream but it was hard to recognize in the bright sunlight; the water was running clear, and there was no snow on the meadow where we had run naked and where the first spring flowers were now beginning to show.

Drvar was as I remembered it, a long straggling main street where every second house was a burnt-out shell destroyed by the Italian Army or by the Croat Ustase during the offensive the previous autumn. However, this time it had the bustle of a general headquarters with Partisans, many in British battledress, hurrying about their business. The British Mission was installed in one of the few undamaged houses and, having handed Perkins over to the officer in charge of repatriating shot-down pilots, I went in search of Fitzroy Maclean. I was told that he was out but was expected shortly to return and meanwhile David Satow and Randolph Churchill found me something to eat. David explained that I had unfortunately arrived just too late for the March moon period and no RAF landing operations were expected for another three weeks. My disappointment was not shared by Randolph who seemed delighted at the prospect of having someone fresh to talk to.

Brigadier Maclean was extremely helpful, approving in principle our plans for establishing a forward headquarters with the Partisan IX Corps in Northern Italy, and promising to commend the plan to Tito in due course. As for Slovene HQ, about which I expressed serious doubts, Maclean said that Jones was due to be relieved and that he was sending one of his senior officers, Colonel Peter Moore, to sort things out. At this point our conversation was interrupted by David Satow who said that a signal had just been received from Bari that a Soviet aircraft was proposing to land that same night at Bosanski Petrovac to evacuate some wounded and some Partisan 'notables'.

Fitzroy offered to lend me his horse which was immediately saddled up. However, it was late in the afternoon before I set off alone, having been assured by David Satow that there was only one road over the mountains and I could not miss my way.

It was a long gentle climb to the summit of the pass through a straggly forest with 6,000-foot mountains on either side. The occasional village proved deserted, the houses blackened and burned by the Italians or the Ustase and I met nobody on the road. Except at the top of the pass the snow had settled and the going was firm enough for me to keep up a steady trot. Even so, it took me over four hours to cover the 20 miles and I did not arrive at Bosanski Petrovac until nearly 9 p.m., just as the advance party were setting off for the airstrip in order to set out the landing lights. Having handed over my horse to be watered and fed and returned to Fitzroy the following day, I snatched a cup of soup and then followed in their footsteps.

The landing strip was in a clearing deep in the forest, the snow reflecting the paraffin goose-necked lamps which marked the runway. I had not long to wait and shortly before 10 p.m. I heard the approach of the DC3. Having circled once, it landed and then, taxiing round in a flurry of snow, came to rest in front of us with its engines ticking over. In a matter of minutes its freight had been unloaded, the wounded on their stretchers hoisted aboard, followed by the Partisan 'notables' and myself. The doors slammed shut and the engines opened up, throwing clouds of snow against the fuselage. Then, bumping and yawing down the improvised runway, we took off. Peering out of my window for a last look at what Alfgar and I had come to refer to as 'Partisania' before we headed south for Italy, I saw that the lamps on the runway had already been extinguished. The whole operation had taken less than fifteen minutes.

This Soviet DC3 had been designed for carrying VIPs and had comfortable upholstered seats. My only anxiety, and it was not one which I seriously entertained, was whether the anti-aircraft batteries at Bari would be familiar with the Russian recognition signals. I need not have worried had I known that our pilot was the celebrated Captain Shornikov, the hero of many landings behind the German lines on the Eastern Front.

Everything had happened so quickly and I had been so continuously on the move that I found it hard to believe that barely twelve hours had elapsed since Perkins and I had been arguing with the village Kommandant at Bobljusk about whether I could find my way up the valley to Drvar without a guide. But it was with a feeling of enormous thankfulness that I settled down in my comfortable bucket seat and went to sleep. I awoke just as we touched down at Bari.

It was past midnight and nobody took any notice of my arrival so I slipped away in the darkness and thumbed a ride into town in an army truck. The sleepy night porter at the Hotel Imperiale seemed unconcerned by my somewhat ferocious and extremely unconventional appearance or the fact that I had neither badges of rank nor identity documents and he showed me up to my bedroom where I thankfully took off my boots and undressed for the first time since leaving Plitvice.

CHAPTER 23

Return to Base

I HAD left Charles Villiers in London as his wife was expecting her second child. Unknown to me while I was with the Partisans, disaster had struck and both she and the newly born infant had died. In great distress, Charles had recently arrived at Monopoli in order to take charge of the Clowder base. Having learned from the RAF that they could not pick me up from Bosnia until the April moon period, he had flown to Malta, ostensibly in search of some new recruits but also to visit his sister, Theresa, who had been devoted to his wife. Charles returned the day after my arrival and he and Gerry Holdsworth insisted that I should lose no time in driving over to Naples to report to HQ Allied Armies in Italy (AAI) at Caserta. I had a heavily infected sinus and a raging headache and would have given anything for a couple of days' rest instead of an eight-hour drive across the mountains in an open jeep. However, I reluctantly agreed and the following morning Gerry and I set off for Naples where we spent the night in Douglas Dodds-Parker's advance headquarters which had a magnificent panoramic view over the Bay of Naples but where the only heating was a single charcoal brazier in the hall.

Next day Gerry drove me out to Caserta and took me to see Brigadier Mainwaring, the BGS (Ops). After listening to my story for about twenty minutes, Mainwaring left the room and on his return said that General Alexander, the GOC-in-C, wanted me to give a presentation to himself and the senior members of his staff in twenty minutes' time. This was not as terrifying a prospect as it might have been, for on my long march south I had rehearsed in my mind, a dozen times or more, the points which I wanted to make in my report, and had I not been half-blind with headache, I should have enjoyed the experience. I spoke for half an hour and was then questioned closely by both General Alexander and his Chief of Staff, General John Harding. The nature of their questions left me in little doubt that what they had in mind was an invasion of the Dalmatian coast or of the Istrian peninsula and I tried to explain that my knowledge both of the topography and of the Partisans' order of battle was very incomplete. However, the prospect of an Allied army landing in Istria and an advance through the Ljubljana Gap to Vienna had immediate implications for future Clowder planning and General John Harding in particular gave me every encouragement.

On my return to Monopoli I found a signal summoning me urgently to London and I set out in a confident mood. I spent forty-eight hours at Algiers. Mr Macmillan was away but I called on Roger Makins, his deputy, at Allied Force headquarters. Then, after a brief stop at Gibraltar, I flew on to the United Kingdom. It was ten months since I had given up my job in Baker Street and flown out to the Mediterranean with Bickham Sweet-Escott. Naturally, many changes had taken place in my absence but I had not expected to find myself almost forgotten. During the six months that he had been CD Colin Gubbins had transformed an essentially civilian organization into one where the techniques and procedures were at least compatible with those practised by the regular army. I had grown to look on SOE as a culture rather than as an organization and I did not find this militarization altogether congenial. Moreover, in the operational sections, and particularly in those dealing with north-west Europe, there had been an infusion of keen young officers straight from the Staff College who seemed to me to spend too much time dictating memos to each other. Noteworthy too was that they answered the telephone giving their surnames and appointments in staccato tones which was at variance with the discreet, and even devious, anonymity in which the older members of SOE had been trained to reply. Having nothing to do with Overlord, I felt rather a fish out of water and, since Colin Gubbins was not expected back from India for another week, I was glad of Douglas Dodds-Parker's offer to lend me his house at Great Missenden where I retired to write my report.

This report was more widely read and aroused more interest in Whitehall than I had expected. I was summoned to see General Ismay at the Cabinet Offices and he later invited me to dine at his flat in Loundes Square. I was also sent for by General Sir Alan Brooke, the CIGS, who questioned me closely about Istria and the Ljubljana Gap. He subsequently noted in his diary for 14 April 1944: 'After lunch Davidson came in … and a Major Wilkinson, just back from Yugoslavia, who was very interesting.'* I also saw a number of senior officials in the Foreign Office and Sir Desmond Morton, writing from 10 Downing

---

* Alan Brooke Diaries, in *Triumph in the West* by Arthur Bryant (Collins, 1959), p. 182.

Street, commented at length on my report (a copy of this somewhat incoherent letter is preserved in the Public Record Office). Finally, there came an invitation from the Prime Minister to lunch at Chequers in company with Bill Bailey who had been a senior BLO with General Mihailovic. Perhaps fortunately for me, I was on a training exercise in Scotland and the summons never reached me, for the Prime Minister gave short shift to ill-briefed officials and I certainly fell into this category. I also received encouraging comments from various academic historians then working in secret government departments, notably David Footman and Elisabeth Barker, and these I particularly valued. Had I realized that my report would be taken to the Yalta Conference, preserved in the PRO and, many years later, published in the United States with a Slovene translation published in Ljubljana, I might have been more careful with my syntax and more fastidious about my sources. However, the facts that it contained, for which I was largely indebted to Florjan, have stood the test of time.

From my various meetings in Whitehall I derived the impression that an outflanking operation from Italy across the Adriatic was being warmly advocated by General Alexander and, to the dismay of the Chiefs of Staff, was supported spasmodically by the Prime Minister. For the record, I should say that on the rare occasions on which I was asked my opinion, I maintained that, owing to the mountainous terrain, a com- bined operation might prove costly unless German morale had entirely collapsed. Secondly, while the Partisans might help in establishing a beach-head, they would have their own agenda and I questioned whether their co-operation could be relied on unless the Western powers had agreed to satisfy Tito's territorial claims, notably the acquisition of Trieste and possibly the incorporation of the Slovene minorities in Venezia Giulia and Carinthia.

Of more immediate interest, General Ismay told me of the intention to create a new command to direct air supply of Tito's Partisans and the operations of the various raiding forces in the Adriatic. Known as the Balkan Air Force, it would be under the command of Air Vice Marshal (Sir) William Elliott to whom he offered to give me an introduction. The establishment of the Balkan Air Force seemed to come as unwelcome news to Colin Gubbins when I reported this development to him and he foresaw that friction was inevitable between Air Vice Marshal Elliott and Major General Stawell who had finally been persuaded to leave Cairo and establish the headquarters of Special Operations (Mediterranean) (SO[M]) at Mola di Bari. Moreover, Gubbins questioned whether it would be possible for Clowder to remain independent of both these organizations and to continue, as at present, to take its orders direct from London. However, I had no difficulty in securing his approval and that of the SOE Council to the Clowder plan of establishing one or more dispatch stations on the southern border of Austria.

The *raison d'être* of the Clowder plan depended on a regular supply of suitable Austrian agents. Ronald Thornley had recruited about a dozen volunteers, mostly Jewish Social Democrats, who had been interned by the British authorities as enemy aliens at the beginning of the war. At his suggestion, I travelled up to Scotland where, under Gavin Maxwell's expert tuition, they were undergoing field training. On an extended night exercise, I was delighted to find that 'on the hill' I could easily outstrip everybody, including the instructors! However, while admiring their courage in volunteering to return to Austria, I feared that both their race and their politics might make this category of volunteer unacceptable to the communist-orientated Partisans. Thornley agreed and said that he was trying to recruit more suitable candidates from the Austrian prisoners of war who had surrendered in North Africa. However, even if this recruitment drive were successful, it would take six months to train the radio operators and by then the winter snows would have fallen, making many of the Partisan courier lines across the Karawanken Alps virtually impassable until the following spring. Meanwhile, anxious to be rid of them, Thornley said he planned to send the present group to Italy as soon as they had finished their training and to administer them he proposed to attach two or three officers from his Austrian section to the Clowder headquarters. This was the sort of administrative commitment that I had been most anxious to avoid. Besides, once they were in Italy, I feared that the pressure would increase to use these agents on missions for which I might consider them unsuitable and for which I would, nevertheless, be held responsible. The initial clear objectives of Clowder seemed to be being compromised and I might be forced to accept the second-best which Alfgar and I had so far always managed to avoid.

Before leaving Italy I had given orders that Edward Renton was to be dispatched to HQ IX Corps to reinforce Hesketh-Prichard as soon as the necessary permits could be obtained from the Partisan authorities. By the time these permits were received, it was already the May moon period and, unfortunately, a few days before his operation was due, Edward Renton fell ill. Although Charles Villiers had broken his leg parachuting only six weeks previously, an immediate decision was necessary and, after consulting Gerry Holdsworth but without consulting me, he decided to take Renton's place. His flight was twice aborted but, at the third attempt on the night of 14 May, he dropped safely in north-east Italy near Chiapovano and established himself at HQ IX Corps in the absence of Alfgar who was making his way eastward along the foothills of the Karawanken Alps in search of a base closer than Cerkno to the Austrian frontier.

I felt personally responsible for Charles as well as for Alfgar, and the former's *fait accompli* raised my stake in Clowder and tied my hands at a time when I was having serious doubts as to whether the game was worth the candle and whether, owing to the absence of suitable Austrian agents, I should not do better to cut my losses and seek employment elsewhere. One thing was certain: it was high time that I returned to Italy and took charge of the situation which was running out of my control. Unfortunately, by now the D-Day restrictions had been imposed on persons flying out of the United Kingdom and, until these were lifted, it was impossible to obtain an air passage to Italy no matter how urgent one's business. I was, therefore, obliged to kick my heels in London until the middle of June.

On 15 April I went to Longcross to stay with Aunt Eleanor for our joint birthday. It was the first birthday that we had spent together for six years and Hetty produced a dinner worthy of pre-war days; the first asparagus was cut and she used a private hoard of sugar to make the meringues which were always a special birthday treat when I was a schoolboy. Wartime life at Longcross was very drab. My aunt Edith was suffering from severe clinical depression though she put up a brave show when I was present. Apart from Hetty, there was no one to help in the house, and the garden on which they depended for vegetables and eggs was looked after single-handed by Eleanor who was now well over seventy. Like everywhere else in rural England, there was endless war work to be done in the village and, as a church warden and an organizer of the Women's Institute, Eleanor had more than her share and hated every minute of it, for she was a very private person. There was no petrol and she went everywhere by bicycle in all weathers. Longcross suffered little from air-raids but an incandescent splinter from an incendiary bomb had fallen in the hall and had been successfully doused by Hetty and by Eleanor with a stirrup-pump and a bag of sand. Both my aunts had aged considerably during the eight months that I had been away and I wondered whether I was seeing them for the last time. After dinner, when I was finishing a bottle of my uncle Claud's 1927 claret, I was reminded with great delicacy that neither my uncles nor my great-uncles had any children living and that I was the last of the line. I did the best I could to reassure my aunts that once the war was over I would think seriously of marriage but, for the time being, I had too much else on my mind.

Nevertheless it was a timely reminder that this was my thirtieth birthday and I remembered how my mother, when I was a spotty *lycéen* in Alexandria in the early 1930s, had insisted on my reading Algernon Blackwood's *Adventures under Thirty* as an example of how a young man should seek enlightenment. I hoped I had not altogether disappointed her. My mother was, in any case, much in my thoughts for she had just received the news that my step-father had died of a heart attack in Beirut. Although aged over sixty and blind in one eye, he had managed, to his great satisfaction, to get himself re-commissioned in the Royal Engineers and had spent eighteen months in the Western Desert re-inforcing the defences of Alexandria as well as undertaking missions to Cyrenaica and Baghdad. For my mother, who had never reconciled herself to the army, to lose two husbands 'on active service' was a trauma from which she never recovered.

The fact that he lived and worked in Egypt meant that I had never seen much of my step-father while I was growing up, apart from the six weeks of my summer holidays. He had always treated me with great kindness and consideration, even when I was a 'tiresome teenager'. However, it was not in his nature, nor was it in mine, to show each other any signs of affection, and when I had taken Alan Brown to stay with my parents in 1939, he had remarked on the old-fashioned formality of our relationship. While I was never conscious of feeling jealous of him in a Freudian sense, I never for a moment looked on him as a substitute for my father. Nor did he make any such pretence, though he did his best to teach me to ride, to sail a boat and the rudiments of trout fishing. Above all, he set an example of good manners and the sort of chivalrous behaviour characteristic of men of his generation, particularly those who had served at the front during the Great War.

I was greatly saddened by his untimely death but my thoughts at this time were mainly with my mother. I hated to think of the misery and loneliness which she must have been suffering as a refugee in Cape Town and now widowed for the second time.

CHAPTER 24

Summer 1944: *Reculer pour mieux sauter*

BEFORE leaving for London I had discussed with Gerry Holdsworth the possibility of establishing in Northern Italy, in the Carnaric Alps, dispatch posts on the Austrian border similar to those which we were hoping to establish in Slovenia. Gerry had acted on this suggestion and, on 14 June, Squadron Leader Count Manfred Czernin, MC, DFC, RAF, and an Italian radio operator were dropped on the Monte Losa in Carnia, some 20 miles south of the Austrian frontier. Czernin lost no time in recruiting a local guide and moved up to Timau to explore the frontier zone. In early July he moved eastwards towards Campo Rosso and discovered another route across the mountains. Meanwhile he dispatched several couriers across the frontier into Austria. Gerry decided to reinforce this initial success and Captain Patrick Martin-Smith and a British radio operator, Sergeant E. C. R. Barker, Royal Signals, were dropped near Ampezzo on 18 July. The party was heavily attacked within a few hours of landing and lost nearly all its stores and personal kit. However, a week later Czernin and Martin-Smith joined the headquarters of the Osoppo, the right-wing Italian resistance group, in the Tramonti area where they established their main base. It was 50 miles by road from the Austrian frontier, but at this time the whole area was liberated and motor transport was available. On 12 August further reinforcements arrived consisting of Major George Feilding, 3rd Hussars, and Major S. F. Smallwood, Intelligence Corps, and four Austrians who were dropped near Tramonti. One of the latter, Giorgeau, set off across the frontier three days later. He returned a fortnight later, on 28 August, and reported that the Austrian people he had met were apathetic, lacking in patriotic spirit and terrified of Nazi reprisals. However, he recrossed into Austria on 9 September meeting Derati, Czernin's chief guide, near Ausser Villdraten. The two were seen in the upper valley of the Drau in January 1945 but they were never seen again.

In the Slovene sector the situation was less auspicious. By the end of May it was clear that the courier lines between the Slovene community in Austria and HQ IX Corps had been irreparably damaged and that the latter's interest was now exclusively directed towards the liberation of Trieste and Venezia Giulia. Villiers had, therefore, decided that there was no point in his remaining in north-east Italy and, after a seventeen-day march along the southern foothills of the Karawanken Alps, he finally joined up with Hesketh-Prichard at Solcava, about 15 miles south of Eisenkappel. I proposed to join them there in August to assess the possibilites and decide whether it was worth continuing the Slovene operation now that Czernin seemed to have found easier lines into the East Tyrol. Meanwhile, the Clowder base at Monopoli had been re-inforced by a detachment from the Austrian section in Baker Street consisting of Major James Darton, RA, Captain John Wedgwood and Miss Betty Hodgson, FANY. The task of this detachment, which received its orders from Baker Street HQ was to take charge of the prospective agents who were now beginning to arrive in Italy from the United Kingdom and the Middle East. Until now Gerry Holdsworth had taken us all under his wing but his Italian operations were extending all the time and, with its latest reinforcements, Clowder was becoming too much of a burden on No. 1 Special Force. It was clear that we should shortly have to look after ourselves, even though this meant recruiting additional administrative staff. However, I was determined to remain tied, as far as possible, to No. 1 Special Force which was originally the advance detachment of Massingham, SOE's HQ with AFHQ at Algiers, and avoid the embraces of Major General Stawell, now installed at Mola di Bari. So far as Clowder was concerned, I was convinced that this embrace would be the kiss of death. These sorts of intrigues, endemic among agencies involved in special operations, had become my speciality but they were very time-consuming and, since the headquarters involved were many miles apart, I spent much time on the road. With one thing and another, the five weeks following my return from London passed very quickly.

I was fortunate indeed in having someone as competent as Edward Renton to assist me and from the third week in July he took virtual charge of the Clowder headquarters at Monopoli leaving me free to make the final preparations for my own return to Slovenia in ten days' time. I cannot pretend that I relished the prospect of returning to the uncertainties and discomforts of Partisan life but I consoled myself with the thought that I should not, this time, have to contend with the rigours of winter and I looked forward to seeing Charles and Alfgar again. It was, therefore, a severe shock when I received, out of the blue, a personal telegram from General Gubbins ordering me to postpone my departure indefinitely. No explanation was given but, shortly afterwards, I received a personal and confidential letter from him dated 30 July, which read as follows:

> I sent you a wire postponing your departure to join Hesketh-Prichard firstly because of the difficult situation on the spot, which there is no need to complicate further and, secondly, because of larger considerations. These are that the sands seem to be running out and I feel strongly that you must now set about your big plan in the event of [German] collapse and tee-up all the arrangements. I think you will be in a better position to deal with such a situation if you are outside rather than if you were within. I want you to stick quite clearly to No. 1 Special Force and Allied Armies in Italy: that is your only chance of the necessary degree of freedom and independence and you will get much better backing that way. Do not, whatever happens, get mixed up with Balkan Air Force, as their theatre is primarily Balkan. However, this is teaching you to suck eggs.

Naturally, I did not question this direct order which made obvious sense.

The 20 July plot and Stauffenberg's unsuccessful attempt to assassinate Hitler had shown that a *Reichswehr* coup aimed at overthrowing the Nazi party was no longer an impossible hypothesis and that the end of the war might be nearer than we thought. However, neither Ronald Thornley nor I shared the general optimism, both of us being convinced that even if Hitler was overthrown the rulers of Germany and the *Reichswehr* would fight to the bitter end within the Reich frontiers to meet the threat of the Red Army. Nevertheless, if there were a general German collapse, a scenario which was code-named Rankin 'C', it was reasonable to assume that there would be some spontaneous Austrian resistance which Clowder would be expected to support. My first task was to set down on paper what I conceived to be Clowder's role under Rankin 'C' conditions and to obtain the approval of AFHQ and HQAAI for these forward plans. The second task was to earmark the weapons and various military stores, including uniforms, which would be needed to equip any Austrian resistance groups which materialized. Fortunately, at this stage in the war there was no shortage of surplus arms and equipment but every requisition had to be argued on its merits and the Clowder headquarters was submerged in paperwork which until now, thanks to the support of No. 1 Special Force, we had been able to keep to a minimum. Although, by training, an operatic conductor who before the war had been a *répétiteur* at the newly opened Glyndebourne opera, Edward Renton proved to be a meticulous logistic planner and he and Pat Winney, our new quartermaster, relieved me of much of this onerous and thankless task. All this Rankin 'C' planning on top of the continuing need to provide the back-up for the Slovene and Italian missions in the field placed a very heavy burden on the limited staff at Clowder headquarters and during the month of August the latter were regularly working sixteen hours a day. Nevertheless, we made good progress in all directions and on 3 September I wrote to Gubbins as follows:

> Mon General: Have now completed most of the subterranean preliminaries to selling a Clowder advance HQ under Rankin 'C' conditions, and am hoping next week to go to AAIHQ and AFHQ to sell the thing on the following lines:
>
> (a) Furnishing communication with Austria which is an essential pre-liminary to any military occupation, if only to give information where the aircraft can land and what reception they are likely to get from the locals. Because on the assumption that there is no Armistice, which there may well not be, and that desperate pockets of resistance remain inside Austria, it may be some time after the complete collapse of all coherent effort before it would be possible to land the small occupying force which is available.
>
> (b) Counter-Intelligence, see AD/P from DH828 Compass 449. This appears to have been welcomed by Ib. AFHQ who have got nothing going in in advance of the regular occupying forces.
>
> (c) Combat propaganda, i.e. armistice terms, instructions to civilians what is expected of them etc. etc. For this I have got a 'Combat Propa-ganda Team' [*sic*] under Sandy Gordon of the Grenadiers, who is an old friend and a first-class soldier. He takes a nicely casuistical view of his responsibilities and feels that, like the mace-wielding bishops of old, in the early stages a pistol and a few hand-grenades are as good a propaganda line as any and his team are all fully trained soldiers. All this is calculated to take place once organized resistance has ceased, but before the situation is sufficiently quiet for the occupying troops to land. A very similar situation recently confronted Charles Mackintosh in Florence, only here it may be weeks rather than days before regular troops arrive.
>
> (d) I have consulted with Louis (who has helped me enormously with advice over all these things), and he and I both feel that the right tactics are to plan only for the first three weeks and after that to see how things make out, and if there is a useful job, which there certainly should be, to persevere with it.
>
> (e) CSM Hughes and the Greenleaves party have just come out. I have only seen Hughes as yet, who is in terrific form and full of fight. We just got him out in time as he has got poisoned knees and abscesses and things, which seem inevitable after you have been in for as long as he

has, which is really why I am so worried about Alfgar. Alfgar need I say has become a legendary figure with the P'zans and is credited by them with 70 Germans to his own gun. He has a rather more modest estimate, but he must have done frightfully well, and is now *inter alia* a P'zan Battalion Commander with full rights and men under command. The whole Clowder stock as chaps, as opposed to their proper mission, is fearfully high, and they are the only BLOs really accepted by the P'zans as part of themselves in the combatant role and trusted with troops. Really very gratifying in a silly sort of way.

(f) How I envy both him and Charles, and wonder whether I mightn't have gone back for a short spell in July, though I suppose the Rankin things would never have been done if I had. The awful part is that I wonder whether Clowder as a fighting patrol mightn't really have added more to the war effort in view of conditions in Austria than all the present messing about, but there it is. We'll try and make a good job of the next thing too, and much as I dislike the present role of non-playing captain, it probably is the most sensible arrangement from the team point of view. Anyhow, I salve my *amour-propre* that way!

Having obtained the approval in principle of HQAAI and AFHQ for Clowder's new and extended role, I flew back to London in the middle of September to discuss the details with Gubbins and Ronald Thornley.

On the eve of my departure for England news came through from AFHQ that I had been awarded an immediate DSO, Alfgar an MC and Hughes an MM for our reconnaissance work the previous winter. Though delighted by this recognition, I could not help thinking that our mission had been strenuous rather than dangerous and could attribute these awards only to the persuasive recommendations composed by Gerry Holdsworth who at one time had been a successful public relations executive. Having time to spare in Naples, I bought a DSO ribbon in the officers' shop and sewed it on myself. However, my blushes were spared on my return to London since it was almost completely hidden by the lapel of my uniform tunic.

CHAPTER 25

Alfgar and Charles

I HAD left Alfgar at Istrian headquarters on 27 February and the following day he had set off on his return to Cerkno where he arrived on 5 March. Here he was shortly joined by CSM Hughes. He remained at this headquarters until 27 April and during this time two stores drops and a body drop were successfully carried out. These operations, organized with exemplary efficiency by No. 1 Special Force, did nothing to improve Alfgar's relations with Captain Davies, the official DLO and representative of Macmis, who resented Alfgar's close friendship with the Kommandant and envied the priority given to Clowder operations. The 'bodies' delivered included two Anglo-Austrian agents, Gardner and Hall, who had volunteered for work in Austria and who had been held in Egypt since the previous autumn.*

On 27 April, Alfgar, accompanied by Gardner and Hall, left HQ IX Corps bound for Austria. The party started off by taking the route which I had followed in February but once again the courier line proved unreliable and they learned that, possibly as a reaction to my abortive attempt to cross into Austria, the Germans had made a clean sweep of the Partisan organization south of Villach and had arrested the members of the organizing committees in both Klagenfurt and Villach as well as leading members of the Slovene community south of the river Drau. There was nothing for it but to recross the mountains in exceptionally bad weather for the time of year and the party then proceeded, rather hazardously, along the southern slopes of the Karawanken Alps until, on 31 May, they fetched up in a Partisan outpost known as the West Korosko Odred in the mountains south of Eisenkappel. When Charles Villiers visited this Odred in June he described it as being 'only forty

---

* Charles Gardner joined the Intelligence Service after the War, was awarded a CBE, and died in 1995.

strong, living most precariously in the woods some five miles inside Austria and penned between the Loibl and Seiberg passes.'*

After two days' rest Alfgar set out again, on 2 June, for the East Korosko Odred which had recently been formed and was now about 250 strong, operating in the area bounded by Eisenkappel, Crna and Jesersko. On 7 June Alfgar signalled the results of his reconnaissance, recommending that the Clowder advance base should be moved from north-east Italy to the area of the Korosko Odreds and that Charles Villiers, who had recently dropped to HQ IX Corps, should join him there as soon as possible.

Three weeks later Charles arrived after a hazardous march across the slice of Slovenia now formally annexed to the Third Reich. He was accompanied by two British radio operators and Sergeant Catoni of the SIS. Charles and Alfgar were a formidable combination and they set about building up the Korosko Odreds' strength so as to secure a reasonably safe advance base for operations into Austria. During the months of June to September 1944, 25 tons of stores were delivered by the RAF and collected by the Partisans which enabled the latter to increase their strength tenfold from a little over 200 to nearly 2,000. Nevertheless, although they carried out a number of raids in the Drau valley, the Partisans resisted Charles's and Alfgar's attempts to engage them in active harassing operations against the enemy, being under strict orders from Slovene headquarters to conserve their resources until the closing stages of the war when they would be required to invade Austria and establish Partisan control over the Slovene community in southern Carinthia. On the other hand, British and Slovene interests coincided in their aim of establishing an outpost north of the river Drau, and Partisan HQ appreciated that such an outpost could be maintained only by supplies dropped clandestinely by parachute operations requiring Clowder's expertise. Alfgar made the crossing of the river Drau his personal responsibility which he pursued with an obsessive single-mindedness, believing it was essential for the development of Clowder's plan in the longer term. This conviction was shared by members of Clowder's HQ staff, who received every encouragement from the Special Operations branch of AFHQ at Caserta. Alfgar was uniquely qualified to carry out this task. His relief was overdue but the intelligence forecast predicted the early collapse of German resistance,

---

* A new headquarters staff improved morale and efficiency and, supported by three Clowder sorties of arms and explosives, the strength of this Odred was raised to over 200 men and women by August 1944.

and that he would be overrun and relieved before the winter weather set in. I therefore decided not to attempt to replace him for the time being.

Meanwhile, life in the Korosko Odreds was extremely hard and insecure. The size of the British presence imposed a serious burden on the Partisan administration and was tolerated only because of the latter's dependence for arms and equipment on parachute drops from Italy. Moreover, the rapid approach of the Red Army and the political differences which had arisen between Marshal Tito and the Western Allies now coloured many of the instructions received from Slovene headquarters. It was, in the words of the official report, 'due only to immense perseverance, determination and to his superior personality that Hesketh-Prichard succeeded in persuading the Partisan leaders to allow him to cross the Drau.' A further set-back was the treachery of an SIS agent, for whom Charles had to accept responsibility, which resulted in the Partisans' refusal to accept under their protection anyone not of British nationality, a restriction which effectively foreclosed the original Clowder plan of introducing Austrian agents with the help of the Slovene Partisan organization. Henceforward our agents would have to be parachuted into Austria 'blind'.

During 1944 the Germans had woken up to the threat posed by Partisan forces, armed and supplied by air from Italy. They had certainly broken the Slovene ciphers which were elementary and they were probably also monitoring the Clowder radio traffic though the latter, being always enciphered on one-time pads, was reasonably secure. They would also have noted the supply drops of *matériel* in remote mountain valleys and though no attempt was made to intercept these sorties, raids by border police and militia interfered with the collection, distribution and storage of these supplies. The treachery of the so-called British agent led to a surprise attack resulting in the burning of the house in the Logan valley in which the British staff had been living and a running fight lasting five days in which both Charles and Alfgar distinguished themselves, the latter being credited with the improbable tally of forty Germans to his own gun. (This legend died hard and was repeated to me when I visited Slovenia forty years later.)

Although German counter-measures presented an increasing threat to the Korosko Odreds, culminating in a full-scale offensive later in the autumn which had disastrous consequences, so far as the crossing of the Drau was concerned an almost equally damaging and far more insidious threat was presented by the formation in Italy of the Balkan Air Force which now determined the priorities to be allotted to the support of special operations. Clowder came off relatively badly compared with the more immediate requirements of special operations behind the Italian front which now absorbed most of the resources of No. 1 Special Force; and the massive task of supplying and re-equipping Tito's divisions in Bosnia and Croatia. Clowder's clandestine supply drops required the services of the highly skilled pilots and navigators of the Special Flight and could not be met by the use of transport aircraft which were now being regularly used for the support of Balkan operations and formed the major part of the aircraft available to Balkan Air Force. In any case, Balkan Air Force was most reluctant to operate north of the Karawanken Mountains for political as well as for technical reasons and, as August progressed, the air support on which Alfgar's project north of the Drau entirely depended became increasingly unreliable.

Although Alfgar's personal reputation had never been higher, by the end of August the Partisan enthusiasm for the crossing of the Drau was visibly dwindling and there was some evidence that the 'go-slow' policy which they adopted was the direct consequence of the difficulties which Tito was encountering in his negotiations with the Western Allies over the future of Venezia Guilia. However, in September the local attitude improved, thanks largely to the arrival of Ales Bebler at HQ IV Zone, which had been established earlier in the summer to co-ordinate the activities of the Korosko Odreds. During the long discussion which Alfgar and I had had with Bebler when we had spent the night with the Primorskan Executive Committee on our way north eight months previously, he had shown himself very interested in Clowder's plan for Austria which he now supported vigorously. However, time was beginning to run out and there seemed little chance of being able to establish a forward base in the Saualpen before the onset of the winter snows or, according to AFHQ's optimistic forecast, before the whole area of southern Carinthia was overrun by the advancing Allies. Without orders from the highest authority, the Korosko Odreds refused to co-operate and without Partisan co-operation the crossing of the river Drau was not feasible. On the other hand, for the British to have called off the operation at this late stage after so much time and effort had been expended on it would have meant a serious loss of face at a time when there were reports that a rival Soviet Mission was planning a similar operation for which they were receiving every assistance. The Partisans' objections were not exclusively political. They did not believe that Alfgar would be able to maintain radio communication with Italy, still less that clandestine supply drops could be guaranteed in all weathers or, indeed, that these were technically possible under the conditions which would be met by a party crossing the river Drau. To overcome these doubts Alfgar succeeded in maintaining continuous radio communication with London during a five days' running fight and he devised a system under which he waited for a drop for only two nights at the same place. To demonstrate the feasibility of all this, he arranged a supply operation inside the Austrian frontier on 26 August when the right stores were dropped, found, distributed and all traces removed twenty-six hours after he had ordered the sortie and given the delivery point. This operation greatly impressed the Partisans and reports of it undoubtedly influenced Ales Bebler in our favour.

The deciding factor, however, was the arrival at HQ IV Zone on 24 September of General Luka (Franz Leskovsek), a very senior member of the Slovene Partisan movement and a former Minister of War. Luka, it will be recalled, was the person who had joined in my midnight discussion with Bebler about Austrian resistance (and for whose benefit we had switched from French to German), and with his very considerable support all local objections to the Drau crossing were finally overridden. Orders were given to prepare a fighting patrol of 100 men who would cross the river Drau in mid-October and take Alfgar with them. However, Luka demanded that the operation should be conditional on the provision of seventy Liberator sorties to support a general uprising of the Slovenes in the Drau valley. On receipt of Alfgar's triumphant telegram reporting these developments, I flew over to Caserta to discuss the situation with AFHQ and sent a signal to London seeking formal approval for the operation to proceed.

Although the Operations Branch at Caserta gave its support to the project, political objections were raised to the mass deliveries of arms and explosives for the Slovene minority in the Drau valley which, it was pointed out, would be included in the British zone of occupation. While accepting that guerrilla raids against the Leoben–Klagenfurt railway and German communications generally might be of short-term tactical value and politically acceptable, the massive air support on the scale envisaged by General Luka might be taken by the Partisans as acceptance of their territorial claims and could not be countenanced. I telegraphed this verdict to Alfgar adding that although the planners were less optimistic about the rate of their advance than they had been six weeks previously, they were still reasonably confident that he would be overrun and picked up before Christmas, though not before the first of the winter snows had fallen. Alfgar replied that HQ IV Zone was not insisting on the Liberator sorties as a precondition but that there was

an immediate requirement for collapsible rubber assault boats to transport the party across the river.*

While AFHQ's reaction had on the whole been positive and we had
been urged to press on with the operation, SOE HQ in London was
less enthusiastic than I had expected. Thornley telegraphed that he had
discussed the matter with General Gubbins and David Keswick and
they had come to the conclusion that the final decision must be left to
Alfgar. On the whole the intelligence community in London shared
AFHQ's optimism that a German collapse was imminent and that, as
Colin Gubbins had written to me earlier in the summer, 'Vienna is the
next stop'. However, he personally was far from convinced that German
resistance was broken and that a collapse was imminent and he advised
me to think very carefully before committing Alfgar to another winter
in the mountains from where it might be extremely difficult to extricate
him if, as indeed happened, the Allied advance was delayed until the
spring. Anyhow, if German resistance was to collapse between then and
Christmas, there would be too little time to organize any effective
Austrian resistance groups and the only organized resistance likely to be
available was that provided by the Slovene Partisans. In these circumstances he thought the long-term political disadvantages would probably
outweigh the short-term military advantages. I shared Thornley's doubts,
particularly as Charles had described Alfgar as looking 'thin, worn and
tired, but driven by fanatic determination on what he himself described
as a one-way journey'. Unfortunately, Charles had been invalided back
to Italy and was not available to give Alfgar the benefit of his advice.
Nor was it possible to present the arguments convincingly in the series
of operational signals which I exchanged with Alfgar who argued that
to cancel the operation at this late hour would cause a totally unacceptable loss of face. I had already received a characteristic signal
from him dated 20 September:

> Personal & Immediate. I read your letter and destroyed the private letters.
> Charles and I talked so much and are so close that there [is] no possibility
> of misunderstanding. I have no illusions as to the risks involved or the
> relative importance of Drau crossing or what I may achieve there but feel
> that even a little first-hand local knowledge and possibly a tiny base free
> from chores of personal security may be of help to you when you put
> your final plans into effect. As far as judgement is concerned, day to day
> Partisan work in the first place is largely a matter of instinct and the
> longer one does this job the stronger the instinct gets. That is why

---

* These were successfully delivered during the first week in October.

Partisans often become senior staff officers but never unit commanders. Trifles too I admit [corrupt groups] but except for the welcome relief of letting go at Charles I do not show it. My judgement remains unclouded on all main issues but I will report facts and also my appreciation and then you must tell me what to do.

Alfgar's last letter arrived some weeks later:

IV Zone 2 Oct. 1944

My Dear Peter,

At last it looks as if I am going to make a little progress. Alas the weather is awful – wet and cold and I don't think I will enjoy myself very much. I do hope however that we do succeed in doing something however little to justify your superhuman effort ... I am signalling the basic 'task' which I explained to Luka and Lindsay. God I miss you and Charles – when Charles was here I could relax and go off the deep end whenever I liked instead of having to keep hold of myself all the time, etc., etc. I am just forced to KGO in Luka's car so must stop but will promise you to do my damnedest. Do write and tell me all the news please ...

Ever yours

Alfgar

At this late stage nothing short of a direct order from General Gubbins or from me could have prevented Alfgar from embarking on this adventure which was the culmination of ten months' effort and on which all hopes for the future of Clowder were now pinned. In the circumstances of October 1944 neither of us felt justified in giving this order which Alfgar would certainly have disputed with all the force at his command, though no one knew better than he the personal risks involved.

CHAPTER 26

The Drau Crossing

ALFGAR had a fighting patrol of eighty hand-picked Partisans and set out from the East Korosko Odred on 15 October. The patrol was commanded by Mirko (Joze Ulcar) a former Kommandant of the East Korosko Odred and an experienced guerrilla fighter. Frank Lindsay, a US major who had been appointed the representative of Macmis at HQ IV Zone, describes seeing Alfgar just before he left: 'As he was leaving he told me he doubted that he would survive because snow was now on the ground at the higher levels, and tracks that could be followed would be left in the snow. But he was determined to make a try. He had spent five months waiting for the Partisans to agree.'* Thirteen Partisans deserted before they reached the river Drau which the patrol crossed in three parties, Alfgar in the second of them, at a point between Bleiberg and Volkermarkt where the river widens out into a sort of lake known as the Volkermarkter Stausee. The crossing was made without incident but the guide lost his way on the far bank and Mirko and Alfgar had to make for the comparative safety of the Saualpen marching on a compass bearing. On 20 October Alfgar reported that the party had reached the top of the Saualpen west of Wolfsberg and asked urgently for a supply drop with food and warm clothes. The spine of the Saualpen, a hogs-back which runs from south to north, is over 5,000 feet high and above the tree-line. Although the recovery of the stores might prove hazardous and hard to repeat owing to the tell-tale tracks in the snow, the actual air drop seemed to offer no technical difficulties and was accepted by the Royal Air Force.

Unfortunately, for the next six weeks a spell of exceptionally bad weather set in and during this time the Royal Air Force considered it impossible to carry out dropping operations north of the Karawanken Mountains. This disastrous failure to drop supplies meant that Alfgar

---

* Frank Lindsay, *Beacons in the Night* (Stanford University Press, 1993), p. 166.

and his Partisans were entirely dependent for food on what they could beg or steal from the local inhabitants. The latter, who were by no means exclusively of Slovene origin, lived in isolated cottages and farmsteads in the forest where they were employed as woodcutters and foresters. Whatever their sympathies, they were terrified of the Partisan bands and even more terrified of the ruthless reprisals which they could expect from the German and Austrian security services if they were caught aiding the enemy. As recently as August 1944 Himmler had declared Styria and Lower Carinthia a special security zone and the presence of sixty desperate Partisans in addition to the other marauders and outlaws who had taken refuge in the Saualpen was insupportable and betrayal was inevitable.

During November conditions worsened; the winter weather set in and the party split up, desperate for food and shelter. The failure of the RAF to drop supplies became the subject of bitter recrimination and Alfgar's relations with the Partisans were not improved when he knocked down one of the party who was plundering a cottager. He was so conspicuous and his identity as an Englishman so widely known that his presence anywhere was a source of danger. Nevertheless he seems to have moved around freely and small actions were carried out against the Klagenfurt–Huttenberg railway and a handful of Austrian outlaws and deserters were recruited, much to the disgust of the Partisans. No contact seems to have been made with the group of fifteen Partisans who had crossed at the end of June and who, early in October, had reported to the East Korosko Odred that they had secured 300 recruits in the Saualpen. What news there was from Partisan sources, which was scanty and unreliable, came from a party of expert couriers who had been dispatched across the Drau in September to keep contact between the Korosko Odreds and the 'June Troop'. As the winter weather grew more severe, it became impossible for Alfgar's party to remain sleeping in the open near the summit of the Saualpen where they were reasonably secure and in sufficient strength to defend themselves if attacked by a German patrol. Instead they were forced to split up and seek shelter in villages lower down the mountain. Here some lived illegally while others built hide-outs in the woods and stole their food from the farmers. During this period Alfgar seems to have spent most of his time in the neighbourhood of Eberstein about 15 miles north-east of Klagenfurt on the western slope of the Saualpen, sleeping rough and living from hand to mouth.

By the middle of November it was clear that the Allied armies had no chance of breaking through the Gothic Line until the spring and

Alfgar's mind turned towards the possibility of stealing a German aircraft from the airfield at Klagenfurt, a few miles away, and flying himself out to Italy. He was achieving nothing and his situation had become desperate. His last signal was received on 3 December. He reported that he was being continually harried by the enemy and concluded: 'Give my love to all at White's. This is no life for a gentleman.' Then his transmitter went off the air.

To begin with Alfgar's radio silence gave no particular cause for anxiety about his personal safety, though it made it difficult to organize the supply drop which was needed so urgently.

There was no prospect of the weather improving and, realizing what was at stake, the Royal Air Force agreed to attempt a daylight sortie with a Beaufighter, a fast two-seater fighter-bomber. Food, warm clothing and two replacement radio transmitters were packed into the external wing fuel tanks, carefully cushioned with sponge rubber in the hope that they would withstand the shock of being dropped without parachutes. It was planned that the aircraft should circle low over the area where Alfgar was thought to be in the hope of seeing some sign of recognition from the ground which, if Alfgar was alive, would almost certainly be forthcoming. However, on his return the pilot reported that he had seen no sign of life and before returning he had jettisoned the stores with his spare fuel tanks. After the war Mirko said that they had seen the fighter drop its wing tanks but it had not occurred to him that the tanks might contain supplies and no effort had been made to recover them. This suggests that by mid-December, when the Beaufighter operation took place, Alfgar was already dead.

The long delayed Halifax drop was carried out on 27 December. Most of the containers were recovered by the Partisans and the stock of food and warm clothing enabled them to survive the winter. Out of the sixty-five men who crossed the Drau in September, forty worn and demoralized Slovenes came down from the Saualpen when the fighting ceased in May 1945. But of Alfgar there was no trace.

What happened to Alfgar? It seems extremely unlikely that he was captured by the Germans. After the war an intensive search of the German and Austrian security and police records revealed no trace of his arrest. Members of the Slovene community who freely admitted having known him would offer no explanation of his disappearance. Mirko reported to Slovene headquarters that Alfgar had been killed on 3 December in a fight with the Germans and he confirmed this when questioned by Frank Lindsay who met him by chance the following July. However, like all the other Slovenes who were interrogated by various British authorities in the months after the war, Mirko pretended to have no detailed knowledge of the circumstances of Alfgar's death. There is much circumstantial evidence that he had become increasingly unpopular with the Slovene community whose lives he put at risk by his mere presence in the vicinity and also of increasing friction with the Partisans who blamed him for the failure of the promised supply drops on which their lives depended. It is possible, though it seems unlikely, that in desperation they murdered him considering that his presence put their own lives at risk. A more sinister possibility, for which there is slight circumstantial evidence, is that he was murdered by the Partisans on the express orders of the Polit Kommisar for the Slovene community in the Drau valley, a fanatical communist, possibly on the instructions of the Soviet Mission whose influence was now dominant at Slovene headquarters or simply because he knew too much.

In January 1945, Major A. C. G. Hesketh-Prichard, MC, Royal Fusiliers, was posted as 'Missing believed killed'. Fifty years later, in 1994, the Austrian authorities gave permission for Alfgar's name to be added to a memorial at St Ruperth near Volkermarkt marking a mass grave containing the bodies of unidentified Partisans. The inscription runs: 'Hier ruht britischer Verbindungsoffizer A. C. G. Hesketh-Richard [*sic*] (Major Cahusac).' The request of the League of Carinthian Partisans that the inscription should also be written in Slovene was not granted.

CHAPTER 27

The End of Clowder

D URING the late summer of 1944 Manfred Czernin's operations in Northern Italy looked more promising than Charles's and Alfgar's efforts in Slovenia. Co-operation with the right-wing Osoppo resistance groups had proved easier and less fraught with politics than relations with the Slovene Partisans and there was more scope for private enterprise. On the other hand, there was no Italian ethnic community in the East Tyrol comparable to the Slovenes in Carinthia with their long tradition of irredentism. However, by the end of the summer we had found no evidence of any active Austrian resistance movement which we could support and, given the lack of suitable agents and the shortage of aircraft, I came to the conclusion that the maintenance of the elaborate infrastructure which we had so painfully built up during the past twelve months was no longer justified. I had to make an immediate decision to evacuate the redundant liaison officers before the onset of winter made it impossible to extricate them; there was, however, some unfinished business. Besides Alfgar Hesketh-Prichard's expedition across the river Drau which required regular air support if it was to survive, there were still two operations to complete in the Italian sector.

SOE London had been left in no doubt of the shortcomings of the Austrian volunteers who had been recruited in the United Kingdom. However, Thornley had been confident of being able to recruit additional volunteers, in particular some trained radio operators, from among the thousands of Austrians taken prisoner in North Africa. These hopes had been disappointed and Jimmy Darton, the X Section representative, had only been able to recruit half a dozen POWs willing to return to Austria. Nevertheless among those he brought to Italy for further training was one outstanding individual: Wolfgang Treichl (alias Taggart).*

---

* His elder brother, Heinrich Treichl, became one of the leading personalities in postwar Austria where he was chairman of the Kredit Anstalt Bank.

Treichl was an ardent Austrian patriot determined to assist the Allies in liberating his country from Nazi domination. As a junior officer in the Reichswehr, Treichl had succeeded in having himself transferred to the Afrika Korps with the sole intention of deserting to the British and volunteering to return to Austria as a resistance leader. He was a young man of great charm and integrity and we had the highest hopes that at last we had found someone of the right calibre to organize an effective Austrian resistance group. Enormous efforts were made to complete his training and procure the necessary forged documents in time for the October moon period when it was planned to drop him to Czernin at Tramonti and for him and a companion to be smuggled over the frontier by one of the courier lines which Feilding had organized from Forni Avoltri. Treichl's destination was Saltzburg where he was confident of finding friends and supporters. The operation took place on the night of 12 October and was a disaster. An inexperienced navigator mistook the lights of the gendarmerie barracks at Tolmezzo for the dropping zone which was some twelve miles distant. No recognition signals seem to have been exchanged and the mistake was inexcusable but the upshot was that Treichl and three other Austrians were dropped into the arms of a German patrol. Treichl was shot and killed on landing; his companion, Huber, escaped in the darkness and succeeded in joining the British Mission some days later; while the two remaining Austrians, Priestley and Dale, were captured. Fortunately they were still wearing uniform and their cover story that they were British officers was believed. Consequently, instead of being handed over to the Gestapo, they were treated as prisoners of war and survived.

Other bad news was to follow. The Germans had woken up to the threat posed by the existence of resistance groups along the Austrian frontier which were receiving Allied support from Italy. As early as August 1944, Himmler had designated Lower Carinthia and Styria as a security zone 'to be defended as resolutely as East Prussia' and the number of search and destroy missions in the Drau valley and in German-occupied Slovenia had been significantly increased. Italy's turn was yet to come, but on 10 October the Germans mounted an offensive in Carnia and Friuli which almost wiped out the local Italian resistance groups. Major Smallwood, who had broken his leg, and Sergeant Barker, who had gallantly refused to desert him, were captured.* A week later the Germans broke through and streamed down into Tramonti, and

---

* Both survived but were badly treated under interrogation by the German security service.

Czernin and Martin-Smith were engaged in fierce fighting. The resistance succeeded in recapturing much of their lost ground and, after the German withdrawal, the dropping zone at Tramonti was found to be undamaged. From here Czernin flew back to Italy by Lysander on 29 October, having handed over command of the Mission to Feilding. By the beginning of November the only agent unaccounted for was Giorgeau, Czernin's original courier, who had recrossed into Austria on 9 September and vanished. During November Feilding made four unsuccessful attempts to contact him, crossing into Austria but being driven back by atrocious weather. On the last of these sorties, he was betrayed, ambushed and slightly wounded.

Since the winter was fast closing in, Feilding sought permission to withdraw the Italian Mission. However, he was told to remain at his post while a last attempt was made to drop a radio operator in to Giorgeau during the November moon period. Nevertheless, life was becoming increasingly difficult in Carnia. The bad weather prevented the RAF delivering supplies from Italy and, with the prospect of yet another winter of war, local morale was suffering. The Germans offered a reward of 800,000 lire for Feilding's capture and the risk of betrayal became serious.

Giorgeau's radio operator, Brenner, was dropped on 17 November but although George Feilding made several determined efforts to put him across the frontier, the weather made the courier lines impassable. On 27 November a new German offensive began and George Feilding was instructed to withdraw the entire mission via Yugoslavia as soon as possible. After many adventures, the party arrived in Italy on 27 December and Feilding was awarded a well-deserved DSO.

Alfgar's radio silence and George Feilding's return to Italy effectively marked the end of Clowder Mission. Frank Pickering still remained at HQ IV Zone to back up Alfgar if he resurfaced, and a small party under Alex Ramsay was standing by in Italy ready to parachute into the Saualpen to reinforce him if opportunity offered. Otherwise, by the end of the year everyone was accounted for and I was faced with the task of finding useful employment for some two dozen highly motivated and specially trained officers. They were to form the nucleus of what was henceforward to be known as No. 6 Special Force with a role more closely resembling that of the SOE staffs attached to units in north-west Europe.

I was not particularly depressed by the failure of Clowder Mission because I had always accepted that the difficulties might prove insurmountable. The principal obstacle to success was that the spirit of resistance as we had come to know it in Western Europe simply did not exist in Austria which remained entirely passive until the Third Reich was in its final death throes. Secondly, though I had not expected that Slovene territorial claims in Carinthia would be taken seriously, I had not thought that their demand for the return of Trieste would be rejected out of hand or that this divergence in our war aims would make it so difficult to allay Slovene suspicions about the motives of the Clowder Mission. These suspicions were reinforced by the understandable reluctance of AFHQ to authorize the delivery of substantial quantities of arms and explosives to dissident elements in the future British zone of Austria. Thirdly, the failure of the Allied armies in Italy to break through the German defences in the autumn of 1944 not only sealed the fate of Alfgar's expedition but shook the confidence of the Partisans in the military competence of the Western Allies compared with that of the Red Army which was advancing relentlessly across Eastern Europe. Finally there was the chronic shortage of aircraft and trained air-crews. Clowder, more than most of the special operations in the Mediterranean theatre, depended on regular air drops of arms and supplies not only for its credibility but, in the case of Alfgar in the Saualpen, for its very survival. These operations with their dropping zones in otherwise inaccessible mountain areas needed to be undertaken by the highly trained aircrews of the Special Flight. With the establishment of the Balkan Air Force in the summer of 1944 these Special Flight air-crews were no longer available and Clowder missions were accorded a lower priority than they had previously enjoyed. Of all the factors affecting Clowder, this lack of air support was the most critical.

On the other hand, Clowder Mission was not a total failure. We had reported in detail on the state of resistance in northern Slovenia and north-east Italy, both areas of major strategic importance which had not previously been reconnoitred by British officers. As early as January 1944 we gave a detailed and balanced assessment of Slovene territorial claims in Carinthia and Venezia Giulia. We organized the delivery of 100 tons of arms and supplies which were dropped by parachute in otherwise inaccessible areas along the Austrian frontier. Finally, the presence of highly trained British officers in this disputed, often dangerous, territory was a source of encouragement and, indeed, of enlightenment to many of the Partisan rank and file whose communist indoctrination gave such a false picture of Britain and its war effort. The conduct of the British officers and their active participation in every aspect of Partisan life made a deep and lasting impression and contrasted favourably with the behaviour of the Soviet liaison officers who insisted on an altogether superior lifestyle to that of the ordinary Partisans and remained in the relative safety of their headquarters.

My chief sadness was that Alfgar should have sacrificed his life on what turned out to be a hopeless venture, though the legend of the British major in the Saualpen has not been forgotten in the fifty years that have passed since his death. Nevertheless his exceptional talents as an entrepreneur as well as a highly skilled expert in the electronics and communications field were a loss which British industry in the post-war years could ill afford. On a more personal level, his death brought home to me, more strongly than ever, how blindly war destroys its victims.

CHAPTER 28

No. 6 Special Force

OUR plans for the employment of No. 6 Special Force in the event of a German collapse, the so-called Rankin situation, which had been approved by AFHQ and SOE London, needed urgently to be brought up to date. There seemed to be three main tasks. First, during the final advance the remaining Austrian agents, organized into Jedburgh parties of three or four, and officers operating in uniform, might usefully be employed in harassing the retreating enemy and cutting communications behind the lines. To co-ordinate these activities I proposed to install Charles Villiers in charge of a No. 6 Special Force Staff Section at HQ 8th Army. Secondly, while I was last in London it had been tacitly agreed that I should have a general responsibility for organized resistance groups operating ahead of the 8th Army, particularly in the approaches to the Ljubljana Gap. Thirdly, I foresaw that during, and particularly in the immediate aftermath of, 8th Army's advance into Austria, British corps commanders were going to be faced with an unholy influx not only of Germans but of Hungarians, Bulgarians, Cetniks and other members of the Axis forces and that No. 6 Special Force with its 'politically aware' and polylingual officers might have a useful role to play in sorting out the confusion. Finally, I was working on a rather vague post-hostilities role in which I saw No. 6 Special Force acting as an undercover branch of the Security Service, pursuing war criminals and cleaning up pockets of resistance. When last in England I had discussed these plans in broad outline with Colin Gubbins and, confident that he approved in principle, I flew over to AFHQ and secured their final endorsement before taking off for London on 15 December.

Facing the sixth winter of the war, London was looking shabbier than ever and everyone, whatever his responsibilities, was desperately tired. By now most of the launching sites of the V2 rockets in north-western Europe had been overrun, but this unpredictable form of bombardment, against which there was no known defence, seemed to have had a more damaging effect on people's morale than had the Blitz, even at its height. Hopes of an early German collapse, so confidently expressed when I had been in London two months earlier, had given place to the grim realization that, as in 1918, we were going to have to slog it out with a determined enemy. The resolute defence of the Gothic Line in Northern Italy and still more the early successes of the German counter-attack at Bastogne were proof that, as yet, the enemy were far from defeated in the West. Nevertheless, the relentless advance of the Soviet Army on the eastern front, already massing for a three-pronged attack on Berlin, meant that a German surrender in the first half of 1945 was now almost inevitable.

Thanks to the contribution of the French Resistance to Overlord, SOE was now accepted by most of Whitehall as a serious and responsible organization. Moreover, the Baker Street headquarters had been brought to a hitherto undreamed of level of efficiency. Unfortunately, there were few peaks left to conquer and I found Colin Gubbins depressed and preoccupied with the search for tasks which would hold the organization together in the post-war years when, he was convinced, Soviet expansionist policy would have, sooner or later, to be resisted with every weapon at the West's command. At dinner with him soon after my arrival, I explained my long-term plans for No. 6 Special Force in which I saw myself occupying a modest appointment in the future British element of the Austrian commission from where, if necessary, I could co-ordinate the activities of other former Clowder officers for whom I was confident of being able to find positions in military government, the security branch and similar post-war oganizations. Gubbins said that he was thinking on very much the same lines in relation to Germany but that everything depended on obtaining the acceptance of SOE as an independent peacetime organization. If provision could be made for a skeleton headquarters in some dark corner of Whitehall, it should not be too difficult for some old comrades' association to hold together the nucleus of at least a European organization with sufficient clandestine radio transmitters to ensure that we were not caught as completely unprepared as we were in 1939 and 1940. I agreed with Colin Gubbins about the importance of keeping contact with our continental friends whose co-operation we had built up so laboriously and at such great expense over the years. However, having a less sanguine temperament than his, I thought that until some major threat to peace had been clearly identified, it would be extremely difficult to obtain approval in peacetime for a skeleton headquarters organization of the sort which he envisaged, and that we should first concentrate on the British Occupied Zones in Germany and Austria. At his request I set out my thoughts in a short paper entitled 'All Dressed Up but Nowhere to Go', which he told me he found 'unhelpful', for he had a far wider vision. However, I was less concerned with these long-term plans than with the role of No. 6 Special Force in the immediate future.

I outlined to Geoffrey Harrison of the Central Department of the Foreign Office the plans which AFHQ had approved for the employment of No. 6 Special Force as a sort of political reconnaissance unit and action group for special operations in the British Zone of Occupation in the weeks immediately after hostilities had ceased. He offered no objection in principle, providing that we were operating under the orders of the British High Commissioner. Believing that we were home and dry, I telegraphed to Edward Renton telling him to confirm 8th Army's approval of Charles Villiers's attachment and to make the necessary administrative arrangements. Then, having dealt with my immediate problems, I travelled down to Serge Hill to see Alfgar's mother, Lady Elizabeth Motion.

It was a sad occasion but she made my task as easy as possible, producing a bottle of Alfgar's private stock of vintage Krug for dinner while I did my best to describe the heroic nature of his mission and what I imagined to be the extraordinary danger and discomforts in which he was now working. Although I said there was no reason to be seriously alarmed about Alfgar's temporary radio silence, I did not conceal the fact that his situation was desperate now that there was no chance of his being relieved before the winter snows set in. Her only comment when I had finished was to say how much it all reminded her of Hesketh, Alfgar's father. I left Serge Hill with a very heavy heart.

I spent a long weekend at Briggens where Charles Villiers was recuperating from an attack of typhoid and then on Christmas Day I travelled down to see my aunts at Longcross. It was not a cheerful visit, for Edith was undergoing one of her bouts of deep clinical depression and Eleanor was exhausted looking after her. They were now living almost exclusively on food produced in the garden and in the village. Eleanor had turned over more of the garden to vegetables and increased the number of chickens but otherwise things went on very much as before. The bread which Hetty continued to bake freshly every day was now made of 'standard' flour and, though a khaki colour, like so much else, tasted as delicious as ever; so did the meringues which she again made in my honour from her private hoard of sugar. Imprisoned in her profound deafness, Hetty was in many ways the least touched by the war. For the aunts, the world as they had known it, already shattered by the Kaiser's War, had now finally fallen apart. Brought up never to complain about their fate, these two old ladies faced a bleak and wintery future that Christmas with quiet resignation. Reflecting on all this while returning to London, I concluded that too many of their meagre hopes were now centred on me and that it was high time that I took stock of my own position, my future career and even my private life which, like so many other men, I had been at such pains to exclude during the war years.

Early in the New Year I received a message that Mr Henry Mack, who had recently been designated the Political Adviser to the future British High Commission in Vienna, wished to see me to discuss the current situation in Austria and particularly Slovene claims to southern Carinthia. I rang up the Foreign Office and asked him to lunch with me at the Connaught Hotel where we had an interesting discussion, and I was delighted to find that he took what I considered to be a very realistic view about the Austrians and the likelihood of their lifting a finger 'to work their passage', which was the current slogan. I gave him a short memorandum prepared by SOE's Austrian Section on the sort of political situation which we might expect to find in Vienna if, as now seemed certain, the Red Army got there first. This paper took a far less optimistic view than the current official line which assumed a considerable degree of co-operation with the Soviet authorities in the formation of a genuinely democratic government. Hal Mack clearly shared our scepticism and later in the meal he asked me whether I would be interested in joining the Political Division of the Austrian Commission. I was dreading the prospect of returning to peacetime soldiering, having had no conventional battle experience and being totally out of touch with modern infantry warfare, and the Political Division sounded the sort of job for which I felt reasonably well qualified. However, I took it as a very tentative offer and I was delighted when, before I left London, he rang up offering me the job of controller of his Political Branch.

Accepting his offer, I sent Mack a copy of the memorandum on the tasks of No. 6 Special Force in the immediate post-war phase which had now been formally approved both by AFHQ and by the SOE Council and which I had already discussed informally with Geoffrey Harrison. This unsolicited action raised a hornets' nest after my return to Italy when Hal Mack forwarded a copy of my memorandum to the Foreign Office. Although Harrison and Troutbeck, his under-secretary, minuted that they saw no objection to the employment of No. 6 Special Force in the suggested role, Cavendish-Bentinck, to whom the papers were marked in his capacity as Chairman of the Joint Intelligence Committee, objected in principle to SOE's activities being extended to the occupational and post-hostilities phase. This drew a magisterial ruling from Sir Orme Sargent, the deputy under-secretary of the Foreign Office, who minuted Troutbeck: 'We must certainly not allow SOE under cover of proposals of this kind to continue operations in the post-hostilities period. They have already tried to do so in the case of Germany under cover of negotiating an agreement with the Russians and we have scotched it. We must do the same in this case.' Gubbins protested that the proposal had been carefully worked out at the direction of SACMED and AFHQ under whose direction SOE in Italy was required to operate. The correspondence lasted until mid-April and by then No. 6 Special Force was fully integrated into the 8th Army and, in the early days of the occupation, was to carry out a number of special assignments of exactly the kind described in the disputed memorandum to everybody's satisfaction.

By mid-January I was ready to return to Italy. While waiting for the Allied spring offensive to begin, I concentrated on getting to know the group of semi-redundant Austrian agents who were now earmarked to form the Jedburgh parties and I organized a skiing course at Terminillo in the mountains north of Rome. Although all were Austrian-born, few had been old enough to learn to ski before coming to England and I amused myself reproducing what I remembered of the basic ski training which I had watched my friends in the 101 Gebirgsjaeger regiment giving their recruits on the slopes of the Zugspitze in 1937. Rather unfairly I won all the downhill races as I was the only person who had a decent pair of skis, but characteristically the Austrians took their handicap for granted.

I was in daily radio contact with my base, hoping against hope for news of Alfgar which never came. His loss had affected me more deeply than I cared to admit and prompted me to volunteer for just the sort of hare-brained operation which I had so often and so roundly condemned in others as unprofessional conduct. I have my submission before me as I write:

SECRET

Commander SO(M)

1. I request you to consider the desirability of sending me on a special mission to VENEZIA GIULIA, with the following objects:-

(a) Making a military report on this area in relation to FREEBORN OPERATION. G-3(Plans) in a conversation said they did not anticipate that we should be likely to reach VENEZIA GIULIA in other than FREE-BORN conditions.

(b) Making a political report on the Italo-Slovene problem.

(c) Briefing the resident BLOs on (a) and (b) above.

2. My reasons for suggesting myself are as follows:-

(a) The strategic and political importance of this area warrants the dispatch of a senior officer.

(b) I have already a good first-hand knowledge of the Slovene aspects of the problem, and have made a second-hand study of the Italian side.

(c) If I am designated as Field Commander for N-E ITALY such a reconnaissance is almost indispensable to enable me to deal with 15 AG and 8 A and to operate the field units concerned.

3. Early or mid-April would appear a good departure date, as this will give me plenty of time and, by then, the snows should have melted.

4. I suggest limiting my party to myself and a WTO.

5. If you agree to this project in principle, will you clear it with AFHQ and 15 AG and issue me with appropriate orders.

> (Sgd) P. A. Wilkinson Lt. Col. Royal Fusiliers HQ, ME 43 CMF
>
> 2 March 45

I did not expect an early reaction and was surprised when my request was immediately approved. I had had quite a tussle with Louis Franck, the current commander of SO(M) over my claim to become field commander in north-east Italy and I dare say he was fed up with No. 6 Special Force and with me in particular, and may well have thought that it would be easier to deal direct with Charles Villiers now at HQ 8th Army. In any case, I was elated rather than disconcerted by the speed of his response and immediately my depression about Alfgar lifted and my energy returned. By now I knew better than to confide in anyone about my personal plans before it was necessary and, while continuing in charge of No. 6 Special Force, I devoted as much time as I could to the secret preparations for this new venture.

Nor was this my only preoccupation. Rather in the same spirit of desperation, on my last visit to Naples I had agreed to get married.

CHAPTER 29

My Marriage

UNTIL now I had not seriously contemplated marriage. Before the war it was not permitted for officers in my regiment to marry under the age of twenty-six and the rule was strictly enforced, even the son of the Colonel of the Regiment being obliged to resign his commission. Marriage allowance was not paid until you reached the age of thirty. This enforced celibacy was relaxed with the outbreak of war but, after my own experiences, I had no wish to leave behind me a young widow and a fatherless child and long wartime engagements all too often seemed to end in tears.

I had first met Theresa Villiers when taken to dine with her at Briggens for the Puckeridge Hunt ball soon after my return from Czechoslovakia in 1939. We had subsequently dined together in London once or twice and I was about to stay the weekend with her parents, Lord and Lady Aldenham, at Briggens early in 1941 when, to my embarrassment, I learned that their house had been requisitioned by SOE as a training school. More embarrassing still, Briggens was allotted to the Polish Section, for which I was directly responsible and although I obtained permission for the Aldenhams to continue to live in the house, not unnaturally they suspected me of being the author of their misfortunes.

Theresa's father, Algernon Villiers, had been killed in action in France in 1917 a few weeks after she was born. His father, Sir Francis Villiers, was the fourth son of the fourth Earl of Clarendon, the Foreign Secretary, and was Ambassador to Belgium. Her mother's father was Herbert Paul, the historian, who had been Parliamentary Private Secretary to Mr Asquith, the Prime Minister. After the war she had married Walter Gibbs who later became Lord Hunsdon and later still Lord Aldenham.

Having damaged her back in a riding accident, Theresa had resigned from the VADs and spent several months living at home, working as an occupational therapist in a local hospital. I used therefore to see her quite often when visiting Briggens on duty, and sometimes when I was escorting VIPs around the school I would catch sight of her making deprecatory gestures from an upper window. In 1941, having been turned down for Bletchley Park on the grounds that her German was not good enough, she had enlisted in the WRNS and had been posted first to the Outer Hebrides and later to South Pembrokeshire, during which time we had few opportunities to meet. After I went abroad in 1943, she managed to have herself posted to the Middle East and had spent the winter as a 'plotter' in Beirut. From there she had transferred to Malta and in December 1944 she was posted to Naples with the exalted rank of Master-at-Arms, looking after a detachment of 100 WRNS working at AFHQ. Out of some private perversity she had refused to take a commission, replying to interviewing officers who failed to detect the irony in her voice, 'I'm not officer class, ma'am.'

In February 1945, on one of my visits to Caserta, she told me that she had finally changed her mind and agreed to take a commission and was shortly to be sent back to England on a course. I had learned that morning in strictest secrecy of the peace negotiations with Germany which were going on in Lisbon and in Switzerland; nevertheless, it was the view of the intelligence community that the war with Japan might easily last until 1947. It was therefore clear to both of us that if Theresa was sent back to England it might be years before we met again. So, somewhat against my principles, we decided to get married as soon as possible.

Our hasty engagement might have ended disastrously but for Theresa's incredible patience and forbearance, for I was the rottenest fiancé imaginable. I gave our wedding a far lower place in my order of priorities than I gave the current operations in which I was now heavily involved. Even Charles felt obliged to protest that marriage was not something I could do on my afternoon off. However, serious matters like marriage have their own momentum and, somewhat to my bewilderment, on 14 March 1945 we were married in the English Church in Rome. Charles gave Theresa away and Gerry Holdsworth was my best man; Edward Renton played the piano for there was not enough electricity to work the organ. Theresa's bridesmaids were Lavinia Lascelles and Delia Holland-Hibbert; both were WRNS officers and, like Theresa, when not on duty had spent most of their spare time with Field Marshal Alexander's ADCs at the Kennels at Caserta, riding the Field Marshal's horses. Our wedding was the beginning of another romance, for Lavinia Lascelles subsequently married Edward Renton. Charles had been sent some money by his mother to provide Theresa with a trousseau but he blew it all on the wedding reception for which the champagne had to be bought on the black market from stocks previously belonging to a German officers' club.

We spent our honeymoon in magical surroundings in a house at Ravello in the grounds of the Villa Cimbrone which belonged to Manfred Czernin's mother. The villa itself, with its famous terrace immediately above our house, was standing empty as its owner, Manfred's cousin Lord Grimthorpe, was serving with his regiment in Northern Italy and we consequently had a free run of the place. From the drawing-room windows of our house, which was perched on the side of the cliff, there was a sheer drop of 200 feet into the sea below. The villa was inaccessible to motor traffic and our provisions, which included 100 eggs, were brought up on the back of a mule; there were also countless tins of spam and other wartime delicacies which we were able to exchange with the villagers for fresh vegetables and fruit. There was an Italian cook who provided us with a succession of delicious meals over which we lingered for hours, having little else to do. The Germans had not plundered the library and there was a grand piano in the drawing room with some Beethoven and Mozart sonatas which Theresa played for me. We knew so little about each other that I had no idea she played so well and this was a fresh delight. It was one of her many accomplishments with which she never ceased to surprise me throughout our thirty-nine years of married life. She was an intensely private person and having been mocked by three brothers in her youth, she tended to keep her talents for her personal enjoyment unaware of the pleasure that they gave to others.

Our ten days' honeymoon was soon up and Theresa returned to her WRNS barracks at Naples and I to my headquarters at Siena. It had been a very make-shift honeymoon and we were both too exhausted to enjoy our surroundings as we should have done in normal circumstances. Nor did we even have time to get to know each other and when we parted we were still partial strangers. It was, in fact, precisely the situation which in my more rational moments I had been so determined to avoid. Nevertheless in those first ten days of mutual discovery I think that we both glimpsed the happiness that was in store.

Inevitably our hasty marriage produced some family recriminations. Theresa's step-father, a banker who was ever fearful of the future, found it harder than her mother to accept the fact that Theresa, of whom he was extremely fond, was marrying a penniless soldier. Her mother, equally practical, bewailed the fact that if we married in Rome none of our friends and relations would give us wedding presents – which proved to be the case. Edward Renton forgot to post my letter to my mother in South Africa telling her of our engagement and the first that she had learned of the matter was reading the announcement in a back copy of *The Times*.

Theresa and I did not see each other again until my thirty-first birthday when I found an excuse to drive down to Caserta and Theresa managed to find a room in a seedy hotel in Naples where we could spend the night. She produced a luxurious breakfast which we had in bed. We then drove back to Caserta where she was on duty that afternoon and I confessed to her somewhat shamefacedly that although the end of the war was obviously in sight, I was committed to one final operation. This was scheduled for the very near future and she was not to worry if she did not hear from me for three or four weeks and that my office in Siena would let her know that I was all right. Theresa knew very well that I should not disclose operational plans and did not question me further, but she could hardly have failed to have been distressed by my lack of candour so early in our married life or that I did not trust her discretion sufficiently to share with her the details of my assignment. I was angry at finding myself in a situation which I had hitherto been so determined to avoid. Moreover, Theresa's calm acceptance of it made me ashamed of the bravado which had caused me to volunteer for this silly operation. It was, I concluded, high time that I grew up.

CHAPTER 30

The Last Round-up

MY operation was scheduled for the April moon period and I had seized the excuse of a final briefing to drive down from Siena to AFHQ. Looking back, I can only remember the excitement of spending my birthday with Theresa. Nevertheless, my new responsibilities as a married man caused me to take a more realistic view of the nature of my operation than I had done hitherto and I found it far from reassuring.

At this distance of time it is hard to recall the utter confusion of those last three weeks of the war in Europe but it is reflected in the following entries in my diary.

16 April: General situation regarding Venezia Giulia still shrouded in conjecture. No answer from Combined Chiefs and Deedes told me Resmin [Mr Macmillan] had signalled Foreign Office saying that if faced with an 'ad hoc' decision, his alternatives were either to give in to Tito without a struggle, or to hold Venezia Giulia by force of arms. Longhi seems to take a 'realistic' view of the Italian chances of retaining Trieste. Birch [Lieutenant Colonel Nigel Birch, GSO1 of the Planning Branch at AFHQ] says that Plans were playing with the use of a brigade group to take over from the garrison immediately on surrender (if there is a surrender). Rumours are rife that the Combined Chiefs are examining the possibility of using Venice to maintain the British zone in Austria, and leaving Trieste to work out its own salvation. (I am sure this can't work.) Birch asked me to write a paper on Venezia Giulia. Nott-Bower [head of the security division of the future British Commission and later Metropolitan Police Commissioner] gave an amusing second-hand picture of Gusev rejecting the quadripartite division of Grau Vienna at the European Advisory Commission. 8 Army attack is essential.

20 April: Returned from flying visit to AFHQ to discuss whether desirable or feasible to stir up resistance in Austria. Managed to brief Birch in advance that answer is clearly no to both. John Clarke [GSO1 of Macmis] said that Trieste's situation deteriorating daily. Fiume was already partially surrounded and he estimated that in ten days' time there might be 150,000

Yugoslav troops in Istria. Meanwhile another 150,000 reinforced with Voroshilov [?] tanks were sweeping westward from the Danube and by the time of surrender Trieste might be invested by 300,000 Yugoslavs. Meanwhile Tito's attitude was hardening daily and Kidric had promised to fight 'any reactionary power, and if necessary the whole world' if they prevented Trieste returning to Slovenia. This attitude also taken by Bewik, Bebler and others. John suspected strong Russian backing. Philip Broad [a Foreign Office counsellor in the resident minister's office] said EAC had now reached the decision over Venezia Giulia. No details yet but the solution will probably be an Anglo-American occupation. While this is theoretically the best solution, cannot help thinking they have no idea what they are taking on. And where do the troops come from, specially the Americans? Jack Winterton [deputy high commissioner designate] and Jack Nicholls [head of the political division of the Austrian Commission] described their plans for the Vienna mission. How this was to be composed only of 'hirers and quarterers', and the work 'ad referendum'. Saw Bob Mathew [a former member of Clowder] who is going on it as G2 representative.

It was already the beginning of the April moon period and my personal kit was stacked in the corner of my office ready to move at short notice. Meanwhile there was a certain amount of routine work to be done as we had dropped six Jedburgh parties into southern Austria and it was important to avoid them becoming entangled with the advancing Soviet troops who had already taken Vienna and were in process of occupying north-eastern Styria. Meanwhile I was in regular contact with London and Caserta about the latest situation regarding Venezia Giulia. I could not know that the Germans had already signed the capitulation on 29 April but it was clear that the sensible thing to do was to stand down my operation which had been overtaken by events. It was, therefore, a great relief when Louis Franck telephoned me to say that my parachute operation had been cancelled and that I was to go forward immediately to HQ 8th Army. Taking Edward Renton with me, I set out at once, driving through the night, and crossing the Apennines and the now deserted Gothic Line. We arrived at 8th Army about 8.30 the following evening and were told to report at once to HQ XIII Corps just north of Venice. It was bright moonlight as we drove through the shattered villages and over a pontoon bridge across the river Adige. We got to Mestre about 10.30 and I reported to the BGS, Sir Harry Floyd. He said the situation was so fluid and the Germans were withdrawing so fast that there was no point in my trying to organize any resistance in the Gemona area. He added inconsequently, 'I remember Mestre; lost my wife here – on my honeymoon.'

Venice was out of bounds but Edward Renton said that he ought to find out how the SOE detachment had fared during the liberation of the city. I was very tempted to accompany him but fortunately did not do so for, no sooner had he left in my staff car, taking with him my sleeping kit, than the Corps Commander, General Sir John Harding, appeared from nowhere and, telling me to get in his jeep, we drove off at a smart pace heading for Monfalcone. 'He is a very thrusting driver,' I later wrote to Charles, 'and we had two collisions on the way'. Harding said that his instructions were to push on to Trieste as fast as he could and he proposed to take me up and hand me over to General Freyberg commanding the 2nd New Zealand Division which had been given the task of securing the port. It was a glorious spring morning and there was a scent of victory in the air. The church bells were ringing in the villages and the men and women in the streets waved to the troops as they drove by. The general was in high spirits, weaving in and out of the long column of trucks, waving to the troops and acknowledging the salutes of the officers as he drove past. Meanwhile he plied me with questions not only about Trieste and the Partisans but also about Theresa and our wedding. Theresa and he had often ridden together at Caserta and when he had heard that she was getting married he had insisted on lending her his official car, though she was only a WRNS rating, so that she could drive into Naples and buy herself a hat for our wedding (though I cannot remember that she ever wore it).

Shortly after crossing the river Tagliamento, we caught up with General Freyberg. While the two generals conferred, I chatted to Geoffrey Cox whom I had last seen in Crete in 1941 when he was living in Ian Pirie's villa in Canea, editing the *Crete News*. He was once again one of Freyberg's intelligence officers and I told him what little I knew of the high-level discussions concerning the future of Trieste and Venezia Giulia. Meanwhile Harding's orders to Freyberg were short and to the point; namely that he was to push on as fast as he could to Trieste and at all costs try to secure the port facilities.

Harding then departed in a cloud of dust leaving me with General Freyberg who motioned me into his jeep and once again we set off at break-neck speed. The reception given to General Harding as we drove up the line had been more demonstrative than I had expected from the New Zealanders, but the reception given to General Freyberg by his own troops was little short of ecstatic. As we drew up behind each truck, waiting to overtake it, the occupants waved and shouted with the wildest enthusiasm. The general waved back in a somewhat paternal way, obviously deeply moved by this demonstration of affection. And so was I; I had never seen anything like it. We drove along the coastal plain with a cool breeze blowing down from the snow-capped mountains to the north of us and with a hot salty smell from the marshes to the south. The column was travelling at speed, raising clouds of dust and rattling over the cobbles in the small towns and villages. The buildings we passed were intact and there were no signs of war. Here and there among the local inhabitants who waved to us were small groups of the resistance, a few of them with green Osoppo flags but the majority were red Garibaldi communists who raised their clenched fists in salute which rather nonplussed the general but he waved back genially.

We reached the river Isonzo about 3 p.m. on 1 May. Here for the first time there were notices written in Slovene as well as in Italian and there was a sprinkling of Yugoslav Partisans among the Garibaldini who waved to us. By now we had reached the head of the column behind the XII Lancers and were bowling along at 35 mph when, just short of Monfalcone, we were flagged down by two Partisans on motor cycles. We were greeted by a small group of Partisan officers including the Nacelnik of IX Corps who recognized me and shook my hand. I knew that he spoke some German and, with Geoffrey Cox and me translating as best we could, General Freyberg explained that he was under orders from General Alexander, the Supreme Allied Commander in the Mediterranean, to secure the facilities of the port of Trieste which were necessary for the support of the advance of the 8th Army into Austria. Somewhat taken aback, the Nacelnik replied that unfortunately he had no authority to allow the British column to enter Monfalcone. He went on to say that the city of Trieste was already occupied by the Yugoslav Army of National Liberation and that he must return to his headquarters and seek instructions. He suggested that a meeting between General Freyberg and the Kommandant IX Corps should be arranged provisionally for 7.30 that evening to discuss these matters. Meanwhile he asked that we should stand fast.

After a moment's hesitation and to my great relief, Freyberg agreed. I feared that he might be tempted to make a dash for Trieste for it was only about 25 miles distant. In this case and if it was true that the Partisans were already in possession of the city, which seemed more than likely, the New Zealanders might easily have come up against General Drapsin's IV Army of at least 100,000 well-armed troops and it was already 4.30 in the afternoon with only three or four hours of daylight left.

Geoffrey Cox and I agreed that, before Freyberg met the Kommandant of IX Corps, we must do our best to brief him. I started by explaining that the Yugoslavs considered they had a strong claim to the territory to the east of the river Isonzo which had only been ceded to Italy at the end of the Great War and which, until then, had been part of the Austro-Hungarian Empire. Although the coastal belt had always contained a strong Italian minority, which Mussolini had turned into a majority between the wars, particularly in the city of Trieste, the hinterland was almost exclusively Slav and composed both of Slovenes and of Croats. I went on to explain that the Slovenes in particular considered the return of Trieste as one of their principal war aims for which they would almost certainly be prepared to fight. During my presentation, which lasted about twenty minutes, General Freyberg's face grew longer and longer and, at its conclusion, he remarked that he hoped he would be able to steer clear of politics and confine the discussion later that evening to strictly military considerations. I expressed some doubts about this but said that I was sure that the meeting would be entirely inconclusive; indeed, I doubted very much whether the Yugoslav commander would turn up. The rapidity of our advance had clearly taken the Yugoslavs by surprise and, faced with a situation which affected the future of Trieste, they would certainly have to consult Tito personally. I thought there was little likelihood of a decision of such importance being reached that evening. In this, at least, I was proved right for 7.30 came and went and there was no sign of the Kommandant of IX Corps.

Meanwhile I had to deal with the Cetniks. During our drive up General Harding had told me that there was a large group of Cetniks north of Gorizia, many of them wearing German uniforms, who wanted to surrender to the British and he asked me what should be done with them. I said that I had no instructions but if the Cetniks were in German uniform, I supposed that they should be treated as prisoners of war, disarmed and interned. But I added that they should be interned well to the west of the river Tagliamento so that there was no danger of them coming into contact with the Partisans; otherwise there would be mayhem. General Harding agreed and I therefore stuck to this line in answering the inquiries received from the forward troops who were having to cope with large groups of Cetniks and White Guards fleeing for their lives from the Partisans. In particular I remember a huge bearded Cetnik brought in by the XII Lancers who in voluble German recited a long tale of murder and rape perpetrated by the Partisans against the Cetnik camp followers which clearly impressed his captors more than me.

With evident disappointment Freyberg had given orders for the division to bivouac for the night west of Monfalcone. There was no sign of Edward Renton who had dallied in Venice and had not yet caught us up with my staff car and my sleeping kit. It was typical of General Freyberg that he personally arranged for me to be given a tent and some bedding and, shortly before supper, he sent round his servant with one of his own pocket handkerchiefs. Small acts of thoughtfulness like this live on in one's memory when events of major historical importance have long been forgotten. Nevertheless I spent an uneasy and sleepless night torn by my awareness of my dual loyalties. Our meeting with the Partisan officers and the warmth of the welcome given me by the Nacelnik of IX Corps reminded me that these were my former comrades-in-arms to whom I owed a special loyalty. Behind the hills which I could see from my tent door lay the Vipava valley and the village of Slap where a farmer's family had risked their lives to give Alfgar and me shelter during a German offensive. Convinced of the justice of their cause, these Slovenes with whom we had lived on such intimate terms had never doubted that we shared their dreams, or that their wartime efforts would be rewarded by the return of Trieste, the indispensable component of a free and independent Slovenia. With my contempt for Italian fascists and a romantic tendency which I had had since my schooldays to identify with the Austro-Hungarian monarchy, I had fully sympathized with these Slovene war aims which I was now destined to do my best to thwart. I remembered how my hero, Colonel T. E. Lawrence, to show his support of the Arab cause had insisted on entering Damascus at King Faisal's side wearing Arab dress. It was not a gesture which seemed appropriate to my present situation, since in any case many of the Partisans were already wearing British battle-dress. However, I felt the falseness of my position intensely and, rising early, I wrote a long and rather emotional letter to General Harding, appealing for a better understanding of the Slovene cause, particularly by the British press, and indeed by many British officers, who tended to dismiss the Yugoslav Army of National Liberation as mere communist brigands.

Shortly after breakfast an orderly brought a message that the Kommandant of IX Corps wished to arrange a meeting with General Freyberg at 11.30 that morning. We duly foregathered at the same farmhouse where we had held our meeting the previous day. General Freyberg repeated that he was under orders from the Supreme Allied Commander to secure the port of Trieste. The Kommandant replied that since the Yugoslavs were already in control of the port facilities, Freyberg's request would have to be referred to General Drapsin, the Commander of the Yugoslav IV Army. Freyberg said that he understood the situation and would like to meet General Drapsin to discuss the means by which he could carry out the Supreme Allied Commander's orders, and that meanwhile he must continue his advance without delay. Though obviously terrified at having to take a decision of this sort, the Kommandant did not dissent. Freyberg said that it might be necessary to 'clean up' any pockets of German resistance encountered on the way. The phrase 'clean up', which I translated as 'reinigen', caused some confusion and the Kommandant replied that there were no German forces, clean or dirty, left between Monfalcone and Trieste and that the whole area was already under Yugoslav military administration. General Freyberg wisely did not dispute this claim, preferring to keep the discussion on strictly military lines, and after about half an hour the meeting broke up. Freyberg immediately gave orders to resume the advance and we were about to set off when a message arrived that General Drapsin would like to meet General Freyberg at 2.30 that afternoon in order to discuss the situation. A source of some embarrassment when it came to drafting a report of the morning's meeting was that, so intent had we been in our interpreting, neither Geoffrey nor I had thought to inquire the name of General Freyberg's interlocutor. In the event General Drapsin never turned up at the rendezvous and, after waiting for him for twenty minutes, Freyberg gave him up and we set off in pursuit of the column.

There were quite a few Partisan troops in Monfalcone and they waved cheerfully to us, saluting with a clenched fist. The civilian onlookers, however, were far less enthusiastic than they had seemed west of the river Isonzo and I saw no sign of any Italian Partisans. On the whole the streets seemed strangely deserted. We caught up with the head of the column a few miles east of Monfalcone where it was temporarily held up. Ahead of us the coastal plain came to an end and the hills ran down to the sea. There were sounds of shelling on the left flank and some desultory small arms fire ahead to which the advance guard was replying. A trickle of prisoners of war and wounded were being brought in, one rather gory New Zealander with a leg wound waving and cheering and shouting to his mates that 'at last he'd got a blighty one'. It seemed bad luck to me, though he was clearly delighted. The firing was very light and I seized a scout car and went forward to see what was going on. There were a few prisoners who had just been overrun, mostly young boys, and a young NCO told me he belonged to a marine detachment which was supposed to be defending the northern approaches to the town. However, the firing was already dying down and the Germans surrendering right and left. After about twenty minutes, although there was still some shooting on the left flank, Freyberg ordered the advance to continue. We had encountered no Yugoslav troops of any kind since leaving Monfalcone.

Rounding the headland, we came in sight of Miramare, the former Austrian Imperial Palace which I had seen so often from the train on my way to Egypt and, stretching ahead of us, the city of Trieste. Here we halted while General Freyberg gave his orders. Geoffrey Cox, slipping behind a bush in order to relieve himself, emerged a moment later marching before him at pistol point a young German with his hands up who confirmed that this was the last defensive position and the way to Trieste was free. So we set off again, the general leading the way in an open scout car while I followed in a jeep with Geoffrey Cox. We drove at walking pace along the Corniche and through the large crowds lining the streets, the windows and the roof-tops and we were cheered loudly mostly, I reckoned, by Italians hoping we would save them from the Yugoslavs. I expected, at any moment, that somebody would throw a bomb or take a pot-shot at the general and, scanning the roof-tops, I kept my finger on the safety catch of my Colt Super. However, nothing happened and we had still not encountered any Yugoslav troops when, after about twenty minutes, the general decided that, having established his presence, he could now withdraw to the castle at Miramare where he proposed to set up his headquarters.

Meanwhile, I had joined a New Zealand brigadier called Gentry and together we set out in my jeep for the centre of the town; I in search of the Yugoslav town Kommandant and he to reconnoitre the port area. There was quite a lot of shooting in the side streets we drove down; none seemed directly aimed at us but the local inhabitants had clearly plenty of old scores to settle and time was running short. My companion, a most distinguished soldier who had survived every campaign in which the New Zealand troops had been engaged, had every intention of returning to New Zealand intact now that peace had broken out. He found all this domestic shooting disconcerting, and said so. However, I was in a high state of excitement and we careered wildly down the deserted streets amid bursts of machine-gun and rifle fire, some of it over our heads. In the centre of the town there were many Yugoslav Partisan flags – the old Royal Yugoslav flag now emblazoned with a red star – hanging from the windows. Eventually we reached the Piazza dell' Unita. This was something of a misnomer for both the Yugoslav Army of National Liberation and the Italian CLNAI (Committee of National Liberation for Upper Italy) had established their headquarters there, united only in their mutual distrust and the claims of each to have liberated the city single-handed. A considerable number of Yugoslav troops, their distinctive forage caps emblazoned with a red star, appeared to be mingling happily with the predominantly Italian-speaking crowd that was milling about the square and there seemed no sign of tension. Not altogether to my surprise, the Yugoslav town Kommandant whom I had hoped to persuade to pay a courtesy call on General Freyberg was not available and while waiting to see him I received an urgent message to go at once to the north end of the town where there was reported to be a confrontation between the Partisans and the New Zealanders over a battalion of Germans who had holed up in a barracks and were refusing to surrender to the Partisans. When I arrived I found both parties glowering at each other about fifty paces distant on opposite sides of the road. In an effort to sort things out, I suggested that if the Germans surrendered to the New Zealanders, the Partisans should be allowed the spoils of war in the shape of the prisoners' watches and cameras. This attempt at conciliation was scornfully rejected by the New Zealand company commander who said, 'What do you think we want with a lot of f—ing Teds? All we want is their f—ing watches.' I do not know how the matter was resolved for I left them to it and returned to Freyberg's headquarters at Miramare. Here I learned for the first time that the war in Italy was over and that the cease-fire had been signed with effect from midday on 2 May. John Clarke, the British Military Missions Liaison Officer with General Drapsin, was now with General Freyberg. The latter was in excellent form. He said he was determined to avoid any political commitment and to keep any discussions with Drapsin on strictly military lines. He had therefore refused to comment on Boris Kidric's statement that the Yugoslavs would fight to the death for the possession of Trieste. Freyberg went on to say that until he received instructions he was unwilling to meet General Drapsin who had sent him a message via John Clarke seeking to arrange a meeting. It was, in any case, clearly undesirable that Freyberg should be seen to call on Drapsin, and I urged that their first meeting should be on neutral ground.

John Clarke's arrival meant that I was relieved of any further responsibility for liaison with the Yugoslavs. The other good news was that Edward Renton had finally arrived with my staff car and my personal kit. Corporal Jewels made up a bed for me in the salon of the palace between two enchanting Winterhalter portraits of the young Franz Josef and the Empress Elisabeth at the time of their marriage; the former a slim, fair-haired youth in the white uniform of the Imperial Guard and the latter a fairy princess. If I had hoped for a decent night's sleep, I was disappointed and there are cryptic references in my dairy to a German officer in plain clothes and a midnight visit by a German general. I have no clear recollection of either.

Having handed over the day-to-day liaison with the Yugoslavs to John Clarke, I was able to spend 3 May sorting myself out. I signalled to Charles Villiers at HQ 8th Army to arrange for No. 6 Special Force to be transferred from XIII Corps to V Corps which was now charged with the entry into Austria, instructed him to attach himself to V Corps HQ and told him that as soon as I could extract myself from Trieste, I would join him at Udine. I had no radio operator or ciphers with me and was, therefore, precluded from reporting my first impressions to London – which was perhaps just as well. However, I wrote a long report for Lord Harcourt, the SOE representative at AFHQ, which I sent down to Caserta by hand. The gist of it was that the rapidity of our advance had clearly taken the Yugoslavs by surprise and they had been unable to present us with a *fait accompli*. However, it was indisputable that the Partisans had occupied most of Trieste, including the port area, by the time we arrived. Freyberg having fortunately been prevented from meeting General Drapsin, relations with the Yugoslavs had so far been kept at a working level and there had been no confrontation. Nevertheless, the latter were in a truculent mood and would certainly resist any attempt to take over the port by force. If we were really dependent on the use of Trieste as a base for the advance into Austria, it could only be with the full consent of the Yugoslavs. However, if we could give an assurance that we would restore Trieste to Yugoslav administration once we had no further use for it, I felt reasonably confident that we would be allowed to operate the port in the meantime. Otherwise I predicted that we would face a severe internal security problem and, possibly, labour troubles organized by the communist underground.

I do not know what action Bill Harcourt took with my report. However, on 5 May General Alexander telegraphed to the Prime Minister: 'I believe that he [Tito] will hold to our original agreement if he can be persuaded that when I no longer require Trieste as a base for my force in Austria, he will be allowed to incorporate it in his new Yugoslavia.' Mr Churchill reacted predictably to this proposal. However, in retrospect it seems noteworthy that General Alexander and Harold Macmillan should have stuck their necks out so far, and I hope I had nothing to do with it.

About dinner time on 3 May, General Freyberg received a protest from the Bishop of Trieste about the behaviour of the Yugoslavs. John and I were not particularly impressed by the bishop's recital of atrocities, remembering what the White Guard and Domobrans, not to mention the Italian Army of Occupation, had done to the Partisans. However, General Freyberg seemed very upset and I was sent to lodge a protest. I was received by the liaison officer with IX Corps at the Kommandatura Mesta who, having listened to my remonstrance, replied disarmingly, 'But surely you expected us to *murder* them!'

The following morning, 4 May, General Harding sent for John and me as he wanted to arrange a formal call from General Drapsin. John agreed to fix this, while Edward Renton and I drove up to Udine. We paused on the bridge at Gorizia where there was a Partisan checkpoint inspecting the papers of a party of priests carrying suitcases and bundles and obviously in full flight from the communists. Udine was *en fête* with Italian Partisans of all colours thronging the streets, the town having been liberated jointly by both Osoppo and Garibaldini. Edward, who fortunately spoke good Italian, inquired after Tom Macpherson, the BLO, and was told that he was up the road at Gemona. There was no sign of any British troops but the Italian Partisans said that the Germans were fleeing as fast as they could in the direction of Austria and that the road was safe as far as Ospidaletto. On a hillside north of Gemona we discovered Tom Macpherson. Tom was a very impressive figure – I think he was wearing his kilt – surrounded by a gang of murderous-looking young guerrillas, many of them dressed in shorts although there was still snow on the hills. They had a variety of Tommy-guns and hand-grenades and were eagerly watching some caves in the mountainside in which some SS were reported to have taken refuge. The latter were now in the process of being smoked out with a flame-thrower and it was obvious that Tom's friends were waiting to shoot them down as they emerged. Tom, who clearly felt badly about their intention, asked me what he should do. I told him that I had long since given up trying to prevent friendly guerrillas from shooting their prisoners. It was, after all, their country and they had many blood debts to settle. I suggested, therefore, that we should leave the SS to their fate and go down to Gemona where he could give me a situation report and we could discuss future plans. On the way down we passed a long column of disconsolate Cetniks in German uniforms making their way south escorted by the Italian Resistance.

Edward and I spent the night at Udine celebrating victory. So far as I remember, there were no other British uniforms to be seen and we were given a triumphant reception. Two of the resistance leaders, Verdi and Mario, insisted that we attend an open-air luncheon which the Osoppo were giving the following day in the town square. I have only a hazy recollection of the seemingly endless speeches recounting local feats of arms, delivered in extremely rapid Italian with melodramatic gestures; and the bottles and bottles of wine and the endless succession of toasts. I envied Edward his command of Italian and as soon as I decently could, I slipped away leaving Edward in Udine to receive Charles Villiers and the main party of No. 6 Special Force which were due to arrive later that afternoon.

Driving south to HQ XIII Corps at Duino I managed to snatch some sleep, arriving just in time for General Harding's meeting with General Drapsin. General Drapsin was rather impressive but the Yugoslavs were clearly under instructions not to give anything away and he did not appear very sure of himself. General Harding, on the other hand, set out the British requirements in very forceful terms. The two generals obviously liked and respected each other but the meeting proved inconclusive and the only outcome was that an international football match was to be arranged.

On 6 May I lunched at HQ XIII Corps and attended Harding's press conference. I then left for Udine where V Corps had already established its headquarters. Charles Villiers had everything under control and took me to see the BGS, Brigadier Toby Low, a close friend of his from his Oxford days, and the Corps commander, General Keightley, and I reported the details of Harding's meeting with Drapsin.

Charles, Edward and I sat up late that night reminiscing. Events had moved so quickly and the German collapse had been so complete that there had been no opportunity to put into effect the elaborate plans which we had made for No. 6 Special Force. Some of the younger members of the team who had not yet been 'blooded' were plainly disappointed but I was thankful to have been spared having to send them into action. It seemed incredible that after all these years the fighting in Italy was over and that the curtain was about to go up on the last act.

CHAPTER 31

Austria: The End of the Road

CHARLES Villiers's close friendship with Toby Low, the BGS of V
Corps, ensured that full use would be made of No. 6 Special Force
during the advance into Austria. The cease-fire in Italy did not extend
to Austria, though it seemed unlikely that an armistice would be long
delayed. It had already been established by others besides Clowder
Mission that Hitler's 'Alpine Fortress' was a myth. Nevertheless, there
was a strong possibility of diehard resistance in the woods and mountains
which might last for weeks, if not for months. However, as we saw it,
the most immediate threat which seemed to us not to have been taken
sufficiently seriously by HQ 8th Army was that, immediately there was
a general surrender, the Yugoslav Army would debouch from the mountain passes and occupy Villach and Klagenfurt as well as the Slovene-
speaking territory south of the river Drau. I had been told as long ago
as December 1943 that this was a major Slovene war aim, and there had
been no signs of any change of heart. At several meetings Charles and
I expressed these fears to General Keightley and Brigadier Low, stressing
that the recent experience in Trieste had demonstrated that Yugoslav
threats of this sort needed to be taken seriously. The point was well
taken and we were assured that, but for German vacillations about the
cease-fire, V Corps would already have been deployed in southern
Carinthia in order to resist Yugoslav incursions. The main axis of our
advance was along the road which ran northward from Udine through
Gemona and Tarvisio and the Yugoslavs using the Wurzen and Seeberg
passes would have far less distance to travel than V Corps.

Early on 7 May I took Captain Bennett and Henri Berger von
Waldenegg with me in a jeep and we drove northwards through Cividale
d. Friuli along the ethnic border in the direction of Plezzo. My diary
reads as follows: 'Saw Dick Fyffe, commanding 2 Rifle Brigade, and had
excellent lunch with the Welch Regiment, Henri passing easily as a

234

British officer. The scenery staggeringly beautiful. General armistice atmosphere and our Sappers peacefully repairing a bridge within easy shot of the enemy.' The latter were holding a ridge at the top of the pass at what must have been very close to the frontier. So far I had seen no sign of Yugoslav concentrations, but suddenly after lunch six Stuart tanks came clattering up through the village, their Yugoslav crews waving and cheering and their destination, Celovec (Klagenfurt), chalked in large letters on their turrets. All I could do was to send an urgent message to Corps HQ reporting what I had seen and saying that they had better look sharp if they wanted to get to Klagenfurt first. I then drove back to Udine as fast as I could.

On arrival at Corps HQ I went with Charles to see Toby Low who said that the bridges had now all been repaired and that the advance into Austria was to take place that night. Providing detachments for the leading troops I sent Charles, Henri Berger and Lochead, a newly joined member of the mission, to go in via Tolmezzo while Alex Ramsey, Birkett, another new member, and I would go with the main body via Tarvisio. Bennett and Gardner I sent back to Plezzo.

I told Ramsey and Birkett to go on ahead and meet me in Tarvisio. I then settled down to drafting situation reports for London and Caserta and to issuing instructions to the six Jedburgh parties who were now operating in Carinthia and Styria. It was, therefore, nearly eleven o'clock before I set off in my staff car for Gemona and Tarvisio. It was, I reflected, extremely satisfactory that No. 6 Special Force was in sufficient strength to head the advance on all three axes and that so far everything seemed to be working according to plan. I reached Tarvisio about midnight where, to my surprise, there was no sign of Alex Ramsey and Birkett. A major in the Rifle Brigade said the road ahead was now clear and that the cease-fire would take effect from 6 a.m. I had half a bottle of whisky and, while we were celebrating victory, a message came in to say that there was a German major in the hospital who wished to surrender to somebody 'of equal rank' but was unfortunately unable to leave his bed. We sent back a heartless message reminding him that surrender was unconditional and promising that one of us would shoot him after breakfast.

I left Tarvisio at 4.30 a.m., noting that the road seemed strangely deserted. However, the absence of traffic did not worry me since I was convinced that the main column was ahead of me and, having had a heavy day, I curled up on the back seat of my staff car and went to sleep. I was woken up by the car braking suddenly and, in the light of the masked headlamps, I saw a barrier across the road and three or four figures in what were unmistakably German uniforms. A sentry was covering us with a machine-gun. I expected that at any minute our car would be riddled with bullets and it flashed through my mind that this was a particularly silly way in which to end the war. However, my fears were short-lived. An officer approached and, having inquired whether I spoke German, he said very politely, 'Wollen Sie bitte 500 meter zuruckfahren. Der Waffenstillstand beginnt erst um sechs Uhr.' ('Would you please pull back 500 metres. The armistice does not begin until 6 a.m.') However, an older companion said, 'Macht nichts. Er darf weiterfahren wenn er will.' ('It doesn't matter. He can drive on if he likes.') It was tempting to be the first British officer to head the advance into Austria, but I had had a bad fright and prudence prevailed. So we withdrew to a lay-by round a bend in the road where, in the cold light of the dawn, we cooked breakfast. Six o'clock came with no sign of British troops and we watched the early morning train puffing up the valley from Arnoldstein, its sleepy passengers apparently oblivious of their momentous circumstances. I waved to the engine driver, and he waved back. And so we waited until eight o'clock when a red-tabbed brigadier arrived with an escort of 27 Lancers. He seemed rather surprised to see us but did not demur when we fell in just ahead of the leading company of the Rifle Brigade and the jeeps of Popski's Private Army who eyed us malevolently. In this order we drove down the valley to Arnoldstein.

At Arnoldstein we met the main column which, to my great surprise and satisfaction, was headed by Charles Villiers. It transpired that the Germans had cratered the main road between Gemona and Tarvisio and the main column had consequently made a diversion crossing the mountain and approaching Villach down the Gail valley from Hermagor. By the time that I had started north, some three hours later, the demolitions had been repaired and the Royal Engineers had waved through the unsuspecting driver Jewels when I had been asleep in the back of the car and, unaware of these developments, we had continued on our way until brought to a halt at the Austrian frontier post.

It was a beautiful May morning with scarcely a breath of wind and the Karawanken mountains were reflected in the calm waters of the Worthersee. The villagers waved to us as did many of the convalescent German soldiers who thronged the hotels and boarding-houses which lay along the north side of the lake. There were a few glum faces but no signs of open hostility. There were some bizarre sights, like the German soldier who came to meet us marching down the middle of the road doing the goose-step but, on the whole, there was an end-of-term spirit in the air as we passed through these lake-side villages.

However, in Klagenfurt itself there were few cheers and, in the streets, the onlookers eyed us glumly. A stream of Germans in uniform driving both military and civilian vehicles, riding bicycles or on foot were heading northwards. There were no Yugoslav troops to be seen in the streets or Slovene flags or inscriptions in the centre of the town. The road from Villach led straight to the Rathaus where we halted. I sent Charles and Henri Berger von Waldenegg, who had just had a touching reunion with his sister and his grandmother whom he had met by chance in the street, to go southwards in the direction of the Loibl Pass and make contact with any Yugoslav forces approaching from the south. Then, accompanied by Alex Ramsey and Birkett, I went up the steps of the Rathaus. It was a fine seventeenth-century building with a classical façade and an open courtyard where I was met by a group of civilians who announced that they were the new provisional government of Carinthia, elected the previous day. After listening to their description of their democratic credentials, I cut them short by saying that they should report to the British Military Government officers who would soon be arriving. Meanwhile I took their names and personal details which I was able to signal at once to London and Caserta knowing that neither would be at all pleased to learn of the existence of this so-called provisional government. Nevertheless, it was something of a journalistic 'scoop' for it was many hours before the representatives of the Military Government arrived and reported these details through the usual channels.*

Meanwhile, Charles and his detachment had run into a lively infantry battle which was taking place around Ferlach between the advancing Yugoslavs and a group of SS troops who were now fighting for their lives. Charles had also come across numerous signs of Partisan activity north of the river Drau in the southern environs of Klagenfurt. We reported our morning's activities to Toby Low who dispatched some troops to cover the bridge over the river Drau and sort out the SS in Ferlach. I then withdrew everybody to a housing estate on the western edge of the town where we had set up our signal station. Here we

---

* In 1970, when I was ambassador in Vienna, I attended a British Week in Klagenfurt celebrating the twenty-fifth anniversary of the town's 'liberation' by British troops. The official programme contained a photograph entitled *Mai 1945: Offiziere der Britischen Besatzungsmacht in ersten Gesprach mit Vertretern des freien Osterreich.* The Landershauptmann was somewhat disconcerted when I told him that the central figure was none other than myself and the other officers were members of No. 6 Special Force which I commanded.

lunched. The working-class family whose house we had commandeered let us use their kitchen to prepare our meal and were surprised and delighted to find that, not only were we not acquisitive as they had been led to expect, but everyone they had encountered spoke fluent German.

I spent the afternoon making up for my lost sleep in the garden of this little house, waking only to listen to the relay of Mr Churchill's announcement in the House of Commons that the war in Europe was ended with an unconditional German surrender.

Epilogue

For the permanent headquarters of No. 6 Special Force Edward Renton succeeded in laying claim to a small late eighteenth-century country house on the road north to St Veit, Schloss Annabichl. It had been a German Air Force officers' mess, and had not only sufficient sleeping accommodation but also a courtyard where we could keep our vehicles as well as outbuildings which we could use for our signals station. The only snag was that, since it overlooked the airfield, it was certain sooner or later to be claimed by the Royal Air Force.

During the first twenty-four hours German troops streamed past the Schloss in every sort of vehicle and on foot along the road to St Veit. In the general panic I watched a staff car with a German officer drive straight over a group of foot-soldiers leaving two bodies lying in the road. In the midst of this *sauve qui peut* there were attempts at normality. I saw to my amazement a solitary tram trying to make its way against the stream, the driver doggedly ringing his bell to clear the road. Among the mass of military vehicles there were occasional civilian cars crammed with refugees and personal belongings; and every now and then one bearing a Yugoslav number-plate. I was reminded of our exodus from Poland on the night of 17 September 1939.

In the town I met some scruffy-looking British prisoners of war. Those that I spoke to had mostly been captured in Greece and Crete. In contrast there was a group of haggard-looking Poles who, though in rags, managed to appear smartly turned out. Most of the shops were closed but the streets were busy and German and British troops as well as the occasional Yugoslav mingled with the Austrian civilians apparently unconcernedly. My record of VE Day ends with an enigmatic entry in my diary: 'Dinner with Tony Warre and 27 Lancers. German soldiers coming in to drink.'

On account of his friendship with Toby Low, I left it to Charles to carry out the special tasks allotted to us by HQ V Corps, while Edward

Renton undertook an intensive search for traces of Alfgar, as well as acting as intelligence officer, writing up reports and political summaries and retrieving the Jedburgh parties. Meanwhile I avoided getting involved in the day-to-day running of the unit. I knew that my own days in Klagenfurt were numbered, for arrangements had already been made for me to be transferred to the Political Division of the Austrian Commission as soon as hostilities ended.

On 9 May I called on HQ V Corps and lunched with Teddy Tryon, a Royal Fusilier whom I knew only slightly, who was the brigadier in charge of administration. Crawley, the intelligence officer, had been with me in Auxillary Units in 1940, so one way and another our relations with V Corps HQ were exceptionally close. After lunch I drove up the road as far as Volkermarkt and Griffen with the 27 Lancers. There were a few Partisans to be seen in Volkermarkt but they looked as though they were members of a local Odred and not an advance party of the Yugoslav Army. At Griffen the Burgermeister said he remembered hearing about Alfgar but had never met him and knew nothing of his fate. I called on the brigade commander and, on returning to Annabichl, found a signal from Louis Franck telling me to get in touch with representatives of 15 Army Group who were coming up to Austria. However, in view of our very close relations with HQ V Corps, I saw no advantage in this and let it go. Meanwhile news kept coming in from Alex Ramsey, whom I had sent to patrol south of the river Drau, that a lively battle was still in progress near Ferlach between SS units withdrawing over the Loibl Pass and the local Partisans but there were no signs of the Yugoslav Army approaching in force.

On 10 May a Ukrainian officer arrived for breakfast and I left it to Ronnie Preston who spoke Russian, to find out what he wanted. During the morning Charles and Alex Ramsey reported that they were keeping the peace between the Germans and the Partisans at Ferlach. I went down there to see what was happening and found the ditches full of German arms which had been thrown away, some abandoned tanks and motor transport and I overtook a column of British troops moving up in order to sort things out. My diary entry concludes: 'Brought back a [wounded] gunner. Hit a German truck. Teddy Tryon for tea.' Charles, who had got back to Annabichl before me, told me that Toby Low had been on the telephone and wanted us to organize the disarming of General Pannwitz's Cossack Corps which had surrendered earlier that day and that he had arranged a rendezvous early next morning with the British commander and proposed to take Lochead to assist him. Fearing that No. 6 Special Force might be given the thankless task of becoming the custodians of these 40,000 Cossacks, I warned Charles that, having acted as a liaison officer and organized the disarming, he was then to hand the business over to V Corps and to have nothing more to do with it without orders in writing from me.

Charles and Lochead set off early next morning and, having made contact with the British troops who were to support him, Charles stationed Lochead on the road and withdrew to a small hill a couple of hundred yards distant to await events. It was not long before the Cossack column appeared, marching five abreast. To Charles's horror the leading horseman ignored Lochead's signal to halt and he disappeared into their midst. Charles started up his jeep and was preparing to go to Lochead's rescue when he realized that it was merely the Cossack's mounted band which had overrun him. When General Pannwitz, who was leading the column in person, came abreast he returned Lochead's salute, raised his hand and the long column came to a rippling halt; it stretched as far as the eye could see. Two hours later when I visited the scene I found the Cossack squadrons proceeding at a walk in half sections, each man throwing his rifle into an open farm wagon as he passed. I noted that as soon as it was full each wagon was removed and carried off into the woods by Tito Partisans under the eyes of the British troops who were supervising the operation and who made no attempt to intervene. Nor did I, for in Slovenia and particularly in Croatia, we had suffered greatly at the hands of the Cossacks who were the cruellest of the cruel and apparently licensed by their German officers to rape and loot at will.

The surrender of the last major mounted formation in Western Europe was a Napoleonic scene. The German officers, who were immaculately turned out and superbly mounted, cantered nonchalantly up and down the line, and I could only admire their arrogance in the face of disaster. The Cossacks themselves with their brightly coloured headgear were reminiscent of earlier and more romantic wars depicted in the coloured plates in history books; their discipline was impeccable. The fact that the Cossacks and their elegant German officers had perpetrated more atrocities in Yugoslavia and Northern Italy than any other enemy unit did not detract from the magnificence of their surrender.

When the winter weather had forced Alfgar down into the forest, he had taken refuge on the western slope of the Saualpen where, as I discovered later, there were scattered Slovene communities. However, the only precise indication of his whereabouts that he had given was his original signal that he had reached the summit of the Saualpen west of

Wolfsberg, and it was therefore in this direction that I went to look for him. It was hard to make headway against the flow of refugees, many of them Hungarian soldiers in uniform who were often accompanied by their families riding in farm carts crammed with their personal belongings. All were fleeing in front of the Soviet troops who by now had occupied the whole of Styria. Just short of Wolfsberg I met some French prisoners, including a group still in their striped concentration camp uniforms. Haggard-looking but deliriously happy, they were dancing insanely and drunkenly down the road as they made their way westward on foot. At various villages on the way I inquired after Alfgar but nobody seemed to have heard of him on the eastern side of the hill. By the time we started home, many of the Hungarians were already bivouacking for the night, brewing up beside the road with their horses hobbled and grazing and the women and children gathering firewood and fetching water. For ten miles or more the scene resembled one vast Gypsy encampment and, to add to the confusion, there was now an influx of fierce-looking Bulgarians. In the valley, the Cossacks were still handing in their rifles as they filed past at the walk. This procession might have been less orderly had they known that the Yalta Agreement had consigned them to be returned to the Soviet Union to meet their fate.

At Annabichl I found a telegram from Jack Nicholls, the head of the Political Division, saying that he was coming up to Austria as a political adviser and instructing me to return to Rome at once to take over from him as acting head of the Political Division of the Commission. However, before I left I wanted to visit the spot where I thought that Alfgar and his party had crossed the river Drau in their rubber boats. Taking Alex Ramsey with me, I drove in a jeep to Volkermarkt, now occupied by a company of the 60th Rifles commanded by John Christian. He said there were rumours that the Bulgarians were shooting at anyone who tried to approach them. Nevertheless we turned south, crossing Volkermarkter Stausee where, according to my diary, the river Drau was 'broad, muddy and fast with deep sloping banks'. It must have been a considerable achievement on Alfgar's part to have got the three boat-loads across without alerting the enemy. Once across the river I turned left for Bleiburg to investigate the story about the Bulgarians. There was a detachment of 27 Lancers in the town square and the sergeant in charge said that I must see Miss Nunn. She proved to be the former English nanny of the Thurn und Taxis family and had spent both world wars at the family castle nearby. She said that she had been subjected to no sort of persecution or even supervision by the Austrian authorities and that the townspeople had always treated her with great kindness and sympathy. The Thurns had done everything possible for her comfort, even sending to Switzerland for her favourite brand of English tea. Alex Ramsey and I listened, spell-bound, to her story and when eventually we tried to escape she implored us to wait and meet her 'children'. These proved to be a man and a woman in their late thirties, both of them literally dressed as children; he in leather shorts and white stockings and she in a short Dirndl skirt and white ankle socks. Both greeted us gravely, he with a little bow and she with a curtsey. To their nanny's evident approval, they then sat like well-behaved children while she described how the Yugoslav Partisans had abducted sixty hostages from Bleiburg, including her best friend, the chemist. The two 'children' remained silent throughout, smiling amiably, and it was only then that I realized that both were dumb and probably profoundly deaf. A few minutes later Count Thurn himself arrived. He was an elderly man, dressed in Austrian country clothes, a Loden jacket and a green hat with a chamois scut in the hat-band. He introduced himself, 'We're only Boches, you see,' and then launched forth into a long complaint about the depredations inflicted on his estate by hungry Cossacks and pillaging Partisans, expressing grave fears about the future, for his castle lay very close to the Yugoslav frontier. Reluctantly we extricated ourselves from this bizarre tea party and, having promised Miss Nunn every support from the British authorities, went on our way.

At Sistersdorf we turned south for Eisenkappel and the Seeberg Pass, the scene of several of Charles's and Alfgar's forays into Austria during the previous summer. The Seeberg Pass was guarded by the Lothian and Border Horse. I failed to recognize their young colonel who had a row of medal ribbons including a DSO and who introduced himself to me as 'Simpson Minor' whom I had last known when he was a small boy in my house at Rugby. There was also a Slovene Partisan town kommandant at Eisenkappel who remembered Charles and Alfgar and, perhaps in consequence, seemed on reasonably good terms with the British. He said that there was a large force approaching from the Yugoslav side but seemed uncertain whether they were friend or foe.

Retracing our steps as far as Eberndorf we turned westward and drove through the Rosental on the south side of the river Drau. This was territory which was over 90 per cent Slovene-speaking and there were signs of an intense recruiting drive being carried out by the Partisans. There were no British troops to be seen but groups of scared German prisoners were being rounded up with kicks and jeers by youthful Partisans and herded towards the Yugoslav frontier. One mild-looking German officer in rimless spectacles appealed to me as a fellow Christian to save him from the Tito Anti-Christ but he was hustled away by his captors before I had a chance to reply. Forest fires were burning quite fiercely on one side of the road and at Ferlach I saw a group of refugee White Guards who, according to my diary, were 'well armed, soldierly and cheerful', though certainly about to be murdered by the Partisans. The main road was thronged with, presumably anti-Tito, refugees who were still streaming over the Loibl Pass. They appeared utterly exhausted and I noticed a child about five years old fast asleep lying across the handlebars of a bicycle. On the bridge over the river Drau there was a British checkpoint manned by the Welsh Guards who, I noted in my diary, seemed 'almost as loot-gorged as the Partisans'. The company commander was Paul Makins who had been a friend of mine at Cambridge.

At Annabichl that evening there was a small farewell dinner for this was my last day in command of No. 6 Special Force.

Klagenfurt airfield was not yet open to transport aircraft and early on 13 May I set off in my staff car on my long drive to Rome. At HQ V Corps where I stopped to say goodbye there was news of continued fighting at Feistritz and of occasional shots being exchanged between the British and the Partisans. This confrontation saddened me and although the shimmering lake looked particularly beautiful in the morning mist, I reflected that, with my divided loyalties, it was just as well to be shot of the whole business. Avoiding the main road to Villach where there was now a continuous stream of military traffic, I travelled south of the lake as far as Arnoldstein, driving along the foothills of the Karawanken mountains. Any one of these isolated villages might have been my base had I succeeded in crossing the Alps in February 1944. In this remote corner there were no traces of war and the only traffic consisted of farm carts bringing in the hay. It was only six days since I had last driven through Arnoldstein, but this time the sun was at my back and the main street was jammed with army trucks bringing up supplies from Italy. So at Tarvisio I left the main road and drove up to the Predil Pass. Here too it was wonderfully peaceful with no longer any sign of military activity, and I drove gently south to Udine where I spent the night with Tom Macpherson.

The following day I drove for the last time following the ethnic frontier through Gorizia to Duino to take my leave of XIII Corps. The castle which dated back to the dark ages had been completely destroyed in the Great War and rebuilt by Count Torre e Tasso, the Italian branch of the Thurn und Taxis family I had met at Bleiburg. General Harding was on a tour of inspection so I continued on my way to HQ 15th Army Group where I had a long session with General Gruenther, the United States commanding general. He showed little sympathy for Slovene claims to Trieste which, as usual, I supported. However, he asked some searching questions about the extent of the Yugoslav threat to Carinthia, remarking that my estimate, based on my personal observation, of the number of Partisans north and south of the river Drau was less than half that contained in the latest intelligence summary. I suggested that part of this discrepancy might be explained by our intelligence people equating the Partisan *brigada*, which numbered anything from 100 to 500 men, with a regular infantry brigade. Gruenther showed interest in this suggestion and agreed that it might be so.

Having completed my leave-taking, we headed south as fast as we could drive.

It was midnight by the time we had crossed the Apennines and the city of Florence lay beneath us, the great dome of the cathedral and the campanile just discernible in the moonlight. The warm May night was heavy with the scent of wild thyme and on the spur of the moment I told driver Jewels that we would sleep where we were by the side of the road. I lay awake most of that night contemplating the immensity of the starry sky and reflecting on the futility of war in general and of my own efforts in particular during the past six years which, at the time, had seemed so desperately important. I was profoundly thankful that, unlike so many of my friends, I had survived, but I was conscious that mine had been in the main a spectator's war and that as a peacetime regimental officer I would always remain something of an outsider. Consequently I reckoned that I had little future as a professional soldier and the sooner that I exchanged my sword for a pen the better. I reached this definitive conclusion just as the first rays of the morning sun were gilding the red roofs that lay below me, and my mind went back to my first view of Florence when, aged twelve, I had thrown open the shutters of my room in the Pensione Maria Pia and gazed entranced across the river Arno at the terracotta dome of the Duomo.

SOE had requisitioned a large house, previously a girls' finishing school, on the road to Fiesole. Here I bathed and breakfasted and then set out for Rome where my wife, who wanted me safe and close, was waiting for me. I was aged thirty-one years and thirty days and, if Freud was right in his assertion that maturity was the capacity to defer pleasure, it was high time that I grew up.

No. 4 Military Mission

Distribution of Duty

Chief   Major-General Carton de Wiart

Staff Officers   Colonel C. McV. Gubbins
                     Lt. Colonel E. R. Sword
                     Captain F. T. Davies

Staff Captains   Captain J. S. Douglas
                     Captain H. J. Lloyd-Johnes

Camp Commandant   Captain R. H. Hazell
                     Captain H. Curteis

Signal Officer   Lieut. C. A. Henn-Collins
                     Lieut. E. Carlton

Order of Battle   Captain P. A. Wilkinson
                     Captain Blake
                     Lieut. Michell

Cypher Officers   Lieut. Parker
                     Lieut. Sedgwick

Transport Officer Lieut. R. J. Wright
                     Captain P. A. Wilkinson (i/c lorries when on move)

Pay and Allowances Captain W. Harris-Burland

With Fronts when Situation Stabilises

NORTH   Captain A. W. Brown
                     Lieut. M. Rowton
WEST   Captain P. A. Wilkinson
SOUTH-WEST   Major C. J. Johnstone
                     Lieut. R. J. Wright
SOUTH-EAST   Captain H. Curteis
SPARE   Captain W. Harris-Burland

Warsaw, 4 September 1939   *Captain A. W. Brown*
                                              For Lieut. Colonel

Index